The Midcentury Minor Novel

Modern American Literature and the New Twentieth Century
Series Editors: Martin Halliwell and Mark Whalan

Published Titles
Writing Nature in Cold War American Literature
Sarah Daw

F. Scott Fitzgerald's Short Fiction: From Ragtime to Swing Time
Jade Broughton Adams

The Labour of Laziness in Twentieth-Century American Literature
Zuzanna Ladyga

The Literature of Suburban Change: Narrating Spatial Complexity in Metropolitan America
Martin Dines

The Literary Afterlife of Raymond Carver: Influence and Craftsmanship in the Neoliberal Era
Jonathan Pountney

Living Jim Crow: The Segregated Town in Mid-Century Southern Fiction
Gavan Lennon

The Little Art Colony and US Modernism: Carmel, Provincetown, Taos
Geneva M. Gano

Sensing Willa Cather: The Writer and the Body in Transition
Guy J. Reynolds

Gertrude Stein and the Politics of Participation: Democracy, Rights and Modernist Authorship, 1909–1933
Isabelle Parkinson

The Regional Development of the American Bildungsroman, 1900–1960
Tamlyn Avery

Exoteric Modernisms: Progressive Era Realism and the Aesthetics of Everyday Life
Michael J. Collins

The Artifice of Affect: American Realist Literature and Emotional Truth
Nicholas Manning

The Midcentury Minor Novel: American Fiction, 1945–1965
Michael Kalisch

Visit our website at www.edinburghuniversitypress.com/series/MALTNTC

The Midcentury Minor Novel

American Fiction, 1945–1965

MICHAEL KALISCH

EDINBURGH
University Press

Edinburgh University Press is one of the leading university presses in the UK. We publish academic books and journals in our selected subject areas across the humanities and social sciences, combining cutting-edge scholarship with high editorial and production values to produce academic works of lasting importance. For more information visit our website: edinburghuniversitypress.com

© Michael Kalisch 2024, 2026

Edinburgh University Press Ltd
13 Infirmary Street
Edinburgh EH1 1LT

First published in hardback by Edinburgh University Press 2024

Typeset in 10/13 ITC Giovanni Std Book
by Manila Typesetting Company, and
printed and bound by CPI Group (UK) Ltd,
Croydon, CR0 4YY

A CIP record for this book is available from the British Library

ISBN 978 1 3995 2686 9 (hardback)
ISBN 978 1 3995 2687 6 (paperback)
ISBN 978 1 3995 2688 3 (webready PDF)
ISBN 978 1 3995 2689 0 (epub)

The right of Michael Kalisch to be identified as the author of this work has been asserted in accordance with the Copyright, Designs and Patents Act 1988, and the Copyright and Related Rights Regulations 2003 (SI No. 2498).

CONTENTS

Acknowledgements vi

Introduction in a Minor Key 1
1. 'A refusal to be great': Lionel Trilling's *The Middle of the Journey* and *The Journey Abandoned* and the Minor Novel of Ideas 40
2. Breaking Into Laughter: Anticommunism, Late Modernism, and Eleanor Clark's *The Bitter Box* 82
3. Changing Form: Jean Stafford and the Limits of New Criticism 123
4. Herzog in Venice: Richard Stern's *Stitch* and Jewish-American Literary History 163
5. A Lost Classic: John Williams's *Stoner* and the 'Rediscovery' of the Midcentury Minor Novel 189
Coda: Towards a Minor Criticism 211

Bibliography 217
Index 235

ACKNOWLEDGEMENTS

I'm very grateful to the Leverhulme Trust for supporting the research and writing of this book. A Robert L. Platzman Fellowship allowed me to spend some time in Chicago looking through Richard Stern's papers at an early stage of the project. Thank you to the staffs of: the Hanna Holborn Gray Special Collections Research Center, University of Chicago; the Rare Book & Manuscript Library, Columbia University; and the Beinecke Rare Book & Manuscript Library, Yale University. Thank you to Martin Halliwell and Mark Whalan for backing the book, and to Emily Sharp and Elizabeth Fraser at Edinburgh University Press for making it happen. This book is dedicated with love to Harriet and to Manny.

Portions of Chapter 1 first appeared in 'Trilling Unfinished', *American Literary History*, 36.1 (Spring 2024), pp. 138–55. An earlier version of Chapter 4 was published as 'Herzog in Venice: Richard Stern's *Stitch*, Ezra Pound, and Jewish American Literary History', *Studies in the Novel*, 53.3 (Fall 2021), pp. 266–84.

Introduction in a Minor Key

As we do of one another, we tend to ask too much of novels, even if we don't know quite what it is we're asking. It's hard to say what we go to novels for, or what we hope to find in their pages; our desire for novels leaves us wanting. The same was true for American literary critics in the middle decades of the twentieth century, who expected a great deal from novels and who, as a result, often came away empty-handed, or feeling short-changed. At times, midcentury critics appeared to have a very clear idea of what the novel was all about, what it should do and how it should do it; but at other times, they seemed less certain quite what they were looking for. They tasked the novel with fulfilling seemingly impossible criteria and described its value in contradictory terms; and they argued powerfully for its continuing cultural importance while announcing its imminent demise. The critical discourse surrounding the novel at midcentury was marked by a curious tension: a deep-rooted pessimism over the future of the novel together with an equally deep-rooted commitment to it. At midcentury, people believed in the novel even if they believed it was doomed. And consequently, the most interesting critics of the period – Lionel Trilling, for example – began to query their own investment in and attachment to the genre, and instead to make something out of their mixed feelings about it.

This book argues that a loose group of American midcentury novelists, Trilling among them, did something similar. Put too simply, the question facing midcentury novelists was how to go on writing novels after the critics had declared that the novel was dying or perhaps already dead. One could try to ignore the critics, of course, and some may never have paid them much attention in the first place; or one could use one's fiction to repudiate them, prove them wrong. But what of the novelists who, whether they liked it or not, were influenced by the critics' ideas about the novel and so couldn't dismiss them out of hand; who perhaps agreed with at least some of their critique of contemporary literature, and perhaps also with the broader cultural and political critique from which their view of the novel emerged? How might a novelist register in their fiction the same odd mixture of esteem for and pessimism about the novel that marked midcentury literary criticism?

The group of novelists discussed in this book did so by imagining the novel as a minor form, defined by its limits rather than its potential. They crafted fictions of modest proportions and seemingly attenuated ambition, fictions that kept to the third person and eschewed formal experimentation. These novelists acceded to the notion of the novel's diminished possibilities and reduced capacities, often positioning their fiction as in dialogue with the work of midcentury critics. And yet, rather than finding the idea of the minor novel stymieing or disillusioning, they discovered in its smaller canvas and reduced palette the grounds for an unlikely kind of aesthetic freedom. In what follows, I suggest that what is distinctive about the midcentury minor novel is the way in which it performs its own failure to live up to the high expectations and complex demands that were placed upon the novel by critics of the time. The midcentury minor novel dramatises the contradictions and ambivalences of the critics' conception of the genre, offering a subtly reflexive engagement with and critique of the period's literary aesthetics and broader intellectual culture. The midcentury minor novel wagers that the ways in which a novel falls short of critics' criteria might be of more aesthetic promise than the ways in which it succeeds in fulfilling them, or the ways in which it simply rejects them; as though, at midcentury, what one might hope to write is an interesting failure.

This book begins with what may at first appear an outmoded account of midcentury literary culture. I focus on the work of the New York Intellectuals and the New Critics, exploring how these two influential critical groups thought about the novel, and what impact their ideas had on midcentury literary culture. Since at least the revisionary interventions of the New Americanist critics in the 1980s, this once familiar critical history has been pushed to the periphery of our conception of modernism and our understanding of twentieth-century American literary culture more generally, and the concerns and ideas of these midcentury critics have come to seem less relevant to the kinds of work we do now. If they are considered, it is usually in relation to the consensus politics of the Cold War (with *Partisan Review*'s 1952 symposium 'Our Country and Our Culture' often invoked as marking the end of efforts to connect literary modernism with radical politics), and the conservative drift of American intellectual culture more broadly after the war. Within American Studies, midcentury critics are remembered, not exactly fondly, for their elaboration and defence of a highbrow tradition of literary modernism, their occlusion of the work of women and non-white writers from that tradition, and their dismissal of (or just plain disinterest in) popular culture.

Over the past four decades, successive waves of scholarship have challenged the 'canonical modernism' promulgated by these midcentury critics and the ideas of literary value that informed it, establishing instead alternative modernisms more attuned to sociopolitical issues of race, class, gender, and sexuality, and more inclusive of a variety of artistic and intellectual traditions, influences, and practices.[1] Important work by Michael Denning, Barbara Foley, and Alan Wald, among others, has sought to decentre the anti-Stalinist aesthetics of the New York Intellectuals, in order to recover overlooked trajectories of radical art and writing in the early and middle decades of the twentieth century.[2] Their work moves away from a focus on a 'coterie of avant-garde authors toward a more expansive view of modern literature's investment in everyday life', including in its 'public institutions'.[3] Building on this, Sean McCann, Mark McGurl, Michael Szalay, and Stephen Schryer, among others, have also considered the institutional contexts and conditions shaping American modernism.[4] More broadly, the trend within the 'new modernist studies' has been towards a conception of modernism as 'prismatic and plural rather than monolithic and static', giving rise to a proliferation of 'modified modernisms', wherein the modifiers are, among others, 'spatial (planetary, global, transnational)', 'temporal (late, inter-, midcentury)', and 'geopolitical (interwar, World War II, postwar, cold war)'.[5]

While the fields of American Studies and the new modernist studies have to some extent defined themselves against the work of the New York Intellectuals and New Critics, a number of scholars have recently returned to the work of these midcentury critics to consider afresh their work and legacy. Ian Afflerbach, Amanda Anderson, Mark Greif, and Benjamin Mangrum, among others, have sought to attend to the 'complex textures' and 'shifting intellectual sands' of midcentury liberalism in order to examine how literary aesthetics became a site for exploring 'a cluster of new political sentiments within American liberal thought'.[6] This book contributes to this reappraisal by arguing that the minor novel was an aesthetic formation distinctive to and reflective of this 'tumultuous' period of intellectual history, shaped by the preoccupations of and crosscurrents within postwar liberal thought.[7]

The Midcentury Minor Novel is also in dialogue with scholarship seeking to reframe midcentury literature more broadly. The new modernist studies has challenged some of the ways in which post-1900 literature has tended to be periodised by emphasising both the variety and longevity of modernist aesthetics. Part of this work has involved a redescription of some forms of midcentury writing as 'late modernist', a term I take up in Chapter 2.[8] According to Tyrus Miller, 'late modernist writing appears a distinctly self-conscious manifestation of the aging and decline of modernism', while at the same time 'strongly anticipat[ing] future developments, so that without forcing, it might easily fit into a narrative of emergent postmodernism'.[9] By contrast, another set of scholars have recently begun to think of the midcentury as a discrete period in literary history, giving rise to the field of 'midcentury studies'.[10] Claire Seiler suggests that 'the new modernist creep across the twentieth century' carries with it the risk that the aesthetic and discursive formations particular to the midcentury period fail to be recognised as such.[11] In *Midcentury Suspension* (2020), Seiler looks 'elsewhere than modernism for purchase on the midcentury', asking what we might 'gain from reading the century not forward from the modernist heave, but outward from its historical middle'. Seiler's important study examines how midcentury writing often reveals and reflects 'the period's profound sense of its own historical middleness, its feeling of suspension amid unclear onsets and outcomes'; indeed, she suggests that 'suspension' is the signature 'trope' and 'ethos' of the period.[12]

The approach adopted in this book draws on insights from within the fields of both the new modernist studies and midcentury studies. Miller's account of late modernist writing as a 'self-conscious manifestation' of the 'decline of modernism' certainly captures something of the reflexive aesthetic project of the midcentury minor novel, which emerges from a similar sense of attenuated artistic possibilities and feeling of belatedness. But Miller's conception of late modernism as prefiguring some of the characteristics of postmodernism runs counter to how I situate the midcentury minor novel in the history of twentieth-century American literature. Echoing Seiler's emphasis on the suspended quality of midcentury culture, I suggest that, rather than a harbinger of future aesthetic developments, the minor novel remains somewhat stubbornly of its 'awkward' midcentury moment, ultimately representing a literary mode not pursued, an aesthetic path not taken, by later writers; its rise and fall therefore amounts only to a minor episode in the history of modern American fiction.[13]

Like Seiler, I look elsewhere than modernism for purchase on the midcentury; but unlike her study, mine draws on the growing body of revisionary work on midcentury liberal thought, by Amanda Anderson and others, in order to re-examine the influence that liberal intellectuals and their literary aesthetics had on midcentury literary culture. This narrower focus means that this book aspires only to be a minor work of criticism – a category I return to and advocate for in the Coda – but it allows me to concentrate more concertedly on the fate of the novel at midcentury. As will become clear, in paying special attention to the novel, I am following the lead of the midcentury critics themselves, for whom discussions about the future of the genre became freighted with a range of political and professional questions and anxieties.

Midcentury Literary Criticism and the Fate of the Novel

The novel has perhaps never been held in higher regard than it was at midcentury. Many critics fostered a 'near-religious belief in the novel's office', Mark Greif writes, tasking it with nothing less than 'the restoration of the human'.[14] In 'Manners, Morals, and the Novel' (1947), one of the key essays in *The Liberal Imagination* (1950), Lionel Trilling describes 'the novel of the last two hundred years' as 'the most effective agent of the moral imagination'. 'It was never, either aesthetically or morally, a perfect form,' Trilling writes, but 'its greatness and its practical usefulness lay in its unremitting work of involving the reader himself in the moral life, inviting him to put his own motives under examination, suggesting that reality is not as his conventional education has led him to see it'.[15] Critics like Trilling believed that the novel could offer exposure to and instruction in moral difficulty and psychological complexity, and so be a site for valuable modes of non-instrumental intellectual reflection, private pleasure, and ethical engagement. Novels might surprise us, Trilling believed, and, in catching us unawares, restore us to a fuller sense of ourselves.

Many midcentury critics came to attach such importance to the novel as a result, in part, of their personal investment in and subsequent disillusionment with radical politics in the 1930s.[16] Scarred by Stalinism, American intellectuals came to distrust narratives of progress, rationalism, and materialism, and grew sceptical of the organisational impulses of any formal politics that attempted to manage or legislate the liberty of individuals.[17] Such impulses were discernible not only at the political extremes of Stalinism and fascism, but also in mainstream liberalism; that there was something totalitarian about liberal democracy was a suspicion shared at midcentury by New York Intellectuals and Frankfurt School theorists alike.[18] In response to what they characterised as liberalism's overly optimistic faith in 'social reform and technocratic progress', midcentury intellectuals placed 'a distinct emphasis on tragic limitation and negative forces', portraying history and politics as prone to irresolution and struggle, and man as beholden to unconscious desires.[19] Intellectuals as different in sensibility as Arthur Schlesinger Jr and Reinhold Niebuhr adopted what Amanda

Anderson calls a 'bleak ethos', attending to the 'contradictions and ironies of modern political life' in an effort to guard against the dangerous naivety and 'misguided progressivism' of what they now described as the 'old liberalism'.[20] The political landscape for these anti-Stalinist intellectuals was one of tempered expectations and existential anxieties, in which man's individual freedom was imagined as always under threat.

The novel, according to these intellectuals, had been among the casualties of 1930s radicalism. This was evident in progressive critics' high regard for literary naturalism, which Trilling and other anti-Stalinists disdained for its 'informing idea of the economic and social determination of thought', or what the critic Richard Chase called its 'necessitarian ideology'.[21] It was also evident in the broader tendency among progressives to judge a work by its adherence to liberal values. 'If we are to talk about literature in its relation with social good and the future of democracy we ought to be aware how harmful literature can be,' Trilling writes, discussing *The Grapes of Wrath* (1939), a novel that he suggests only 'cockers-up the self-righteousness of the liberal middle class: it is so easy to feel virtuous in our love for such *good* poor people!'[22] Rather than bolster our beliefs, or tell us something we already know, a novel should be an encounter with uncertainty and contradiction. Reading a novel, we should become less, not more certain what we think.

In response to what they judged to be the crude politicisation of literary culture in the 1930s, midcentury literary critics sought to reimagine the relation between the novel and society. Social reform was not a criteria and a novelist's politics were beside the point; indeed, as Trilling would observe, most of the writers midcentury anti-Stalinist intellectuals admired had decidedly undemocratic politics, a point I take up in Chapter 4 when discussing the controversy over Ezra Pound's receipt of the first Bollingen Prize for Poetry in 1949. The task of the novel was not to 'depict social conditions' but to record the 'continual, dialectical clash of values and ideas' that Trilling and others believed characterised 'social reality'.[23] Dismissing the notion of a programmatic link between literature and social progress, midcentury critics instead suggested a more 'indirect' relation between the novel and society, exploring 'the role the aesthetic might play in registering the complexities of political and moral life'.²⁴ '[L]iterature was to be about society but not subject to it,' David Hollinger writes, '*of* the world, but not *in* it'.²⁵ The novel might act as 'a kind of dynamic refuge from formal politics', in Amanda Anderson's phrase, in which 'specific aesthetic energies' could foster the 'capacity to live with paradox, to keep contraries in play without resolving them', a capacity necessary to better confront the 'incompatible moral values and irreducible conflicts of political life'.²⁶ As Ian Afflerbach explains, midcentury intellectuals reconceived of the 'liberal subject' as 'constitutively tragic' and tasked them with 'call[ing] guiding principles into question', 'balanc[ing] antithetical values and [. . .] recogniz[ing] the ineradicable conflicts' shaping political life. What this new tragic liberal subject needed was 'not just legal rights but an aesthetic sensibility' attuned to complexity.²⁷ The novel could allow for the cultivation of such a sensibility and therefore act as a guardrail against political simplicity, checking the progress of totalitarianism. Or, as Richard Chase put it:

> if one had read and understood Melville one would not vote for Henry Wallace [. . .] because Melville presents his reader with a vision of life that is so complexly true that it exposes the ideas of Henry Wallace as hopelessly childish and superficial. Literature tells us that life is diverse, paradoxical, and complicated, a fateful medley of lights and darks [. . .]²⁸

The reconstitution of the relation between the novel and society imagined by critics like Trilling and Chase was a kind of aestheticising of the political. Often enough, David Russell writes, 'the aesthetic has seemed the sphere into which political freedom is translated only so it may be betrayed'.²⁹ Nevertheless, midcentury anti-Stalinists came to think of aesthetic experience as a way to imagine the conditions and limits of individual freedom and then, following on from this, as a way to orient our sense of how we might live with one another. Up to a point, their work resembled the literary formalism of the New Critics, who emerged in the 1930s and came to prominence the following decade. In their practice of close reading, the New Critics conceived of the poem as a non-propositional, internally coherent unity distinct from history and society, and so potentially a site of the sort of non-instrumental experience prized by the New York Intellectuals. The New Critics 'imagined carving out space for the self in a world anxious about the advent of centralized managerial authority and the mechanisms of expanding federal bureaucracy,' Benjamin Mangrum writes, and held literature to be 'the only remaining counterweight to the triumph of technical rationality within the welfare state'.[30] Though they came from very different political and cultural traditions – a topic I return to in subsequent chapters – the New York Intellectuals and the New Critics shared a belief in the importance of setting literature at a critical distance from liberal society.[31] New Critics were more likely to stress certain formal and technical features of a work they presented as ahistorical (symbolism, mythic patterning), but some of their key vocabulary (tension, difficulty, paradox) was shared with the New York Intellectuals.[32]

The midcentury critical discourse of the novel I have begun to sketch was articulated and consolidated through two closely related though seemingly somewhat incompatible projects of literary historiography. The first was the construction of a canon of literary modernism. This was associated with the New York Intellectuals and especially with the group of writers connected to *Partisan Review*, as I discuss in more detail in Chapter 2. Affiliated in its early years with the American Communist Party, from the late 1930s *Partisan* broke ranks and 'established itself as a center for anti-Stalinist intellectuals', rejecting Popular Front aesthetics in favour of a mostly European, cosmopolitan tradition of avant-garde writing, including Dostoevsky, Kafka, Malraux, Joyce, and Gide.[33] These writers were celebrated in *Partisan* for embracing formal innovation and intellectual complexity, and for their radical or adversarial relation to society. The magazine's championing of modernist difficulty formed part of its critique not only of the Popular Front but also of mainstream liberal progressivism and its organisational impulses, reflecting the 'bleak ethos' and chastened radicalism of the broader anti-Stalinist left. Thus, in the pages of *Partisan*, Kafka was admired for his understanding that 'a man caught in the bureaucratic machinery is already condemned', while Dostoevsky was heralded as an 'analyst of contradictions'.[34] Over time, the modernist canon was expanded through a series of revivals of 'previously unrecognized or undervalued authors'.[35] This extended to some American writers. In 1946, Malcolm Cowley's *Portable Faulkner* helped spur a re-evaluation of the author of *The Sound and the Fury* (1929); the following year, *Partisan* editor Philip Rahv described the 'revival of Henry James' as 'a phenomenon as surprising to his devotees as his detractors', noting that 'in the last three years more of his work has been reprinted in this country than in the entire quarter of a century following his death in 1916'.[36]

While James and Faulkner were recruited into an international genealogy of modernism, a second project of literary historiography emerging at midcentury sought to recover a distinctively national literary tradition. Works of criticism by F. O. Matthiessen, R. W. B. Lewis, Richard Chase, Leo Marx, and Leslie Fielder, among others, were foundational texts in the field that became American Studies, each setting out in different ways to portray US literary culture as distinct from its European counterpart in both its aesthetic formations and its underlying cultural conditions.[37] They often did so in terms that 'validat[ed] a common array of New Critical notions of irony, balance, tension, and ambiguity', and that endorsed the ideas of difficulty and tragedy that were also common to anti-Stalinist aesthetics.[38] Midcentury Americanists, that is to say, made their literary history in their own image (as all critics do), championing works they felt to embody the concepts of irresolution, contradiction, and tragic struggle highly valued in the bleak liberalism of their moment.[39] As part of this project, they sought to emphasise the inherently democratic character of a 'hybrid' American literary past enriched by 'an element of romance', in contrast both to a European history of naturalism (besmirched by its association with 1930s radicalism) and an English tradition of 'staid', conservative realism.[40]

As the New Americanists pointed out some decades ago, the 'myth and symbol' approach of this earlier generation of Americanists perpetuated a version of US exceptionalism that chimed with the ideological imperatives of the Cold War.[41] Thus one of the tensions between the two projects of literary historiography underway at midcentury had to with the claims and commitments of universalism and nationalism. The canonisation of an international tradition of literary modernism arose, in part, as a rejoinder to the jingoism of Popular Front 'Americanism'.[42] Anti-Stalinist intellectuals drew on European existentialism to explore in their work the possibility of a kind of revisionist, attenuated universal humanism, elaborated in aesthetic experience and attuned to the conditions of anxiety, alienation, and pessimism widely felt to define the postwar moment – what Hannah Arendt, a frequent contributor to *Partisan*, called 'the modern feeling of homelessness in the world'.[43] But while the cosmopolitan *Partisan* crowd concerned themselves with the 'condition of man' – a phrase that Mark Greif shows circulated surprisingly widely and variously in midcentury intellectual culture – Americanist scholars sought to identify a native literature exemplifying a distinctively American democratic ethos and embodying a recognisably national character, a project that aligned with the early Cold War effort to define and export a brand of American idealism rooted in democratic plurality which could be contrasted to Soviet totalitarianism.

The midcentury critical discourse of the novel became widely influential as intellectuals migrated from little magazines into university English departments as part of a broader expansion in higher education in the postwar period.[44] The discourse circulated through university reading lists, student textbooks – such as the New Critical anthologies *Understanding Poetry* (1938) and *Understanding Fiction* (1943), discussed in Chapter 3 – academic conferences and symposia, and institutionally affiliated journals such as the *Kenyon Review* and *Southern Review*, as well as *Partisan* and other smaller magazines.[45] Intellectuals had a new kind of cultural authority, prestige, and influence in the period. They provided students drawn from a rapidly expanding middle class with an evocative critical vocabulary for discussing literature, and this vocabulary gradually made its way, in somewhat simplified forms, into weekly reviews and magazines, while the paperback revolution underway in this period allowed newly canonised novels to move from reading lists and college libraries to bookstores and newsstands.[46] This combination of institutional and market conditions helped the midcentury critical discourse of the novel to travel quickly and widely, and to gain an unlikely currency in 'the mainstream of American culture'.[47] In literary circles, meanwhile, criticism rivalled creative work in importance and cachet. 'You waited for their essays,' recalled Robert Lowell, who was greatly influenced by the New Critics early in his career, 'and when a good critical essay came out it had the same excitement of a new imaginative work.'[48]

But just as they had seemed to secure the novel's history, these same midcentury critics began to cast doubt on its future. Surveying the landscape of contemporary fiction, midcentury critics were nearly unanimous in their negative appraisal of what they found. While individual writers were sometimes celebrated – most frequently Saul Bellow and Ralph Ellison, and more occasionally Jean Stafford – the field as a whole was usually condemned.[49] 'One is tempted to say of the creative effort of our decade: It is largely abortive,' the leading New Critic John Crowe Ransom declared in a 1948 *Partisan* symposium on 'The State of American Writing', the same year another New Critic, Mark Schorer, in an influential essay, wrote that, 'In the United States during the last twenty-five years, we have had many big novels but few good ones'.[50] In his widely read 1951 study, *After the Lost Generation*, John Aldridge also bemoaned the quality of recent fiction, suggesting it displayed 'little evidence of new developments'.[51]

In explaining what they characterised as the inferiority of contemporary fiction, critics suggested that the conditions that had given rise to the newly canonised traditions of high modernism and, reaching further back, 'classic' American literature were now at an end. The New York Intellectuals' conception of modernism rested upon the idea of the writer's adversarial relation to society, but it seemed to many commentators that such a relation was no longer possible in midcentury America. 'Alienation is usually taken to be the condition of the modern writers,' Ihab Hassan noted in his 1961 study *Radical Innocence*, 'but the nature of that alienation has changed with the rise of mass culture.'[52] Writing in 1956, John Aldridge also decried the 'conformist tendencies now dominant in the American intellectual life', suggesting that 'our democracy in its current form' gives writers 'neither a dogma which might provide a basis for heretical action nor an opportunity to discover [. . .] way of life which would represent a heresy of democracy'.[53] In his 1961 study of midcentury fiction, Marcus Klein similarly argued that the modernist idea of an 'organised isolation' was now 'outmoded', no longer affording the contemporary writer 'that negative usefulness which should be his justification'.[54] Americanist critics, meanwhile, tended to draw a contrast instead between nineteenth- and twentieth-century American culture. 'The contemporary picture [. . .] remains curiously frozen in outline,' R. W. B. Lewis concludes in *The American Adam* (1955), suggesting that, unlike the period that produced Melville and James, the midcentury 'is anything but dialectal and contains within it no opposite possibilities on which to feed and fatten'.[55]

Critical discussions of the state of contemporary fiction often widened to consider the fate of the novel more generally. No sooner had critics argued for the crucial importance of the novel to the culture, and developed a range of interpretative tools and criteria for evaluating it, than they suggested it was in grave danger. Prophecies and pronouncements of the death of the novel are as old as the novel itself, but they emerged with particular frequency and forcefulness at midcentury.[56] Granville Hicks – in a collection of essays pointedly titled *The Living Novel* (1957) – complained that one heard 'this solemn assertion, repeated every few weeks by somebody or other, that the novel was dying if not quite dead'.[57] Hicks perhaps had most immediately in mind Yvor Winters, the rather idiosyncratic but influential formalist critic to whom I return in Chapters 4 and 5, who in a recent essay had written that 'most intelligent critics and even novelists are aware' that 'the novel in our time is nearly dead', before openly admitting to no longer bothering to read contemporary fiction: 'I have better ways of spending the few years remaining to me'.[58] Like Hicks, Trilling observed how insistent discussion of the death of the novel had become. 'It is impossible to talk about the novel nowadays without having in our minds the question of whether or not the novel is still a living form,' he writes in 'Art and Fortune' (1948), and although he does 'not believe that the novel is dead', he does wonder whether:

> we are at the close of a cultural cycle, that the historical circumstances which called forth the particular intellectual effort in which we once lived and moved and had our being is now at an end, and that the novel as part of that effort is as deciduous as the rest.[59]

There were institutional reasons that allowed midcentury critics to dismiss contemporary fiction and openly query the future of the novel. The canonisation of a genealogy of high modernism and a tradition of 'classic' American literature had given these critics plenty of material to work with and little professional need for new talent; if they ever did want to freshen up a reading list or find a subject for their next critical study, they could always launch another revival of a neglected earlier writer. In his contribution to *Partisan*'s 1948 symposium on 'The State of American Writing', John Berryman responded to the editors' prompt, 'What is the meaning of the literary revivals?', by suggesting that, 'The question apparently wants me to say that these novelists are being revived mainly because we have no fiction of our own; so I will, but it's obvious'.[60] But Berryman perhaps gets things the wrong way round: it wasn't that the revivals were indicative of the state of recent fiction, but that they represented a more valuable resource than contemporary literature for the disciplinary work in which midcentury critics now found themselves engaged. To mark an end to modernism – or even to the novel as a living form – was to define a specialism, and to provide a still fledgling field an institutional coherence and integrity. 'Scholars and critics are curiously like property owners', as Saul Bellow put it in 1957. 'They have their lots surveyed. Here the property begins and there it ends. A conservative instinct in them [. . .] resists extension, calls for limits [. . .] "Thank God," they say, "it's over. Now we have a field. Now we can study"'.[61]

But the relation between the institutionalisation of literary studies on the one hand and the disregard of recent fiction on the other was more complex than this. To some, it seemed that, in elevating the status of modernist writers, midcentury critics risked placing their work beyond the imaginative reach of a younger generation of novelists, interfering with the usual passage of literary influence. Such was the view, in any case, of critics like Aldridge, who placed the blame of what he thought to be the dearth of good contemporary fiction squarely at the feet of meddling professors:

> The leaders and apostles of the movement whom the younger group had thought of as their natural and at least spiritually living mentors appeared now to have been embalmed and mummified [. . .] and set up in niches to commemorate the grandeur of a vanished cult, while their works had

come to be looked upon, not as models to be admired and imitated but as sacred canonical treasures to be studied as objects of research.[62]

This view was widely echoed, including by Robert Gorham Davis in a *Partisan* symposium: 'If the imaginative writing of the forties is less ambitious and interesting than that of the twenties and thirties,' writes Davis, 'it is partly because of the inhibiting effect of current aesthetic and academic theory.'[63] Institutionalising modernism had effectively brought it to a close as a living literary movement; how could avant-garde rebellion remain a provocative pose for a writer to strike, Marcus Klein asked, when it was 'taught in midwestern colleges'?[64] Midcentury fiction writers thus found themselves 'at the end of a tradition' which was now the preserve of critics rather than novelists; 'the avantgarde has been professionalized', as Clement Greenberg put it in *Partisan*, 'organized into a field for careers'.[65] Critics' tendency to fold the end of modernism into a broader narrative of the end of the novel made matters worse. And because of the new prominence and prestige these critics enjoyed in midcentury literary culture, their opinions were hard to dismiss. 'I should like to disregard them,' Bellow wrote of the death-of-the-novel critics, 'but that is difficult because they have a great deal of power.'[66] Furthermore, many felt that the revitalised genre of criticism now seemed to be doing some of the intellectual and imaginative work that had once been (according to these same critics) the domain of fiction; in what Randall Jarrell called the 'Age of Criticism', the role of the novel in the culture became less certain, even as Trilling and others argued that 'there never was a time when its particular activity was so much needed'.[67]

To summarise, as American literary studies professionalised at midcentury, it did so in terms that, on the one hand, elevated the status of the novel as a literary form crucial to the development of what Trilling called the 'moral imagination', but that, on the other, precipitated the critical disavowal of most contemporary fiction. As the discipline organised itself around the twin canons of international modernism and nineteenth-century American literature, contemporary US writing paled in comparison and became surplus to the institutional requirements of critics, who often framed what they declared to be the absence of major new works of fiction as indicative of the decline of the novel itself as a viable form, a 'shrinkage of the aesthetic horizons' reflecting the attenuated political imagination and bleak tenor of midcentury liberal thought more generally.[68]

But midcentury critics' disillusion with contemporary fiction, and their apparent readiness to announce the death of the novel, also betrayed a certain unease as to how their discipline had come into being, the terms by which the novel had been historicised and canonised, and by which they themselves had achieved their cultural prominence. Firstly, critics who held university positions now had to contend with the irony that they were seeking to portray the novel as a site for private moral engagement from within one of the postwar period's most successful public institutions.[69] 'We critics,' Trilling wrote worriedly to Ransom in 1948, 'ha[ve] by now become institutionalized [. . .] the danger comes that all that was won with difficulty will turn into academic cliché, given back to us by almost all the students who are at all bright.'[70] 'Trilling implied that the modern canon [. . .] needed to be protected from the popularization and vulgarization that is a risk of trying to teach it,' David Hollinger writes.[71] Put another way, the problem for critics was how one could hope to offer a course in non-instrumental reflection.[72] A similar ambivalence as to how the values of literature (as described by midcentury critics) could be reconciled with the imperatives of the classroom also appeared inherent to the New Critical approach to textual analysis. 'While one aspect of the New Criticism seemingly democratized literary studies through close reading,' Benjamin Mangrum writes, 'another of its main sensibilities simultaneously construed the interpretive task as a decisively difficult one.'[73] This was the early gatekeepers of American literary studies not simply pleading the case for the necessity of their expertise, but also wondering whether what was valuable about literature was the sort of the thing that could be communicated at all; a truly 'active' literature, Trilling felt, consists of works that exist 'happily [. . .] beyond our powers of explanation' – a slightly surprising conclusion for a critic and university professor to reach.[74]

Secondly, and much more speculatively, midcentury critics' disillusionment with contemporary fiction and their pessimism about the future of the novel could also be said to have revealed a doubt as to whether the novel as they had described it ever in fact existed – that is, a doubt as to whether the terms by which they had come to define the novel's relation to society, and the criteria they had established by which it was to be judged, were the right ones, or whether they had mistook the novel all along.

Among the New Critics, there had in fact always be a touch of puzzlement about and condescension towards the novel. 'How we are to deal with the novel remains a problem for us,' Arthur Mizener writes in an essay published in *Kenyon* in 1950. 'It is our drunken, disreputable cousin, never mentioned when the subject can be avoided but forever turning up on the front porch at the most embarrassing times.' 'And yet,' Mizener continues, 'novels must be dealt with, not because of any passion we may have for an orderly aesthetic of the novel, but because we have to talk about them, in print, in the classroom, and among our intelligent, unprofessional friends', and because 'the novel is the last of the verbal forms to retain wide popularity'.[75] A similar reluctance to engage with the novel is discernible in essays of the period by other leading New Critics such as R. P. Blackmur and Allen Tate, the latter of whom suggested that a serious criticism focused on fiction might be impossible simply because a novel is so much harder to grasp in its entirety than a poem. 'Who can remember, well enough to pronounce upon it critically, all of *War and Peace*, or *The Wings of the Dove*, or even *Death in Venice*,' Tate asks in a 1944 essay. 'I have read all three of these books in the past year; yet for the life of me I could not pretend to know them as wholes, and without that knowledge I lack the material of criticism.'[76] Tate's essay is indicative of how the New Critics tried to apply a formalist approach developed for poetry to the study of prose – exemplified in Mark Schorer's essay, 'Technique as Discovery' (1948) – and found it to be at best an imperfect fit.[77] Tate writes that 'it has been through Flaubert that the novel has at last caught up with poetry', a judgement that only serves to show how the New Critics always saw fiction as playing second fiddle to verse.[78]

But even among critics apparently devoted to the novel there is discernible an ambivalence as to how the literary form had come to be so highly regarded and successfully institutionalised.

Trilling was 'caught up in the mystique of the canon', according to David Hollinger, and 'his investment [. . .] in the modern texts was simply prodigious'.[79] But while Trilling often referenced the same international roster of modernist novelists celebrated in the pages of *Partisan* – and expressed admiration for Melville, Hawthorne, and other nineteenth-century authors now deemed 'classic' American writers – his personal literary tastes were rather more idiosyncratic and not a little contrarian. The books he liked best belonged neatly neither to the modernist nor Americanist traditions discussed above, but to what he called the school of 'the novel of manners', a mostly European strain of realist fiction flourishing in the nineteenth century and preoccupied with 'the investigation of the problem of reality beginning in the social field'. This kind of novel 'has never really established itself in America' because of an American 'resistance to looking closely at society'.[80] Elsewhere, Trilling suggests that, 'In this country the real basis of the novel has never existed – that is, the tension between a middle class and an aristocracy which brings manners into observable relief as the living representation of ideas.'[81] Characterised by 'moral realism' – Trilling's term for 'the perception of the dangers of the moral life itself' – the novel of manners provides readers with an education in 'the extent of human variety and the value of that variety'. This echoes what Trilling, in the preface to *The Liberal Imagination*, defines as 'the job of criticism': 'to recall liberalism to its first essential imagination of variousness and possibility, which implies the awareness of complexity and difficulty'.[82]

The novel of manners therefore exemplifies the ambiguous cultural work that Trilling and other anti-Stalinist critics demanded of fiction – even though Trilling suggests that the conditions which had given rise to it were not to be found in America, and never had been. In any case, what Trilling often seems to value most about reading novels is something simpler, more 'primitive': their appeal to what Henry James called, in a phrase Trilling liked, 'the blessed faculty of wonder', or the experience of being held by a good story.[83] And he queried whether 'the novel was better off when it was more humbly conceived than it is now', as he wrote in a 1948 essay, before the novel was tasked by professional critics with the 'renovation of the will'.[84] "To recapture the love of telling a story, of wonder and suspense,' Trilling wrote to novelist Eleanor Clark, 'that, it seems to me, is what modern writers need'; as though the novel were altogether more ordinary than midcentury critics, including Trilling himself, were making it out to be; or as though it shouldn't be taken quite so seriously.[85]

Even as he outlined a tradition of the novel of manners, Trilling tended in his critical work to focus less on canonical authors and texts and more on peripheral figures and overlooked works. He devoted a book to E. M. Forster's fiction, wrote major essays on the ways in which the talents of Sherwood Anderson and William Dean Howells had gone astray, and penned a lengthy defence of the unfashionable F. Scott Fitzgerald; his landmark essay on Henry James, meanwhile, took as its subject what many held to be among the novelist's least significant books, *The Princess Casamassima* (1885). Trilling, in other words, was always drawn to marginal cases, such that we might say he was less concerned with the canon than he was with its exceptions, or more interested in how a novel could fail to fulfil its promise than in how it succeeded in doing so. I pursue this idea in Chapter 1.

A similar ambivalence is also discernible in the work of critics focusing more narrowly on American literary history. In *The American Novel and its Tradition* (1957), Richard Chase follows Trilling in suggesting that, 'In America, with the exception of Henry James, the novelists of manners are among the writers of second or third rank'.[86] Rather, the American novel has, according to Chase, 'worked out its destiny and defined itself by incorporating an element of romance'. This 'amalgamation' produces 'an imaginative world of radical, even irreconcilable contradictions', making American literature rich in the sort of complexity and conflict prized by midcentury critics, a fiction of 'literary hybrids' 'less interested in incarnation and reconciliation than in alienation and disorder'.[87] And yet Chase ultimately presents the tradition of the American novel as a curious one – secondary, certainly, to its European counterparts and perhaps most similar to what he describes, quoting F. R. Leavis, as the 'minor tradition' emerging out of Emily Brontë's *Wuthering Heights* (1847), a novel that the author of *The Great Tradition* (1948) describes as 'a kind of sport'.[88] That there was something constitutively 'minor' about the American novel was echoed elsewhere, with a different emphasis, in early Americanist criticism: in Leslie Fiedler's suggestion, for example, that American fiction seems 'unfallen in a disturbing way, almost juvenile' or 'pre-adolescent', unable to 'develop'; or in the stress placed by R. W. B. Lewis, Leo Marx, and Ihab Hassan, among others, on the 'innocence' of US literature and culture.[89]

In different ways, then, midcentury critics sought to elevate the novel – to historicise, canonise, and institutionalise it – but did so in terms that cast doubt not only on whether the conditions that had given rise to the novel were still available at midcentury, but also on whether the novel as they variously described it ever existed in the first place. Often the novel appears in midcentury criticism not so much as an object of study as an horizon of possibility. No sooner had midcentury critics conjured the novel into being than they made it disappear.

Trajectories of Postwar American Literature

The most influential account of the effect that the midcentury critical discourse of the novel had on the fiction of the time remains Thomas Hill Schaub's *American Fiction in the Cold War* (1991).[90] Paralleling the approach adopted by the New Americanist critics, Schaub frames his study as a critical history of the transformation of postwar liberalism told through the prism of literary aesthetics. He portrays the formalism of the New York Intellectuals and the New Critics as indicative and facilitative of the conservative drift of American intellectual culture and the emergence of the 'consensus politics' of the early Cold War. Central to his argument is the claim that the literary aesthetics of the late 1940s 'exerted a paralyzing effect upon American narrative fiction'.[91] Midcentury literary criticism's stress on craft, technique, and form, together with its ambiguation of the relation between aesthetics and politics, created a 'prescriptive atmosphere', Schaub suggests, which served to 'erode further the authority of the writer already weakened by the literary history of the thirties and early forties, when the ideological impulse behind naturalism and social realism was both discredited and displaced' by modes of literary formalism that presented themselves as 'ideologically neutral'. The loss of a clear connection between aesthetics and politics, and the erosion of the writer's adversarial relation to society, 'amounted to the removal of an entire and habitual point of view,' Schaub writes; 'in this vacuum the postwar emphasis upon formal craft acted as a tourniquet' upon midcentury novelists.[92]

Fiction writers often positioned themselves 'in direct opposition' to the opinions and directives of midcentury critics, Schaub notes. He quotes Ralph Ellison (whose work I discuss in Chapter 2) complaining how 'the nineteenth-century novel of manners is held before us as final evidence of our futility and the novel's point of highest glory and swift decline'.[93] Schaub also cites Saul Bellow's reflection that his second novel, *The Victim* (1947), had been written too much in thrall to what he called 'the Flaubertian standard' admired by these critics, a standard he came to find 'repressive' and which he would disregard in *The Adventures of Augie March* (1953).[94] But Schaub is also careful not to take at face value 'the oppositional point of view assumed by many writers'; in fact, he shows, the 'interaction between the serious young writers' and the critics was more complex than this, and contends that the work of many midcentury novelists was 'guided and shaped' by the same set of ideas 'which informed the thinking and assumptions of the critical community'.[95] Indeed, Schaub argues that the effect of the midcentury critical discourse of the novel, and the bleak liberalism that underpinned it, was so detrimental to American fiction precisely because so many writers had imbibed it so deeply, and accepted many of the aesthetic commitments of the critics: he points, for example, to the commonplace dismissal of naturalism; the widespread sense of the inadequacy of nineteenth-century realism, and yet, simultaneously, the unavailability of avant-garde experimentation; and the pervasive feeling that the adversarial position adopted by modernist writers was impossible in a 'mass culture'.[96] Further, Schaub suggests that many writers of the period also accepted 'the definition of the novel as an outmoded form repeated in the influential essays of Richard Chase, Ian Watt, Lionel Trilling, Philip Rahv, Irving Howe, and José Ortega y Gasset'.[97]

Schaub suggests that a crucial way in which writers responded to the negative influence of critics was through a decisive turn to first person narrative. The 'invention of first person voices,' Schaub writes, was 'a form of resistance' to pressures 'for political conformity and controlled, crafted form'. First person narrative 'embodied a point of view [. . .] issuing from the unimpeachable authority' of the writer's 'consciousness and perception', thereby reflecting the emphasis placed by midcentury literary aesthetics on the priority of private experience and judgement; but, at the same time, this kind of narrative allowed writers a greater formal freedom, a release from the imperatives of Jamesian craft. 'Such narrators as Holden Caulfield, Augie March and Invisible Man were meant to be a kind of Strether Unbound,' Schaub writes, alluding to the protagonist of *The Ambassadors* (1903), 'liberated from both social convention and aesthetic orthodoxy.' Because he frames the literary aesthetics of the late 1940s as essentially conservative in character, Schaub is particularly interested in how first person narrative allowed writers to reimagine the relation between aesthetics and politics, noting that 'the significance of the first person was consciously debated by writers, and is especially apparent in the remarks of those writers who nurtured a commitment to some form of socialism'.[98] In Schaub's telling, first person narrative represented a 'new form' through which writers could recapture the 'adversarial stance' constitutive to the idea of the modern artist they had absorbed from the critics. Such a point of view was 'best exploited by writers who conceived of themselves as minorities or outsiders,' Schaub argues, suggesting that this 'accounts in some measure for the fact that much of the most interesting writing of the forties, fifties, and sixties was written by blacks, Jews, women, members of the drug world, and disaffected youth'.[99] The widespread embrace of first person narrative by these minority writers was 'the result of a generation's need to find its own way, freestyle,' Schaub concludes, beyond the confines of the dominant critical discourse of the novel.[100]

Schaub's suggestion that minority writers attempted to free themselves from the 'tourniquet' of midcentury literary aesthetics by experimenting with 'idiomatic voices' parallels, to some degree, Mark McGurl's more recent history of the interrelation of postwar fiction and the rise of the creative writing program, a history I return to in subsequent chapters. In place of a linear development from modernism to postmodernism, McGurl charts the emergence of two major modes of post-1945 American prose writing, 'technomodernism' and 'high cultural pluralist' fiction.[101] In the latter, 'the high literary values of modernism' are joined with 'a fascination of cultural difference and the authenticity of ethnic voice'.[102] 'The high culture pluralist writer,' McGurl writes, is called upon to combine 'a rhetorical performance of cultural group membership' with the 'elevated idiom of literary modernism'; among his prime examples are Ellison and Philip Roth, who also feature prominently in Schaub's argument.[103]

More so than McGurl, Schaub focuses on the strong influence that midcentury critical discourse had on the period's broader literary culture, evidencing the high if sometimes hostile regard in which critics were held by writers. In the history Schaub tells, the impact that critics had on midcentury fiction was largely negative: 'paralysing', 'prescriptive', 'inhibiting'. But in what follows, I show that writers responded to the authority of midcentury literary intellectuals in ways other than Schaub charts and produced other forms of fiction than those he describes. His account of the turn towards 'idiomatic' first person narrative in midcentury fiction accords with most recent accounts of the trajectory of postwar literature, and with the direction of the new modernist studies and the disciplinary habits of mind of the academy more generally (a history McGurl also sketches): away from an institutionalised high modernism towards 'high cultural pluralist fiction'; away from an elitist canon dominated by a few white male authors towards a broader literary field sustained by the work of non-white writers, in which the line between high and popular culture is increasingly blurred. But there were, I want to suggest, other kinds of novels being written in response to midcentury criticism that do not neatly fit into this history and that cannot be straightforwardly read as prefiguring later developments in the postwar field.

Indicative of this is that, while Schaub convincingly suggests that first person narrative became a crucial resource for writers seeking ways to move beyond the constraints of midcentury aesthetics, none of the midcentury novels I discuss in this book are written in the first person. This may seem an incidental point of difference of limited critical purchase, but it is suggestive of a more fundamental distinction between Schaub's account and my own. Rather than turn inwards, the writers I consider stuck to the third person familiar from nineteenth-century realism and the 'novel of manners' – closer, that is, to the 'Flaubertian standard' Bellow would later reject. They tried to practise the novel according to the terms laid out by the critics, even as those terms seemed sometimes to place conflicting demands upon them, and, indeed, to describe quite different kinds of novel. The novelists I survey drew, often quite explicitly, on the principles and concepts of midcentury formalism and accepted the broader critique of liberalism and American culture than underpinned them.[104] Their work emerged from the same 'bleak' cultural climate that gave rise to the midcentury critical discourse of the novel, and their fiction is in dialogue with the ideas of craft, difficulty, tragedy, moral realism, myth, and so on that shaped how the novel was understood and discussed at midcentury. But these writers sought not so much to fulfil as to trouble the idea of the novel handed to them by the critics. Their novels internalise and dramatise the discussions of and doubts about the novel pervasive in the period's literary culture, including the idea that the novel was in crisis or decline; and yet, paradoxically, they make this deep-lying ambivalence about the novel the very basis of their aesthetic project. That is to say, these novelists were animated, not 'paralysed' by the midcentury critical discourse of the novel, creating fictions that accede to the notion that the contemporary novel might be a literary form of diminished possibilities, but in so doing reflexively explore and query the critical debates surrounding the history and future of the genre. To write fiction in the wake of midcentury criticism, these authors suggest, is to reckon with the possibility that the novel might now be a minor form, and to wonder what imaginative opportunities this might foreclose but also, perhaps, make available.

Becoming Minor

In beginning to think of the minor novel as a distinctive mode of midcentury writing, it is useful to turn briefly to Gilles Deleuze and Félix Guattari's influential concept of a minor literature.[105] In its majoritarian mode, Deleuze and Guattari suggest, 'literature presents itself as the expression or representation' of an established, pre-existing subject, identity or discourse – for example, national identity.¹⁰⁶ A minor literature, by contrast, is a literature of a subject, identity or discourse in the process of becoming, or of that which 'is not already recognisable'.¹⁰⁷ A minor literature becomes a site for the 'not yet given' characterised by a 'deterritorialisation' of language, in which the usual modes of expression and representation demanded of language are disrupted.¹⁰⁸ A key example for Deleuze and Guattari is 'Kafka's practice as a Prague Jew writing in German'. 'Separated from a naturalizing, integrating ethnic German speech community', Kafka's German 'had undergone numerous deformations through its proximity to Czech, and its impoverishment had forced a limited vocabulary to assume multiple functions, each term taking on an intensive and shifting polyvocality'; in such a linguistic atmosphere one might be 'a stranger *within* his own language'.¹⁰⁹ Their other examples of deterritorialisation involve more radical forms of linguist breakdown rather than restriction or multiplicity: Antonin Artaud's 'cry-words [*mots-cris*] in which all the literal, syllabic and phonetic values are replaced by *values that are exclusively tonic* and non-written'; or e. e. cumming's practice of 'agrammaticality'.¹¹⁰ The minor is thus imagined by Deleuze and Guattari as a kind of creatively disruptive capacity inherent to language, a capacity in which the dislocating of the ways that language usually operates allows new forms to be evoked or gestured to while remaining as potentialities. The new forms that most interest Deleuze and Guattari are political and specifically anti-colonial; they focus on how the deterritorialising of language allows one to 'find points of nonculture or underdevelopment, linguistic Third World zones by which a language can escape'.¹¹¹ But importantly, a minor literature is 'not necessarily a literature of minorities,' Claire Colebrook writes, and certainly not a literature of high cultural pluralism as described by McGurl, in which writers are 'called upon to speak from the point of view of one or another hyphenated population'; such an expression of an established identity would be antithetical to minor literature's attention to 'becoming and *non*-recognition'.¹¹²

The project of the canonisation and institutionalisation of the novel undertaken by midcentury literary critics would appear to be, in Deleuze and Guattari's terms, 'majoritarian' in its ambition, most overtly in the effort to outline a specifically national history of American literature. And yet we have also seen how these same critics came to portray contemporary fiction as inferior to the traditions of the novel they had recently established, and that this led them to consider the novel as in a possibly terminal state of decline; no sooner had midcentury critics made the case for the novel as a major literary form, in other words, than they suggested it was becoming irrevocably minor. The midcentury novelists I discuss in the book explored whether there were other ways of the novel becoming minor that weren't simply a kind of decline, and whether a certain dislocation or troubling of the concepts of midcentury literary criticism might yield new aesthetic potentialities. To put it in Deleuze and Guattari's terms, these novelists do not repudiate but rather deterritorialise the language of the midcentury literary critical discourse of the novel, so as to gesture to the possibility of a new novel aesthetics captured neither in the critics' description of the novel in its canonical formations nor their narrative of its midcentury nadir. What forms might the novel take, the writers discussed this book wondered, once it has relinquished its major ambitions and given up on greatness, and become instead a genre of limited possibilities and lapsed significance?

There were of course other ways of being minor at midcentury. As suggested above, one convincing way to tell the story of the development of the post-1945 American novel is in terms of the rise of cultural pluralism and the coming to new prominence of previously marginalised literary voices and styles – the story told, in different ways, by Schaub and McGurl. Indeed, as I argue in Chapter 2 in my discussion of Ralph Ellison's work, the novel became the major mode through which minority writers entered the literary mainstream in these decades. But part of my argument here is that although this critical narrative captures much that is crucial to our understanding of the main trajectory of postwar literature, it obscures from view some of the short-lived, less influential aesthetic projects of the period, especially those which are not so easily parsed in terms of sociocultural issues of identity. This book is an attempt to recover one such project.

Certain literary modes were also considered minor by midcentury critics. Popular genres such as detective fiction were dismissed out of hand by the New York Intellectuals and New Critics as being of minor importance because of their association with mass culture.

But other modes played a more complicated role in the midcentury critical discourse described here. Chief among these was literary regionalism, associated at midcentury with Southern fiction, and therefore often looked on kindly by the New Critics.[113] On the one hand, the vital sense of place that characterised Southern fiction was portrayed as an imaginative strength, indicative of a still-living connection to history, tradition, and a religious culture rich with symbolism and moral complexity; but on the other hand, it was also evidence of the reduced 'reach' and narrowing perspective of midcentury fiction. Often historical in its setting, Southern fiction's close proximity to the past was read as symptomatic of a retreat among writers from the complexities of contemporary culture. Southern regionalism was most closely associated with the short story (in the work of Eudora Welty, Katherine Anne Porter, and Flannery O'Connor, for example), a form well-suited both to a focus on place and to the kind of close reading practiced by the New Critics, though regionalism was also a mode experimented with by novelists, such as Caroline Gordon and her husband, Allen Tate. In Chapter 3, I consider regionalism in my analysis of Jean Stafford's engagement with Southern literary culture. Sometimes discussed as a regional writer, I suggest that Stafford's interest in place can be read alongside her preoccupation with symbolism and religious experience as representing a facet of her complex relation and response to New Critical formalism.

Recently, critics have suggested that other, less familiar modes of minor fiction were emerging at midcentury. Mary Esteve has drawn attention to a strain of postwar American fiction engaging with 'liberalism's formal yet pragmatic horizon of redistributive justice', in contrast to the anti-institutional impulse of much midcentury intellectual culture.[114] Texts belonging to the genre of what Esteve calls 'incremental realism' create 'a symbolic economy in which referential figures of liberal activism and welfare-state happiness circulate, albeit inconspicuously and in a minor key'.[115] Incremental realist texts are characterised by an apparent modesty of aesthetic ambition, mirroring the tempered, reformist aspirations of the managerial liberal state, their style gesturing 'toward the near, possible future in which equitable wealth distribution, expansion of public infrastructure, and individual flourishing function as operative ideals'. In this sense, Esteve extends the argument of Michael Szalay's *New Deal Modernism* (2000) by demonstrating the range of ways in which literary fiction engaged with and responded to the apparatus of the liberal state. Although this focus departs from my own interest in the influence midcentury intellectuals had on novelists, I share her aim of tracing the variety of experiments in realist fiction emergent in this period, including 'modest' modes of the novel that appear to reflexively engage with a midcentury sense of limited possibilities, whether aesthetic or political.

My thinking is also in dialogue with the work of critics tracing more recent iterations of minor fiction.[116] Mark McGurl describes how 'modesty of ambition becomes visible as [a] literary mode' in Philip Roth's late quartet of novels, 'Nemeses', which McGurl suggests are characterised by a 'carefully calibrated muting of the outrageous energy' of Roth's earlier fiction. These short novels mourn the death of a particular version of American individualism together with the 'death of a certain historical conception of literature itself,' McGurl argues. Roth's late novels employ 'pointedly traditional literary forms' and suggest that these forms are 'no longer understood, as they were in Roth's youth, and in the youth of literary modernism itself, as forms of enclosure that need to be shattered in the search for an authentic expression of desire', but are instead 'offered as fragile, already-failing vehicles that can carry us, but only for a short while, through the encompassing onslaught of time'. The writers I discuss practised something akin to what McGurl calls 'aesthetic moderation', and in the chapters that follow I also pursue the question of how 'deliberately minor works' might be understood not 'simply [as] a sign of waning creative energies', but rather 'read in [a] more positive or, better, positively negative, light', as purposively self-defeating, or 'already-failing' aesthetic experiments.[117]

Thom Dancer, meanwhile, describes a 'minor mode' of recent Anglophone fiction at odds with 'theories of the contemporary novel that emphasize its capacities to capture and master' the globalised world of the twenty-first century.[118] 'Unlike the global or cosmopolitan novel, the minor novel envisions a more humble function for twenty-first-century fiction,' writes Dancer, 'one that [. . .] values the novel as a form that is explicitly limited, partial [and] provisional.' Building on Deleuze and Guattari's work – and on Leela Gandhi's conception of 'minor globalisation' – Dancer argues that 'by embracing its limited place, its minor function, the contemporary novel regains a kind of oblique or indirect relevance better attuned to the limited ways that the novel might actually make a difference today', faced with the complex catastrophes of globalised injustice and anthropocenic breakdown.[119] While I am less invested in the political stakes of the minor novel, I share Dancer's interest in how a more 'modest' or smaller-scale fiction might 'mak[e] conscious its own profound limits', and how by doing so register a form of 'resistance' to the dominant aesthetics of its historical moment.[120]

The Midcentury Minor Novel

The distinctive project of the midcentury minor novel is perhaps best exemplified in its tendency to stage scenes or instances of aesthetic impasse, wherein the limits of the novel as imagined by midcentury critics are dramatised. In these, what we might call, 'minor moments', the midcentury minor novel performs its own failure, revealing the shortcomings, contradictions, and ambivalences of the midcentury critical discourse of the novel with which it appears to be in concert. In so doing, the novelists discussed in this book engage with the complex textures of midcentury aesthetics, in the process creating fictions at once characteristic and critical of the period's literary culture. These moments of aesthetic impasse take different forms in the novels surveyed in the following chapters.

In Chapter 1, I describe Lionel Trilling's efforts to write a 'minor novel of ideas', in which the value of the novel and the value of ideas are themselves held up to scrutiny. In *The Middle of the Journey* (1947), Trilling explores whether the novel might at once be a cultural form for cultivating the kinds of complex emotional and moral responses celebrated in his criticism, and also a more 'primitive' form, made for the telling of a good story, fit for all kinds of not-so-serious pleasure. His unfinished second novel – posthumously published as *The Journey Abandoned* (2008) – suggests the difficulty in reconciling these two conceptions of the novel, as well as revealing Trilling's ambivalence regarding the changing relationship between universities and literary critics in the immediate postwar period.

In Chapter 2, I explore Eleanor Clark's attempts to both conform to and move beyond the anti-Stalinist aesthetics of the influential *Partisan Review*. Although Clark is best remembered for her travel writing, her fiction, and especially her debut novel *The Bitter Box* (1946), shares the magazine's political outlook and is shaped by the same tradition of European modernism and existentialist thought celebrated in its pages, particularly the work of Kafka. But the novel also offers a critique of the New York Intellectuals' canonical high modernism, breaking free from *Partisan*'s midcentury mood of pessimism and anxiety by breaking into laughter. Drawing on Tyrus Miller's account of late modernist laughter, I compare the role of humour in Clark's novel to that of African-American laughter in the high cultural pluralist aesthetics of Ralph Ellison's *Invisible Man* (1952), a novel concerned, like *The Bitter Box*, with the fallout of 1930s radicalism and the dangers of political progressivism.

In Chapter 3, I move away from the *Partisan* crowd to consider the influence of the New Critics on the work of Jean Stafford, situating her fiction in relation to the midcentury renaissance of another minor mode of fiction – regionalism. Stafford's fiction plays with the ideas of scale and proportion so important to Southern regional writing, while dramatising the limits of the New Critics' quasi-religious conception of symbolism; often, I suggest, her characters fail to develop or function symbolically in quite the ways these critics would have expected. I consider how Stafford's fiction works within and against the interpretative framework not only of the New Criticism but also of psychoanalysis, discussing how her novels *The Mountain Lion* (1947) and *The Catherine Wheel* (1952) at once invite and resist the kinds of symbolic and symptomatic readings these two dominant midcentury intellectual discourses tended to produce.

In Chapter 4, I turn to Richard Stern's neglected 1965 novel *Stitch*, which takes as its subject a series of encounters in Venice between a rudderless Jewish-American writer and a revered elderly sculptor, loosely based on Ezra Pound. Unlike his close friends Saul Bellow and Philip Roth, Stern was always uneasy about embracing the idiomatic first person voice that came to define the postwar 'breakthrough' of Jewish-American fiction; instead, Stern's writing suggests the influence of Yvor Winters and other midcentury formalist critics. But *Stitch* also reveals Stern's ambivalence about formalism, and the high modernist literary values that unwrote it, in its allusions to Pound's antisemitism. In this novel of the 1960s, Stern looks back to the furore of the late 1940s surrounding the decision to award Pound the Bollingen Prize for *The Pisan Cantos* (1948), an episode which became the subject of much debate among Jewish-American intellectuals and a test case for midcentury formalism.

In Chapter 5, I consider John Williams's *Stoner* (1965), by far the best-known of the minor novels discussed. I suggest how the novel reflects the interest pervasive at midcentury in tragedy, both as a mode of thought and as an aesthetic form perhaps no longer available to the contemporary imagination – as though the death of the novel and the death of tragedy, announced by George Steiner in 1961, might somehow be linked. As well as being concerned with the fate of tragedy, *Stoner* captures other intellectual crosscurrents at work in the minor novels discussed in earlier chapters – in its preoccupation with the relation between universities and literary culture, for example, and in its engagement with midcentury formalism. But *Stoner* is also unique among the novels discussed because of its remarkable 'rediscovery' in the early 2000s. I focus on the institutional conditions that gave rise to *Stoner*'s recovery, surveying the changing landscape of late twentieth-century publishing and the impact that reissue series and imprints such as the New York Review Book Classics series have had in reshaping our understanding of midcentury literature.

I have chosen to focus on this set of writers – some of whom will likely be familiar to many readers, others likely not – because each of them engages with a different strand of midcentury thought and aesthetics: Trilling is thinking about the possibility of a kind of 'ideological novel of manners', while Clark is reckoning with the influence of the *Partisan* crowd; Stafford is working through her relation to the New Critics and to Southern literature, while Stern is working through his to high modernism and the emerging field of Jewish-American fiction.[121] Williams, meanwhile, is concerned with the themes of tragedy and institutionality that arise throughout the book, and *Stoner*'s reappraisal allows me to consider the 'afterlife' of the midcentury minor novel. This set of writers is, quite purposefully, not a school or coterie, but a sort of nongroup, for part of my argument is that the midcentury minor novel emerged from not one particular corner of the literary field, but rather across the work of a variety of writers attempting to respond creatively to the commanding influence of midcentury criticism. Although, as will become clear, there are multiple and sometimes surprising points of biographical connection between these writers, they are brought together here because each came in their own way to a version of the same project for the novel, a project that took as its unpromising starting point the notion that the novel may no longer be what it once was. The midcentury minor novel was, I conclude, a kind of failed experiment, one that was ultimately of only marginal importance to the passage of postwar American fiction. But, as I suggest in the Coda, such marginal cases might nonetheless be a useful subject for a more modest sort of literary criticism to pursue.

Notes

1. See, for example, Walter Kalaidjian, *American Culture Between the Wars: Revisionary Modernism & Postmodern Critique* (New York: Columbia University Press, 1993). For an overview of developments in modernist studies, see Mark Wollaeger, 'Scholarship's Turn', in Douglas Mao (ed.), *The New Modernist Studies* (Cambridge: Cambridge University Press, 2021), pp. 41–64.
2. See Michael Denning, *The Cultural Front: The Laboring of American Culture in the Twentieth Century* (London: Verso, 1996); Barbara Foley, *Radical Representations: Politics and Form in US Proletarian Fiction, 1929–1941* (Durham, NC: Duke University Press, 1993); Alan Wald, *Writing From the Left: New Essays on Radical Culture and Politics* (London: Verso, 1994).
3. Ian Afflerbach, *Making Liberalism New: American Intellectuals, Modern Literature, and the Rewriting of a Political Tradition* (Baltimore: Johns Hopkins University Press, 2021), 9.
4. Sean McCann, *A Pinnacle of Feeling: American Literature and Presidential Government* (Durham, NC: Duke University Press, 2008); Mark McGurl, *The Program Era: Postwar Fiction and the Rise of Creative Writing* (Cambridge, MA: Harvard University Press, 2009); Michael Szalay, *New Deal Modernism: American Literature and the Invention of the Welfare State* (Durham, NC: Duke University Press, 2000); Stephen Schryer, *Fantasies of the New Class: Ideologies of Professionalism in Post-World War II American Fiction* (New York: Columbia University Press, 2011).
5. Claire Seiler, *Midcentury Suspension: Literature and Feeling in the Wake of World War II* (New York: Columbia University Press, 2020), 34.

6. Amanda Anderson, *Bleak Liberalism* (Chicago: University of Chicago Press, 2016), 26; Benjamin Mangrum, *Land of Tomorrow: Postwar Fiction and the Crisis of American Liberalism* (Oxford: Oxford University Press, 2018), 2. See also Afflerbach, *Making Liberalism New*; Mark Greif, *The Age of the Crisis of Man: Thought and Fiction in America, 1933–1973* (Princeton: Princeton University Press, 2015).
7. Mangrum, *Land of Tomorrow*, 2.
8. On late modernism in the US context, see Robert Genter, *Late Modernism: Art, Culture, and Politics in Cold War America* (Philadelphia: University of Pennsylvania Press, 2010). For the British context, see Marina MacKay, *Modernism and World War II* (Cambridge: Cambridge University Press, 2007); Jed Esty, *A Shrinking Island: Modernism and National Culture in England* (Princeton: Princeton University Press, 2003); Julia Jordan, *Late Modernism and the Avant-Garde British Novel* (Oxford: Oxford University Press, 2020); Doug Battersby, *Troubling Late Modernism: Ethics, Feeling, and the Novel Form* (Oxford: Oxford University Press, 2022).
9. Tyrus Miller, *Late Modernism: Politics, Fiction, and the Arts Between the World Wars* (Berkeley: University of California Press, 1999), 7.
10. Oxford University Press's 'Oxford Mid-Century Studies Series', edited by Marina MacKay and Lyndsey Stonebridge, was established in 2016, with a focus on British midcentury literary culture. See also Marina MacKay and Lyndsey Stonebridge (eds), *British Fiction After Modernism: The Novel at Mid-Century* (London: Routledge, 2007).
11. Seiler, *Midcentury Suspension*, 35.
12. Ibid., 26.
13. MacKay and Stonebridge describe the midcentury period as 'a critically awkward phase of twentieth-century writing'. 'Introduction: British Fiction after Modernism', in MacKay and Stonebridge (eds), *British Fiction After Modernism*, pp. 1–16 (1).
14. Greif, *The Age of the Crisis of Man*, 114, 106.
15. Lionel Trilling, 'Manners, Morals, and the Novel', in *The Liberal Imagination: Essays on Literature and Society* [1950] (New York: New York Review Books Classics, 2008), pp. 205–22 (222).
16. 'Trilling probably exaggerated only very slightly,' David Hollinger writes, 'when he observed in 1967 that the experience of participating in, or responding to Stalinism, "created the American intellectual class as we know it"'. Hollinger, *In the American Province: Studies in the History and Historiography of Ideas* (Bloomington: Indiana University Press, 1985), 67. See Lionel Trilling, 'A Novel of the Thirties', in *The Last Decade: Essays and Reviews, 1965–75* (Oxford: Oxford University Press, 1982), pp. 3–24.
17. The New York Intellectuals 'held a deep-seated distrust of the programmatic commitments of liberal bureaucracy,' Benjamin Mangrum writes. 'This distrust came in part from [their] debts to Leon Trotsky and his critique of the Soviet Union's Stalinist bureaucracy. They were allergic to most types of organizational authority.' Mangrum, *Land of Tomorrow*, 23.

18. On affinities between the Frankfurt School and midcentury American intellectual culture, see Greif, *The Age of the Crisis of Man*, 57–9. On connections between Trilling and Adorno, see Anderson, *Bleak Liberalism*, 103–7.
19. Afflerbach, *Making Liberalism New*, 104; Anderson, *Bleak Liberalism*, 28. On the widespread interest in tragedy – as both a mode of thought and a dramatic form – emerging in the 1940s, see Deborah Nelson, *Tough Enough: Arbus, Arendt, Didion, McCarthy, Sontag, Weil* (Chicago: University of Chicago Press, 2017), 23–39; Afflerbach, *Making Liberalism New*, 103–36; Cornel West, 'Pragmatism and the Sense of the Tragic', in *The Cornel West Reader* (New York: Basic Civitas Books, 2000), pp. 174–82. See also Reinhold Niebuhr, *Beyond Tragedy: A Christian Interpretation of History* (New York: Scribner, 1937).
20. Afflerbach, *Making Liberalism New*, 104; Anderson, *Bleak Liberalism*, 25.
21. Lionel Trilling, 'Reality in America', in *The Liberal Imagination*, pp. 3–21 (3). Richard Chase, *The American Novel and its Tradition* (Baltimore: Johns Hopkins University Press, 1957), 186.
22. Lionel Trilling, 'Artists and the "Societal" Function', *Kenyon Review*, Vol. 4, No. 3 (Autumn 1942), pp. 425–30 (428). Emphasis original.
23. Schryer, *Fantasies of the New Class*, 9.
24. ibid., 6; Anderson, *Bleak Liberalism*, 101.
25. Hollinger, *In the American Province*, 85. Emphasis original.
26. Anderson, *Bleak Liberalism*, 113; Schryer, *Fantasies of the New Class*, 4; Afflerbach, *Making Liberalism New*, 104.
27. Afflerbach, *Making Liberalism New*, 105.
28. Richard Chase, 'Art, Nature, Politics', *Kenyon Review*, Vol. 12, No. 4 (Autumn 1950), pp. 580–94 (590–1). Wallace was the Progressive Party's presidential nominee in 1948.
29. David Russell, *Tact: Aesthetic Liberalism and the Essay Form in Nineteenth-Century Britain* (Princeton: Princeton University Press, 2017), 4.
30. Mangrum, *Land of Tomorrow*, 44; Schryer, *Fantasies of the New Class*, 30, quoted in Mangrum, *Land of Tomorrow*, 45.
31. See Mangrum, *Land of Tomorrow*, 25–6.
32. On the similarities between the two critical camps, see Thomas Hill Schaub, *American Fiction in the Cold War* (Madison: University of Wisconsin Press, 1991), 25–49.
33. Terry Cooney, *The Rise of The New York Intellectuals: Partisan Review and Its Circle* (Madison: University of Wisconsin Press, 1986), 144. On the cosmopolitanism or 'antiprovincialism' of the *Partisan* crowd, see Hollinger, *In the American Province*, 60–5. For an alternative take on the relation between European émigré intellectual and American mass culture, see Will Norman, *Transatlantic Aliens: Modernism, Exile, and Culture in Midcentury America* (Baltimore: Johns Hopkins University Press, 2016).
34. Hannah Arendt, 'Franz Kafka: A Revaluation', *Partisan Review*, Vol. 11, No. 4 (Fall 1944), pp. 412–22 (414); Philip Rahv, 'Dostoevsky and Politics', *Partisan Review*, Vol. 5, No. 2 (July 1938), pp. 25–36 (27).
35. Hollinger, *In the American Province*, 79.

36. Philip Rahv, 'Henry James's America', *New York Times Book Review*, 2 March 1947, 4. On the influence of Cowley's *Portable Faulkner*, see Greif, *The Age of the Crisis of Man*, 116–19. Morton Zabel's *Portable Conrad* (1948) did something similar for the author of *Under Western Eyes* (1911), a novel that became widely admired at midcentury.
37. On the rise of American Studies, see Russell Reising, *The Unusable Past: Theory and the Study of American Literature* (London: Routledge, 1986); Morris Dickstein, *Double Agent: The Critic and Society* (Oxford: Oxford University Press, 1992), 136–42.
38. Reising, *The Unusable Past*, 116.
39. '[T]he American Renaissance writers were reshaped into modern writers, bristling with irony, ambiguity, and the tragic sense of life'. Dickstein, *Double Agent*, 142.
40. Chase, *The American Novel and its Tradition*, viii. Chase suggests that American romances are 'literary hybrids' (14). Jed Esty observes, 'The hoary Cold War idea that America is a land of contradictions and Britain one of staid compromise is the taxonomic bedrock for Chase's coding of romance and realism as American and British, innocent and imperial, respectively.' Esty, 'Realism Wars', *Novel: A Forum on Fiction*, Vol. 49, No. 2 (August 2016), pp. 316–42 (327).
41. For an overview of the New Americanist critique, see Johannes Voelz, *Transcendental Resistance: The New Americanists and Emerson's Challenge* (New Hampshire: Dartmouth University Press, 2010).
42. See Cooney, *The Rise of the New York Intellectuals*, 85–6.
43. Hannah Arendt, 'What is Existenz Philosophy?', *Partisan Review*, Vol. 13, No. 1 (Winter 1946), pp. 34–56 (35). 'Nothing was more clear about the modern movement to most of its American commentators than its international character,' writes David Hollinger, suggesting that the *Partisan* crowd aimed to outline 'a distinctly modern literature that spoke to universal human concerns'. Hollinger, *In the American Province*, 88. The midcentury discourse of anxiety is discussed in Claire Seiler's *Midcentury Suspension*, and I take it up in Chapter 2. On alienation in relation to modernism and the modest Jewish backgrounds of some of the New York Intellectuals, see Dickstein, *Double Agent*, 91–100. Marcus Klein argues that alienation 'is the defining attitude of our "modern" literature' but one which he suggests loses its intellectual purchase and imaginative pull at around midcentury. Klein, *After Alienation: American Novels in Mid-Century* (New York: World Publishing Company, 1964), 20.
44. See Gerald Graff, *Professing Literature: An Institutional History* [1987] (Chicago: University of Chicago Press, 2008), 162–79.
45. See Cooney, *The Rise of The New York Intellectuals*; John Duvall, 'New Criticism's Major Journals', in Peter Brooker and Andrew Thacker (eds), *The Oxford Critical and Cultural History of Modernist Magazines: Volume II: North America 1894–1960* (Oxford: Oxford University Press, 2015), pp. 928–44; Loren Glass, 'From Consensus to Conflict: Little Magazines in the 1950s', in Steven Belletto (ed.), *American Literature in Transition, 1950–1960* (Cambridge: Cambridge University Press, 2017), pp. 299–312. I discuss the *Southern Review* in Chapter 3.

46. See George Hutchinson, *Facing the Abyss: American Literature and Culture in the 1940s* (New York: Columbia University Press, 2018), 15–42.
47. Schryer, *Fantasies of the New Class*, 1.
48. Robert Lowell, 'Robert Lowell, The Art of Poetry', interview by Frederick Seidel, *Paris Review*, Issue 25 (Winter–Spring 1961). Available at: https://www.theparisreview.org/interviews/4664/the-art-of-poetry-no-3-robert-lowell
49. R. W. B. Lewis mentions Bellow and Ellison as exceptions to his general negative opinion of contemporary fiction in the conclusion to *The American Adam: Innocence, Tragedy, and Tradition in the Nineteenth Century* (Chicago: University of Chicago Press, 1955), 96. The tendency to frame *The Adventures of Augie March* and *Invisible Man* as turning points in the fortunes of the American novel continues in recent work on the period's literary culture. See, for example, Greif, *The Age of the Crisis of Man*. In 1948, John Berryman singled out Stafford as 'the one new writer who [. . .] will not disappoint us'. Berryman, et al., 'The State of American Writing, 1948: A Symposium', *Partisan Review*, Vol. 15, No. 8 (August 1948), pp. 855–93 (860). Stafford often featured in later discussions of the 'New Fiction' of the 1940s. See Chester Eisinger, *Fiction of the Forties* (Chicago: University of Chicago Press, 1963), 294–305.
50. John Crowe Ransom, 'The State of American Writing, 1948: A Symposium', 880; Mark Schorer, 'Technique as Discovery', *Hudson Review*, Vol. 1, No. 1 (Spring 1948), pp. 67–87 (80).
51. John Aldridge, *After the Lost Generation: A Critical Study of the Writers of Two Wars* (New York: McGraw-Hill, 1951), 88.
52. Ihab Hassan, *Radical Innocence: Studies in the Contemporary American Novel* (Princeton: Princeton University Press, 1961), 107–8.
53. John Aldridge, *In Search of Heresy: American Literature in an Age of Conformity* (New York: McGraw-Hill, 1956), 4. On a similar theme, see Irving Howe, 'The Age of Conformity', *Dissent*, 1 January 1954. Available at: https://www.dissentmagazine.org/online_articles/irving-howe-voice-still-heard-this-age-of-conformity
54. Klein, *After Alienation*, 20, 22.
55. Lewis, *The American Adam*, 195–6.
56. See Greif, *The Age of the Crisis of Man*, 104–7.
57. Granville Hicks, 'Foreword', in Hicks (ed.), *The Living Novel: A Symposium* (New York: Macmillan, 1957), pp. vii–xii (viii).
58. Yvor Winters, 'Problems for the Modern Critic of Literature', *Hudson Review*, Vol. 9, No. 3 (Autumn 1956), pp. 325–86 (352, 353).
59. Lionel Trilling, 'Art and Fortune', in *The Liberal Imagination*, pp. 255–80 (255, 263). See also Lionel Trilling, 'The Novel Alive or Dead', in *A Gathering of Fugitives* (Boston: Beacon Press, 1956), pp. 125–32.
60. Berryman, 'The State of American Writing', 860.
61. Saul Bellow, 'Distractions of a Fiction Writer', in Hicks (ed.), *The Living Novel*, pp. 1–20 (16).
62. Aldridge, *In Search of Heresy*, 16.
63. Robert Gorham Davis, 'The State of American Writing, 1948', 866.
64. Klein, *After Alienation*, 24.
65. Greenberg, 'The State of American Writing, 1948', 876.

66. Bellow, 'Distractions of a Fiction Writer', 6.
67. Trilling, 'Manners, Morals, and the Novel', 222. Malcolm Cowley suggested that 'the really new development' in literary culture 'since 1940 has been in the field of criticism'. Cowley, *The Literary Situation* (New York: Viking, 1954), 4.
68. Robert Seguin, *Around Quitting Time: Work and Middle-Class Fantasy in American Fiction* (Durham, NC: Duke University Press, 2001), 135.
69. Stephen Schryer suggests that midcentury critics' curious position relied upon them 'ignoring or mystifying the "sphere of strategy" within which they work – the institutions of the post-New Deal state. As a result, [the critics] embraced simultaneously impotent and exaggerated models of intellectual agency'. Schryer, *Fantasies of the New Class*, 6.
70. Lionel Trilling, Letter to John Crowe Ransom, 21 September 1948, in Adam Kirsch (ed.), *Life in Culture: Selected Letters of Lionel Trilling* (New York: Farrar, Straus and Giroux, 2018), pp. 171–5 (173).
71. Hollinger, *In the American Province*, 82.
72. On this problem, see Lionel Trilling, 'On the Teaching of Modern Literature' [1961], in Leon Wieseltier (ed.), *The Moral Obligation to be Intelligent: Selected Essays of Lionel Trilling* (New York: Farrar, Straus and Giroux, 2000), pp. 381–401.
73. Mangrum, *Land of Tomorrow*, 46.
74. Lionel Trilling, 'The Meaning of a Literary Idea', in *The Liberal Imagination*, pp. 281–303 (292).
75. Arthur Mizener, 'The Novel of Manners in America', *The Kenyon Review*, Vol. 12, No. 1 (Winter 1950), pp. 1–19 (1, 2).
76. Allen Tate, 'Techniques of Fiction', *The Sewanee Review*, Vol. 52, No. 2 (Spring 1944), pp. 210–25 (211).
77. 'The virtue of the modern novelist – from James and Conrad down – is not only that he pays so much attention to his medium, but that [. . .] he discovers through it a new subject matter [. . .] [Technique] not only [. . .] *contains* intellectual and moral implications [. . .] it *discovers* them.' Schorer, 'Technique as Discovery', 73–4. Emphasis original.
78. Tate, 'Techniques of Fiction', 225.
79. Hollinger, *In the American Province*, 82, 83.
80. Trilling, 'Manners, Morals, and the Novel', 212.
81. Trilling, 'Art and Fortune', 261.
82. Trilling, 'Manners, Morals, and the Novel', 219; Trilling, 'Preface', in *The Liberal Imagination*, pp. xv–xxi (xxi).
83. Trilling, 'The Princess Casamassima', in *The Liberal Imagination*, pp. 58–92 (64, 65). Trilling quotes James's phrase again in *Sincerity and Authenticity* (Cambridge, MA: Harvard University Press, 1972), 134.
84. Trilling, 'Art and Fortune', 279.
85. Lionel Trilling, Letter to Eleanor Clark, 5 June 1939, Box 33, Folder 486, Eleanor Clark Papers, Beinecke Rare Book & Manuscript Library, Yale University.
86. Chase, *The American Novel and its Tradition*, 158.
87. Ibid., viii, xii, 7, 14, 11.
88. Ibid., 5; F. R. Leavis, *The Great Tradition* [1948] (Harmondsworth: Penguin, 1972), 39.

89. Leslie Fiedler, *Love and Death in the American Novel* [1960] (Funks Grove, IL: Dalkey Archive Press, 1997), 24. Chase's argument is more directly echoed by Daniel Hoffman, who suggests that 'the realistic fashion emerging in late eighteenth-century fiction made small impact in America. Instead, our prose writers were attracted to a fiction mode which in England flourished briefly as a minor, obverse reaction to the dominant realism of Defoe and Fielding.' Hoffman, *Form and Fable in American Fiction* [1961] (Charlottesville: University of Virginia Press, 1994), 7.
90. Schaub's study is often cited by critics discussing midcentury literary culture, including Afflerbach and Greif. See also Sam Reese, *The Short Story in Midcentury America: Countercultural Form in the Work of Bowles, McCarthy, Welty, and Williams* (Baton Rouge: Louisiana State University Press, 2017).
91. Schaub, *American Fiction in the Cold War*, 50.
92. Ibid., 50, 51.
93. Ralph Ellison, 'Society, Morality and the Novel', in John Callahan (ed.), *The Collected Essays of Ralph Ellison* (New York: Modern Library Classics, 2003), pp. 698–729 (713).
94. Saul Bellow, 'The Art of Fiction: Saul Bellow' [1966], interview by Gordon Lloyd Harper, in Gloria Cronin and Ben Siegel (eds), *Conversations with Saul Bellow* (Jackson: University Press of Mississippi, 1994), pp. 58–76 (63).
95. Schaub, *American Fiction in the Cold War*, 55.
96. Ibid., 55–62.
97. Ibid., 70.
98. Ibid., 69–70.
99. Ibid., 73.
100. Ibid., 81.
101. Technomodernism is 'best understood as a tweaking of the term "postmodernism", in that it emphasizes the all-important engagement of postmodern literature with information technology'. McGurl, *The Program Era*, 32.
102. McGurl, *The Program Era*, 32.
103. Ibid., 57.
104. In this regard, my argument echoes that of early literary historians of midcentury fiction, such as Chester Eisinger. In *Fiction of the Forties*, Eisinger argues that the 'New Fiction' of this period was influenced by both 'the new criticism and the tradition of romance in the American novel'. He suggests that 'the preoccupation with technique, represented by the new criticism, had its impact on the followers of Henry James, the writers of the new novels of manners', while 'the heavy cargo of symbol and myth shrouded in a gothic ambience, represented by the tradition of romance, made the new fiction positively glow in its distorted brilliance' (19–20).
105. Other recent studies draw on Deleuze and Guattari's account of minor literature to describe forms of midcentury writing. See Reese, *The Short Story in Midcentury America*, 44–6; Nicholas Spencer, 'Late Modernism and the Minor Literature of Weldon Kee's Poetry', in Daniel A. Siedell (ed.), *Weldon Kees and the Arts at Midcentury* (Lincoln: University of Nebraska Press, 2003), pp. 147–86.

106. Claire Colebrook, *Gilles Deleuze* (London: Routledge, 2001), 122.
107. Ibid., 103.
108. Gilles Deleuze and Félix Guattari, *Kafka: Toward a Minor Literature* [French, 1977], trans. Dana Polan (Minneapolis: University of Minnesota Press, 1986), 18.
109. Ronald Bogue, *Deleuze on Literature* (London: Routledge, 2003), 95, 96; Deleuze and Guattari, *Kafka*, 26.
110. Gilles Deleuze, *The Logic of Sense* [French, 1969], trans. Mark Lester with Charles Stivale (New York: Columbia University Press, 1990), 88; Gilles Deleuze and Félix Guattari, *A Thousand Plateaus* [French, 1980], trans. Brian Massumi (Minneapolis: University of Minnesota Press, 1987), 125, both quoted in Bogue, *Deleuze on Literature*, 101.
111. Deleuze and Guattari, *Kafka*, 27.
112. Colebrook, *Gilles Deleuze*, 104, 118.
113. A turn to regionalism at midcentury wasn't just a Southern, nor even an American phenomenon. Scholars of modern British literature have re-evaluated the move towards the regional, local and provincial in late modernist and midcentury English writing. See Jed Esty's discussion of midcentury provincialism in his analysis of a 'transition in English literature from metropolitan modernism to a minor culture'. Esty, *A Shrinking Island*, 105. See also David James, 'Localizing Late Modernism: Interwar Regionalism and the Genesis of the "Micro Novel"', *Journal of Modern Literature*, Vol. 32, No. 4 (Summer 2009), pp. 43–64.
114. Mary Esteve, *Incremental Realism: Postwar American Fiction, Happiness, and Welfare-State Liberalism* (Stanford: Stanford University Press, 2021), 5.
115. Ibid., 4.
116. See also Jennifer Soong, 'The Minor Poet: A Case of John Wieners', *Textual Practice*, 7 December 2022.
117. Mark McGurl, 'Philip Roth's Modest Phase', *Post45*, 12 April 2019. Available at: https://post45.org/2019/04/philip-roths-modest-phase/.
118. Thom Dancer, *Critical Modesty in Contemporary Fiction* (Oxford: Oxford University Press, 2021), 151, 154.
119. Ibid., 154.
120. Ibid., 153, 150.
121. Anderson, *Bleak Liberalism*, 32.

CHAPTER 1

'A refusal to be great': Lionel Trilling's *The Middle of the Journey* and *The Journey Abandoned* and the Minor Novel of Ideas

'E. M. Forster is for me the only living novelist who can be read again and again,' Lionel Trilling wrote in 1942.[1] *E. M. Forster* (1943) was Trilling's second book, following another single-author study, an intellectual biography of Matthew Arnold, based on his doctoral thesis and published in 1939. Unlike the Arnold book, the study of Forster was written in a 'concentrated rush' of just a few weeks and might be described as a work of minor criticism of a kind no longer much in vogue: a series of close readings of individual novels brought together under a broad thesis – a method not entirely unlike the one I adopt in this book.[2] In 1964, in the preface to the second edition, Trilling looked back to the book's origins, suggesting that he had tried to recruit Forster in 'a quarrel' he was having in the early 1940s 'with American literature as at that time it was established, and against what seemed to me its dullness and its pious social simplicities I enlisted Mr. Forster's vivacity, complexity, and irony'.[3] The Forster book is best remembered for its introductory chapter, in which Trilling sets out an early iteration of the argument he will put forward in *The Liberal Imagination* (1950). For Trilling, Forster embodies what he will call in that later work a 'flexibility of mind', an awareness of the 'contradictions, paradoxes and dangers of living the moral life'.[4] Trilling's Forster is 'deeply at odds with the liberal mind', despite the fact that 'all his novels are politically and morally tendentious and always in the liberal direction'.[5] Forster seems to be playing the liberal 'game' but is in fact 'at war with the liberal imagination' in his worldly insistence on the 'inextricable tangle of good and evil', in his always hedged endorsement of liberalism's faith in progress and organisation.[6]

Much of Trilling's discussion of Forster in fact prefigures the tenor and direction of his argument in the essays of *The Liberal Imagination*. He admires Forster's portrayals of liberal characters caught in the ironies produced by their attachment to cherished though often woolly political ideals ('a "cherished goal" forbids that we stop to consider how we reach it, or if we may not destroy it in trying to reach it the wrong way' – 'Reality in America' [1946]).[7] He also praises Forster for his plots involving characters of different social classes struggling to understand each other, and for his refusal to treat working-class characters as paragons of virtue ('The literature of our liberal democracy pets and dandles its underprivileged characters' – 'The Princess Casamassima' [1948]).[8] He admires Forster's unembarrassed treatment of finance and commerce, which Trilling thought of as the oil that greased the wheels of the novels he liked best ('every situation in Dostoevski, no matter how spiritual, starts with a point of social pride and a certain number of rubles' – 'Manners, Morals, and the Novel' [1948]).[9] And he approves of Forster's recognition of man's tragic limitations, in contrast to 'liberalism's incompetence before tragedy'.[10]

Trilling is also drawn to Forster's treatment of friendship. He never quite says this in the Forster book, but he does focus on the theme of friendship in his discussion of *The Longest Journey* (1907) in 'Manners, Morals, and the Novel'. Trilling describes Stephen's friendship with a local shepherd, noting that Stephen 'outrages the feelings of certain intelligent, liberal, democratic people in the book by his treatment of this friend' when the shepherd fails to repay a loan and reneges on a bargain:

> Stephen cannot think of the shepherd as the poor, nor, although he is a country laborer, as an object of research [. . .]; he is rather a reciprocating subject in a relationship of affection – as we say, a friend – and therefore liable to anger and required to pay his debts. But this view is held to be deficient in intelligence, liberalism, and democracy.[11]

Most of Forster's novels are plotted around attempts at friendship, often between men, and often reaching across boundaries of class or ethnicity. As others have noted, Forster explores the idea of friendship as a proto-political relationship, an idea informed by the Aristotelian tradition in which the demands of friendship are conceived of as preparation for the demands of democratic citizenship.[12] There is also an interest in Forster in friendship as an alternative to organised politics, an escape from nationalism and other forms of non-voluntary community.[13] Forster sometimes wonders in his fiction about the possibility of a 'friendship office', but part of friendship's appeal to him is of a relation in which moral values related to politics – justice, equality, a recognition of the other's rights – can be instantiated beyond the reach of any institution.[14]

This is also part of the appeal of friendship for Trilling; like many midcentury intellectuals, he was distrustful of institutions. In the preface to *The Liberal Imagination*, he acknowledges the 'necessity' of the liberal state's 'organizational impulse' as part of its effort to arrange 'the elements of life in a rational way'. But he cautions that 'organization means delegation, and agencies, and bureaus, and technicians, and that the ideas that can survive' this institutional apparatus 'incline to be ideas of a certain kind and of a certain simplicity'.[15] The institution Trilling knew best was the university. During his long association with Columbia, the university changed dramatically, and so too did the study of literature, mostly in ways Trilling felt displayed the same liberal proclivity for simplification.[16] 'I wonder if you ever get a notion of how established the critical idea has become,' Trilling wrote to John Crowe Ransom, the leading New Critic, in 1948, worrying that 'we – I mean we critics – ha[ve] by now become institutionalized [. . .] the danger comes that all that was won with difficulty will turn into academic cliché, given back to us by almost all the students who are at all bright'.[17] Trilling was never quite at home at Columbia, certainly not in the way Forster was at home at Cambridge. His private journals – extracts from which were published posthumously in *Partisan Review* – reveal how, early in his career, he fought for his job as an instructor, calling out the not-so-subtle antisemitism that lay behind attempts to fire him.[18] These journals also show his disillusionment with university life, even as he achieved professional success. In 1948, on learning he had been promoted to the rank of full professor, he recorded that the title seemed like a 'great hoax'.[19]

Trilling was also wary of friendship, however, especially when he felt a relationship mixed the personal with the professional, as was often the case in Morningside Heights. In February 1948, he wrote to his Columbia colleague Richard Chase to apologise for his 'inarticulacies and rigidities in personal relationships', explaining how, despite his 'appearance of a fairly easy communicability', he often 'rears back in the face of affection and praise'.[20] William Phillips, a *Partisan* editor and long-time friend, suggested that Trilling 'was able to preserve his working self by disassociating himself from the draining and time-consuming entanglements of human relations'.[21] Morris Dickstein, a former student, recalled that Trilling had 'an aloof but gracious amiability that did not make him particularly accessible'.[22] To Chase, Trilling describes how he finds it difficult to give an honest assessment of a friend's work because of an 'inadequacy of *affectionate aggression*' and a 'fear of his displeasure at my displeasure'.[23] This mirrors the explanation Trilling gives in the preface to the second edition of *E. M. Forster* as to why he has not revised the book. In the years since it first appeared, Trilling writes, he and Forster 'have become – I hope Mr. Forster will allow me to say – friends', and though 'friendship, I am sure, does not make disinterested criticism impossible', it does 'sometimes make it difficult'.[24] Arnoldian disinterestedness is incompatible with Forsterian friendship, then; as though Trilling couldn't conceive of a friendly sort of criticism. Or as though, because institutional relations were always getting in the way of personal ones, it was wise to try to separate the two as best you could. Friendship does, however, as we shall see, play a role in Trilling's fiction, and, as in Forster's work, its promises and failures become attached to the promises and failures of political organisation and institutionality, Trilling replacing Forster's focus on Oxbridge, public schools and the apparatus of empire with an attention to the midcentury bureaucracy of the modern university, and to the new private foundations that would sponsor it.

'Yes – oh, dear, yes – the novel tells a story'

Trilling suggests that the qualities he admires in Forster's work stem from Forster's particular conception of himself as a novelist: his 'refusal to be great'. Forster's refusal to be great can be 'sometimes irritating', Trilling admits, but it embodies an important 'moral intention'. For Forster, 'Greatness in literature [has] some affinity with greatness in government and war, suggesting power [. . .] a touch of the imperial and imperious'.[25] Instead, Forster exhibits a 'relaxation' of will and style that accepts 'the human fact as we know it', acceding to the limitations of human possibility.[26] Like Keats's negative capability – the urge to take 'the dialectical view of any large question' and avoid any 'final judgment', as Trilling puts it in his essay on Keats – Forster's refusal of greatness became for Trilling a model for the moral imagination.[27] The giving up of greatness matched the chastened political mood of the postwar years; refusing to be great could mean the negation of both an imperialist will to power and a liberal belief in progress. 'If, as some think, ours is an "interregnum" period, then the Forster-Trilling perspective would seem natural and appropriate,' Irving Kristol suggested in a review of *E. M. Forster*. 'It is a restrictive and somewhat alien focus, unwarmed by the expansive enthusiasm we have been accustomed to expending on matters of salvation.'[28] Forster's refusal of greatness involved the acceptance of such restrictions, an acceptance that might appear to be a kind of quietism but which Trilling suggests might be quietly liberating.

In refusing to be great, Forster also refuses to conceive of the novel as a major form, or to take the art of the novel entirely seriously. 'What does a novel do?' Forster asks in *Aspects of the Novel* (1927), to which the answer is an embarrassed, 'Yes – oh, dear, yes – the novel tells a story [. . .] That is the highest factor common to all novels, and I wish that it was not so, that it could be something different – melody, or perception of the truth, not this low atavistic form.'[29] Forster's novels are crammed full of story. Characterised by a 'judicious imperturbability,' as Trilling puts it, his fiction 'delights in surprise' – a good, mithridatic inoculation for complacent liberals who are 'always being surprised' by events.[30] Forster's 'addiction to sudden death' in his novels suggests how he happily 'plays with his genre', though it is a serious kind of play.[31] Nor is he 'above an explanatory footnote', feeling no obligation to keep to what Trilling calls – with a nod to Percy Lubbock's *The Craft of Fiction* (1921) – 'the sacred doctrine of "point of view"'.[32] Instead, as another midcentury critic writes, Forster looks back to a nineteenth-century model of the novel wherein the 'relation between author and reader [. . .] was frank and friendly'.[33]

Trilling was ambivalent about greatness. He had 'sympathy with the ambition of the great novelists,' Adam Kirsch writes, but he also suspected that the novelist's aspiration to greatness was a kind self-aggrandising madness.[34] In an entry in his private journal from around 1966 – after he had all but given up his own ambitions to be a novelist – Trilling, surveying the success of the slightly younger Jewish-American fiction writers who came to prominence at around midcentury, reflects that:

> [T]he artist derives his powers [. . .] from a species of insanity, from megalomania, from his absurd belief in his own myth. This is what accounts for the achievement of Mailer and Bellow and even Malamud. They believe they are great men [. . .] To impose, to impose: this is their single aim [. . .] I defeated myself long ago when I rejected the way of chutzpah and mishagass in favor of reason and diffidence.[35]

The slip into Yiddish is interesting, to be sure, and speaks to the contrasting ways in which Trilling and this younger generation of writers construed the relation between their writing and their Jewishness – a topic I return to in Chapter 4, in my discussion of Richard Stern's fiction.[36] Here, we might note how, rather like his suggestion that in Forster's fiction there is only ever 'good-and-evil', greatness for Trilling is always a mixed bag; there is only ever achievement-and-disappointment, victory-and-defeat, informed always by a sense of the costs involved either in embracing the grandeur of one's ambition or in repudiating it ('Hyacinth recognizes what very few people wish to admit, that civilization has a price, and a high one' – 'The Princess Casamassima').[37] Trilling was attracted and repelled by greatness (a little like he was by Jewishness). His uncertainty is nicely captured in the unlikely strength of feeling he had towards Ernest Hemingway. In a 1933 entry in his journal, he describes a letter he has seen from Hemingway to the critic Clifton Fadiman. 'A crazy letter [. . .] self-revealing, arrogant, scared, trivial, absurd: yet [I] felt from reading it how right such a man is compared to the "good minds" of my university life [. . .] how his life

[. . .] is a better life than anyone I know could live, and right for his job. And how far-far-far I am going from being a writer.'[38] Greatness as the reckless abandonment of restraint, then, in contrast to the institutionalised rationalism and sobriety of the life of the critic in the university.

Forster gave Trilling a way to think of the repudiation of greatness as a kind of hard-won victory, or a noble sacrifice ('"Life's nothing," Henry James wrote to a young friend, " – unless heroic and sacrificial"' – 'The Princess Casamassima').[39] Or, as Adam Phillips puts it, 'Forster is Trilling's opportunity [. . .] to find a respectable, legitimate decadence for himself', a more temperate model to follow than Hemingway.[40] And crucially for my argument, the identification with Forster was generative not only because it spoke to Trilling's ambivalence about greatness and personal ambition, but also because it connected to his ambivalence about the novel form itself. Trilling was uncertain what and how much we should expect from novels; he didn't know if we should look to a novel for greatness. He certainly never had much time for what he called the 'legend' of '*the* Great American Novel, which was always imagined to be as solitary and omniseminous as the Great White Whale'.[41] And although he was never really a 'death of the novel' kind of critic, Trilling did wonder whether 'the novel was better off when it was more humbly conceived than it is now'.[42] On the one hand, *The Liberal Imagination* suggests that the novel can be 'a kind of dynamic refuge from formal politics', as Amanda Anderson argues, through which one might cultivate an aesthetic sensibility that could help 'to reorient moral and political thought' (much like friendship might be the proto-political site for the elaboration of civic virtues).[43] The force and appeal of much of Trilling's criticism is the idea that literature can be the arena in which 'flexibility of mind' and an appreciation of 'variousness and possibility' are fostered.[44] But on the other hand, Trilling, like other midcentury critics, was uncertain as to whether the contemporary novel could still perform this cultural work – and indeed whether the novel had in fact ever done so in America.

Trilling worried that American culture had come to 'overvalue' the novel by 'demand[ing] that it change the world'.[45] 'One of the things I feel is that literature has been injured by being made to do more work and of a different kind than is proper,' he wrote to Newton Arvin in May 1942, shortly after his essay on Forster had been published in the *Kenyon Review*.[46] He had chiefly in mind the ways in which literature had been put in the service of progressive politics in the 1930s – not just in the promotion by Marxist critics of the naturalism of proletarian fiction, but also in the broader tendency to judge literary works by their adherence to progressive values. Such a tendency was, Trilling argued, apparent in the high estimation of John Steinbeck's work, and in the preference among liberal critics for Theodore Dreiser over Henry James. Trilling argued that this tendency was indicative of the poverty of the liberal imagination: its inadequate conception of reality, in which the world is crudely separated from 'mind'; its reductive understanding of ideas, hamstrung by a rigid belief in scientific rationalism, which fails to recognise ideas 'as living things [. . .] susceptible of growth and development by their very nature'; and, relatedly, its misperception of culture as 'a flow' or 'a confluence', rather than a dynamic 'struggle'.[47] Trilling worried that the novel belonged to a 'cultural cycle' now at a close, and that its place in the culture had already been usurped by other kinds of writing, including criticism and sociology ('I felt all the time I was reading that I was getting now what I used to get or think I was getting from novels,' he wrote to David Riesman, after reading *The Lonely Crowd* [1950]).[48]

Like other critics connected to *Partisan*, Trilling suggested embracing a mostly European tradition of modernism to counter not only the liberal tendency towards simplification that characterised the radical 1930s, but also a more deeply rooted inclination in American society to oppose material reality with intellectual culture. Yet, in his critical essays, Trilling tended not to focus on the modernist writers or their precursors esteemed by other New York Intellectuals. While Philip Rahv wrote on Kafka and Dostoevsky, Trilling wrote on William Dean Howells and Sherwood Anderson. While some of his *Partisan* peers celebrated modernist experimentation, Trilling preferred a nineteenth-century mode of 'moral realism', of which Forster was an inheritor. If the novel were to survive, Trilling argued, it would need to recapture something of the complex connection to manners, society, and ideas that sustained it in the previous century, just as, if liberalism were to prosper again, it would need to be recalled to 'its first essential imagination of variousness and possibility'.[49] In his essays, Trilling often simply lists the writers belonging to the anti-Stalinist canon of difficult modernists celebrated at midcentury – Gide, Kafka, Dostoevsky, Lawrence, Joyce, sometimes Malraux – rather than write about them. He was more likely to focus on an unfashionable writer – Norman Podhoretz couldn't understand Trilling's 'somewhat disproportionate interest in F. Scott Fitzgerald' – or on a neglected work by a celebrated writer.[50]

This last approach is exemplified in his essay on *The Princess Casamassima* (1886), one of James's least critically admired novels.[51] Trilling claims that the novel yields 'a kind of social and political knowledge which is hard to come by': a knowledge of how 'sometimes society offers an opposition of motives in which the antagonists are in such a balance of authority and appeal that a man who so wholly perceives them as to embody them in his very being cannot choose between them and is therefore destroyed' – that is, a knowledge of tragedy. Trilling celebrates James's portrayal of Hyacinth Robinson as a tragic hero whose 'mind is in perfect equilibrium, not of irresolution but of awareness'.[52] This hard-to-come-by knowledge emerges together with James's appreciation of 'the contrivances of the novel' and his delight in the 'primitive' origins of the novel in folklore and 'magic', a delight he shares with Forster.[53] Even some of Trilling's admirers questioned whether James's odd book warranted such attention. But that a minor novel should have produced arguably Trilling's best essay is itself telling; as though Trilling is saying that the novel is best when it fails, or when its 'roughness of grain' is most visible; or that we can get the most out of a novel when it doesn't quite realise what it set out to do, or when a novel refuses – or sabotages – its own potential greatness.[54] In any case, Trilling was always suspicious of those adjudicating literary greatness. In a 1963 entry in his journal, he defines the term 'Masterpiece':

> typical of the self-important humanism of the 19th century: it has in mind an *artist* who *achieves*, no doubt by *struggle* or *toil*, one or another *great* work; it proposed a hierarchy of grandiosity in the arts and it pretty clearly implied that only the best is good enough for *us*.[55]

The Idea of a Novel: *The Middle of the Journey* (1947)

During the period in which he was at work on the Forster book and the essays that would form *The Liberal Imagination*, Trilling was also writing fiction: *The Middle of the Journey* (1947), his only published novel, the title of which is a nod to Forster; some short stories; and a novel he never finished, published in 2008 as *The Journey Abandoned*.[56] In recent years, a 'kind of critical orthodoxy' has emerged, writes Adam Kirsch, 'that Trilling was, at heart, not a great literary critic but a failed novelist'.[57] This reconsideration is based in part on the posthumously published extracts from his private journal alongside the publication of his selected letters in 2018, which together reveal the extent of Trilling's thwarted ambition. Jotting down ideas for stories he would never get around to writing, Trilling repeatedly expressed his desire in the 1940s and 1950s to concentrate more on his fiction. Kirsch disputes the characterisation of Trilling as a failed novelist, but it was Trilling himself who laid the groundwork for such a reinterpretation of his career. In a talk to graduate students delivered in 1971, four years before his death, Trilling told his audience that he was 'always surprised when I hear myself referred to as a critic'. Even 'after some thirty years of having been called by that name,' he said, it 'takes me a little aback [. . .] and raises an internal grin'. Criticism, he continued, had only ever been an 'afterthought'; what he had 'envisaged was the career of a novelist'.[58] Trilling then writes of how his 'work in criticism took its direction from the novel', by which he means the novel's 'tendency to occupy itself [. . .] with moral questions'. He continues:

> So far as the genre of the novel can be thought of as having, in some large part of its sense of itself, a degree of bias against accepted literary forms and attitudes, to the extent that some part of its impulse might be called *anti-literary*, I would discover in this position the source, or the encouragement, of a tendency which I am aware of in my critical writing, which is to be a little skeptical of literature, impatient with it, or at least with the claims of literature to be an autonomous, self-justifying activity.[59]

Trilling suggests that his ambivalence about the novel and about literature in general – about what its proper relation to ideas, society, and politics should be, about how seriously we should take it – reflects an ambivalence internal to the novel itself; as if the novel were always suspicious of making too much of itself, or of moving too far from its 'primitive' function of telling a story. W. H. Auden, who worked with Trilling for two popular subscription book clubs, 'told friends that Trilling didn't like literature'.[60]

But 'it isn't that I don't like literature,' Trilling wrote in his journal, 'it's that I don't like my relationship to literature'.[61] 'I find myself in a very odd relation to myself as a critic,' he confided to Ransom, dissatisfied with his 'pedagogical role' and 'alienated from the English teaching profession'.[62] If Trilling's 'anti-literary' stance takes its cues from the novel itself, then the implication here might be that his odd relation to himself as a critic and teacher also reflects something he takes to be integral to the novel form. 'Skeptical' or 'impatient' both of claims that literature is a 'self-justifying activity' and that literature can be critiqued and studied, Trilling suggests that whatever we might learn from the novel won't be gleaned from literary criticism and can't be taught in an English department.

In his critical writing, Trilling fashioned a grand style out of his ambivalence. His dialectical method meant he 'could not argue a point without finding arguments for its antithesis', which gave the impression of a fine intelligence in constant modulation.[63] 'Trilling's best essays are in two movements,' Edward Mendelson writes: 'A long fugal adagio winds its way through a novel's sources and details [. . .] Then a brief soaring presto praises the novelist for virtues that exist only in Trilling's [mind].'[64] If this method can give the impression of mastery, it also reflects a deeply divided critical perspective, corresponding to Trilling's Freudian sense of the divided self and his characterisation of culture as a back-and-forth 'struggle'. In his fiction, Trilling similarly dramatises his ambivalence about the novel and its future – his divided view that, on the one hand, the novel is a genre that can speak to moral issues and political questions, and, on the other, that the novel is a genre to be played with, and from which we shouldn't expect too much, a form perhaps already eclipsed by other modes of writing, and one not well-suited to the contemporary turn of mind.

Something of Trilling's ambivalence regarding the novel form is apparent in the contradictory accounts he gave of what his own novel was about. In 1953, responding to a letter from Devette Havez, a French schoolteacher, asking about his work, Trilling describes *The Middle of the Journey* as 'a natural history of the intellectual liberal class as I understand it – its movement to communism, its wish to deny variousness and complexity in life'.[65] By contrast, in a letter to journalist Evelyn King Gilmore the previous year, Trilling writes of his regret that 'the book was frequently called coldly intellectual', and that 'what people seemed to respond to was what I might call the critical cogency of the book, its general cultural, even political, implications'. 'What I liked about it,' he writes to Gilmore, 'were the human touches and the humor, for which, in a way, the larger considerations were an excuse.'[66]

The Middle of the Journey has generally been read along the lines of the account Trilling gave of it to Havez, rather than that which he shared with Gilmore, its serious political and historical theme emphasised over its 'human touches'. The novel certainly invites such a reading. Set in the late 1930s sometime after the Moscow trials, it is the story of a liberal character confronting the ideological blindness of his fellow-travelling friends while acknowledging his own past political naivety. John Laskell, an urban housing planner, has his complacent belief in rational progress challenged by two traumatic experiences. The death of his fiancé and his own near-deadly bout of scarlet fever force upon him 'an overriding sense of the radical *contingency* of existence,' Anthony Hutchison writes.[67] During his initial convalescence, Laskell cultivates a new attention to the world around him, characterised by a kind of tranquil aesthetic appreciation, evident in his 'love affair' with a flower by his bedside: 'gazing at it', he feels 'something like desire; but it was a strange desire which *wanted* nothing, which was its own satisfaction' (19, emphasis original).[68]

Trilling himself had had a similar experience. Laid up ill in bed in the summer of 1928, he reported having 'had the strangest love affair [. . .] with a flower. Someone sent me some roses [. . .] One of them opened into one of the very few perfect things I have ever seen.' Trilling writes of the 'affair' in a letter to Henry Rosenthal, thanking him for sending a copy of *The Possessed* (1871) during his illness – though he admits, 'I didn't read it, *The Magic Mountain* did quite enough for me'.[69] Laskell is also sent a copy of *The Possessed* by a well-meaning liberal friend, but like Trilling he doesn't finish it: 'Laskell could not keep the characters in their places and the intensity of the emotions alienated him' (51). In the hands of Philip Rahv, *The Possessed* became one of the central texts in the anti-Stalinist revisionary reading of Dostoevsky, and so the fact that Trilling and Laskell don't get through it speaks to Trilling's uneasy relation to *Partisan*-style modernism, despite his novel's explicitly anti-Stalinist theme.[70]

The novel retains the air of convalescence, or of the sanitorium, even as the action moves from Laskell's city apartment to the countryside, where he will continue to recover in the company of his friends, Arthur and Nancy Croom, both of whom are sympathetic to the Communist Party. Like Mann's Castorp, Laskell will mediate a set of conversations between characters who are 'representatives and messengers of intellectual realms and worlds', as Mann described the central characters of his novel.[71] Arthur Croom, 'the man of the near future', is a professor of economics, though he 'quite destroyed the notion of donnishness with its meaning of retreat and isolation'; rather, armoured with 'idealism', Arthur is 'the political man whom the nation had not had in sufficient numbers' (64). With Laskell, Arthur represents the organisational impulse of liberalism, his career trajectory suggesting the university's entanglement with government institutions. The central drama of the narrative is how Laskell and the Crooms react to Laskell's brush with death; then how they respond to the defection from the Communist Party of their mutual friend, Gifford Maxim; and finally, how all the characters react to the tragic death of a local child, Susan Caldwell, near the end of the novel.

The Crooms' inability to speak of death reveals the brittleness of their progressivism and the potential inhumanity of their 'passionate expectation of the future' (16). Nancy, more politically radical than her husband, doesn't have a 'language' (17) for death, and acts as though it were 'politically reactionary' (131). Their inability to believe Maxim's account of the brutal methods of the Communist underground represents another failure to accept reality, while their incredulity when Susan is struck down and accidentally killed by her father, Duck – who they romanticise as 'a high manifestation of ordinary life' (109) – reveals their naivety. Maxim's sudden embrace of an apocalyptic religiosity, meanwhile, is not so much a Niebuhrian recognition of irony and tragedy as it is a desperate bid to clear his conscience, obfuscating his personal responsibility for crimes he has committed for the Party by preaching a doctrine of universal guilt. Laskell 'looks instead for a middle way,' Geraldine Murphy suggests, 'between the destabilizing extremes of left and right', achieving something resembling the 'equilibrium' prized by Trilling in *The Princess Casamassima*.[72] Laskell's balanced conclusion, 'An absolute freedom from responsibility – that much of a child none of us can be. An absolute responsibility – that much of a divine or metaphysical essence none of us is' (351), provokes the ire of his friends, which he recognises as 'the anger of the masked will at the appearance of an idea in modulation' (352). 'Rejecting his friends' apocalyptic appeals, he is presented as the only one capable of perceiving the nuances of responsibility' and the only one able to 'endure tragic experience', according to Katie Fitzpatrick, who argues that Laskell's 'willingness to dwell in ambivalence makes him a paragon of the liberal imagination'.[73]

The novel thus shares many of the same preoccupations as Trilling's essays of the period. Indeed, for many readers, its close affinity to Trilling's critical work is part of the problem of the novel. Robert Warshow's review in *Commentary* was famously damning. '[N]ot even in the simplest of Forster's novels is it safe to take any character as the author's mouthpiece,' Warshow writes, 'but Mr. Trilling's identification with Laskell is unmistakable.' 'The novelist's function is not to argue with his characters,' Warshow continues, 'or at least not to try too hard to win the argument', suggesting that Trilling neglects this in his endorsement of Laskell's 'flexibility of mind'. In this reading, the novel ironically comes to be characterised by something of the ideological rigidity it had sought to critique. Trilling is 'finally reduced to the level of his subject', and, Warshow concludes, 'like the Stalinists themselves, he can respond to the complexity of experience only with a revision of doctrine'.[74] Mark Krupnick similarly judges that, in 'striving for a fiction of ideas', Trilling in fact produces an 'excessively schematic' narrative in which his 'characters *are* their ideas'.[75]

But this perhaps is Trilling's point: that our attachment to our ideas diminishes us; or, our overidentification with our ideas distorts our characters. We might read *The Middle of the Journey*, in other words, as a novel of ideas sceptical of our faith in ideas. Late in the novel, Laskell comes to the realisation that the 'idealism of Nancy and Arthur [. . .] raised to a higher degree, had served for some years now the people who demanded ideas on which to build their lives', the implication being that there might be people who wish to build their lives on something other than ideas; or that any idea around which one could imagine building a life is not an idea worth having – because a life is not the sort of thing that can be built, or because the best ideas are always on the move (for Trilling, there should always be room for second thoughts). Laskell the urban planner learns that ideas aren't blueprints. Describing *The Middle of the Journey* as 'a distinctive adaptation of E. M. Forster's novelistic art', Amanda Anderson similarly argues that, 'at its most suggestive, Trilling's novel intimates a new form of the novel of ideas, something like an ideological novel of manners, where individuals are differentiated according to [. . .] their relation to ideas'.[76] 'Trilling seems to imagine we are at a point in history,' Anderson continues, 'where ideas and ideology, as self-consciously held conceptions, are a fundamental part of the identity of certain individuals and classes of individuals.'[77] In Anderson's reading, the novel is especially attuned to the dangers of ideas becoming 'fixed ideologies'.[78] But at times, I want to suggest, the novel portrays a wariness towards not only ideas that harden into ideological beliefs, like the Crooms', but all ideas, including even those of Laskell which seem close to Trilling's own critical positions, as Warshow observes. When read in the light of Trilling's ambivalence about the novel form itself – his suggestion that the novel might be better off 'more humbly conceived than it is now' – then *The Middle of the Journey* begins to resemble a more distinctive adaptation of the novel of ideas than even Anderson intimates: a kind of minor novel of ideas exposing the limits of the form, in which the value of the novel and the value of ideas are themselves held up to scrutiny and thrown into doubt.

Friendly Conversations

A scepticism towards ideas is connected in the novel to a distrust of intellectual discourse more generally. For Anthony Hutchison, 'it is not in the action but in the dialogue, the exchange of political-philosophical opinion [. . .] that *The Middle of the Journey* comes into its own'.[79] But though it is structured around a series of long exchanges of the kind Hutchison describes, the novel sometimes seems a little exhausted by all the talking, or curious about the possibility of having other kinds of conversation. Amanda Anderson similarly suggests that, although for Trilling 'argument is absolutely vital to the life of ideas, including political ideas', it 'also has crucial limits'.[80] These limits are especially clear in Laskell's conversations with the Crooms. Their discussions about politics become 'very heavily charged' (126), Laskell feels, in ways that none of them quite understand. As post-Freudian intellectuals, they are able to 'exchange anecdotes of their own childhoods, trying to explain how they had become the people they were today' (87), but Laskell admits he doesn't know how to talk with the Crooms about 'difficult personal matters' (171). His conversations with Maxim, meanwhile, retain the flavour of an interrogation, reflecting Maxim's career in the communist underground, despite Laskell's efforts to address him with 'friendliness' (148). Even as he grows frustrated at Maxim's techniques of manipulation, as a long-time fellow-traveller Laskell still feels that 'a man who had so much to do with the tempo of events had the right to dictate the tempo of conversation' (142). He is in equal parts horrified and impressed when Maxim talks with his nurse, seemingly innocently; in fact, he is 'establishing contact' (136), and making sure the nurse remembers him so that he might have a witness if he 'disappears'.

The limits of intellectual discourse are also exposed in the novel when characters slip between different registers of conversation or styles of talk. Nancy and Laskell are together in the garden when Nancy asks, 'Are you fond of flowers, John?', prompting a long, faintly Forsterian narrative commentary:

> It was one of those things that one friend can say to another [. . .] while one of them worked and the other idled [. . .] with plenty of time ahead, with no particular concentration on each other, not wanting any special answer [. . .] It came like a greeting and suggested how valuable life could be without struggle, or ideas, or commitments. A hundred, thousand other questions could be asked that would have the effect of making two people

as simple and without strain as Laskell suddenly felt he and Nancy to be. It seemed to him that such conversations could go on forever. (123–4)

The question about flowers inaugurates the possibility of a conversation that has something of the quality of Laskell's convalescent interest in his bedside rose. In both, there is an aimless, objectless desire – a desire without consummation and which is its 'own satisfaction' (19). The novel implies that there was, to be sure, something unhealthy about Laskell's enjoyment of his illness, as though he became rather too enamoured by his own mortality. But the experience also provides him with a capacity for 'contemplation' (19), for the practice of a new kind of attention, the ability to turn to the world with 'no particular concentration'. This releases him from the obligation he has felt to make himself 'useful' (40, 44) to the world, as he tries to do in his professional life, and it releases him from any concern with the future. The Crooms are impatient to 'hurry [. . .] the reality of the better future into being' (111), but this idle conversation allows for a kind of Forsterian relaxation, an unhurried pleasure akin to that of Laskell's affair with the flower. In the passage above, the qualities of the conversation are connected to a practice of friendship, a relationship without consummation or teleology that might take root beyond struggle, ideas, and commitments, beyond intellectual and political life and institutional structures. There is something 'imbecile' (124) about this kind of conversation, Laskell acknowledges (much as there is sometimes thought to be something childish about friendship), and if it were the only kind of conversation one could have it might be its own kind of death (it 'could go on forever'). But there is also the flicker here of the possibility of a life built on something other than ideas, a picture of a life that begins in an idle greeting of friendship, of being welcomed into a relation which is its own satisfaction. Laskell wishes to make explicit the link he has started to form between his love affair and Nancy's question, and he begins to share with her something of the experience of his illness. But the conversation soon takes on a political hue, any talk of death being anathema to Nancy's faith in progress. She teasingly calls Laskell 'quite a Ferdinand', a reference to Munro Leaf's 1936 children's story of 'a young bull who liked to look at flowers and did not charge around like other bulls', and so was 'disgraced but safe' (125), spending the rest of his life in blissful obliviousness of the world around him.[81] 'A good many political feelings became attached to the story and people chuckled over it as if it were a piece of folk-wisdom' (125). The life of contemplation is really a life of emasculated naivety, Nancy mockingly suggests, and Laskell hears the hostility in her comment, which will become more explicit in their later political disagreements.

Laskell has a similar conversation with Arthur when he helps his friend paint the clapboard on the Crooms' house. 'Tom Sawyer stuff', Laskell jokes, but he is soon 'drawn into it' (207) – both into the work and the Twainian idyll of childhood friendship it conjures. After working 'side by side for a while' (207), Laskell reflects that:

> It was an oddly gratifying kind of work, and it took more skill and attention than one would suppose. But beneath the attention he had to give, Laskell felt a glow of relationship to Arthur. They did not talk but now and then they made curt comments to each other on the progress or the problems of the job. They fell into the same rhythm of painting and occasionally paused to inspect each other's work with the eyes of indulgent criticism. (208)

There is the pleasure of paying the attention necessary to do the job, and the pleasure of how this attention provides the conditions for the relationship; the work becomes the work of friendship, much as Nancy's idle talk becomes a kind of friendly invitation. As the pair share 'the warmth [. . .] hidden and expressed by the brisk, masculine language of cooperation' (209), the language necessary for other kinds of conversation is abandoned, the struggles, ideas, and commitments of intellectual and political life suspended. It's hard not to think of this scene of 'oddly gratifying [. . .] work' in relation to Trilling's work as a critic, which he seems never to have found terribly gratifying; or to contrast the friends' 'indulgent criticism' of each other with Trilling's difficulty in responding to the work of those close to him. As with Laskell's conversation with Nancy, however, the possibility of relaxed sociability soon disappears, as the pair begin to talk of the university and politics. Arthur expresses his fear that he could lose his job because of his political activism, a fear that strikes Laskell as absurd: 'Your only danger is that they'll decide to make you a dean or something' (209). He is a 'little disappointed' to realise that Arthur wishes to imagine himself 'at the center of the drama of these troubled times' (209–10), rather than securely at the heart of the liberal bureaucratic state.

During his time in the country, Laskell stays with not the Crooms but the Folgers, a local family who represent a working-class socialist tradition which Nancy is quick to patronise.[82] Near the start of his stay, Laskell hears from his bedroom a wordless voice, 'beginning very low and reasonable, a colloquial utterance, very social', but which rises to 'a high pitch of querulousness', a voice which sets off a 'miserable' (33) growl from the Folgers' dogs. Laskell convinces himself this 'terrible' voice has a universal resonance, 'expressing the grievance of others', making an 'appeal, as it were, to justice' (33). Laskell assumes that the Faulknerian 'vocal idiocy' (34) is coming from the elderly and apparently senile Mr Folger. But, when he rushes downstairs, he discovers that it belongs to the younger Mr Folger, Alwin, and that the sound is a howl not of injustice, but of Alwin merrily imitating 'a good-natured and even witty dog who had somehow just been learning human speech, and of the dogs responding the best they could', in an 'ecstasy of affection, communication and hunger' (34–5). Laskell, we are told:

> would come to listen to this 'mad' conversation with the greatest pleasure. Alwin Folger talking to his dogs, to his old horse Harold, to his cows, was something that would never fail to delight him. [. . .] that endless conversation that had in it the perfect comic belief that all the animal creation could be communicated with. (35)

At the Folgers', then, Laskell enjoys a kind of 'strange cheerful talk' quite different from the sort of conversation he hears at the Crooms', and there is the suggestion that this 'endless conversation' has something of the quality of his talk in the garden with Nancy, which also seemed as though it could 'go on forever'.

This scepticism towards ideas and argument connects to the novel's ambivalence about the value of literature and education. When Laskell's aesthetic sensibility is offended by nine-year-old Susan

Caldwell's interpretation of Blake's 'Jerusalem' – in reciting it, she accompanies each line with an 'illustrative' gesture – he cannot resist offering some instruction; this throws her confidence, and, indirectly, leads to her death. The effects of aesthetic education might not always be so catastrophic, but throughout the novel Trilling queries what good comes from reading well, cautioning that even a refined interpretation or literary idea can be distorted. We see this in the set piece in which the Crooms and Laskell discuss Maxim's essay on Melville's *Billy Budd* (1924), written shortly after Maxim's defection from the Party and his apparent conversion to Christianity. As others have noted, *Billy Budd* was read a great deal at midcentury, and a great deal was read into it; the story became a 'site of struggle,' Geraldine Murphy writes, 'between the old and new liberalism' in America, a text onto which a range of political anxieties were projected, and which was the subject of a number of critical reassessments by prominent critics: from F. O. Matthiessen's religious, metaphysical reading in *American Renaissance* (1941) to Richard Chase's analysis in *The American Novel and its Tradition* (1957).[83] (In 1948, on the other side of the Atlantic, Forster was also thinking about Melville's tale, beginning work on the libretto for Benjamin Britten's adaptation of the story; the opera of *Billy Budd* reached the stage in 1951.) It chimes with the anti-Stalinist politics of the novel that the Crooms, as ideologues, should read Melville's story and Maxim's article in such a way as to suit their political beliefs. Nancy reads the story rather literally (a little like Susan reading Blake), transposing the story's central moral dilemma onto contemporary politics and quickly seeing 'the analogy with the Moscow trials'.[84] Arthur, meanwhile, reads Maxim's article in the way we would expect a liberal 'administrator' (65) to do: he approves of the article's 'core of realism', concluding that 'the great danger to the progressive movement' is that citizens begin 'shouting for immediate political democracy, forgetting the realities of the historical situation' (185). By contrast, Laskell withholds his judgement. After reading the essay, he initially feels 'a disgust for the whole world of ideas that allowed such shifts as Maxim's to be made so easily' (184), but then, after listening to the Crooms' interpretations, wonders whether he should give the piece another look.

In the standard interpretation of the novel, Laskell's suspended judgement models the kind of poised equilibrium Trilling endorses in his essay on *The Princess Casamassima*. But the scene is complicated by the fact that it isn't Laskell but Maxim who invokes one of Trilling's key terms: tragedy. This would seem to counter the idea put forward by Warshow and others that Laskell is simply a 'mouthpiece' for Trilling. At least part of Maxim's interpretation of Melville's story – his reading, for example, that 'we cannot understand Vere's suffering choice because we do not understand tragedy. And we do not understand tragedy because we do not understand love' (183) – sounds like 'vintage Trilling', as one critic puts it, very close to the terms and tenor of 'The Princess Casamassima'.[85] Tragedy, Amanda Anderson writes, is 'the term that Trilling's oeuvre conspicuously adds to the group of terms favored by the New Critics'.[86] We have seen how much of Trilling's thought is inflected with tragedy, and the Introduction suggested how widespread 'thinking tragically', to borrow Deborah Nelson's phrase, was at midcentury; I return to tragedy again in my discussion of John Williams's *Stoner* (1965).[87] In Maxim's article we see how the idea of tragedy might be misappropriated, the novel gesturing to the possibility that tragic reading might become as easily routinised as New Critical close reading – a 'technique' to be administered. Maxim's article weaves a 'crooning litany' of the terms 'tragedy' and 'love', such that Laskell feels 'an intellectual nausea' (183). Trilling's critical style relied heavily on the multiple valences of a few key terms, including 'tragedy' and 'love'; but he was also wary of the power of an evocative vocabulary, and of how important concepts could be travestied by popularisation in a mass culture. 'Maybe I jib a little at even your restrained notion of responsibility,' Trilling wrote to R. W. Flint in 1946, alluding to another key term in both his critical lexicon and his novel, 'perhaps only in reaction from all the bad talk about responsibility that you and I dislike. I begin to think that the very use of the word, and the debate about it, suggest something very wrong with our culture.'[88] That something similar could happen to the idea of tragedy is suggested in an earlier discussion of Oswald Spengler's *The Decline of the West* (English ed., 1926). The Crooms and Laskell cringe at the outdated and simplistic interpretation of Spengler's thesis offered by Emily Caldwell, Susan's mother and Duck's wife. 'How could he explain' to Emily, Laskell wonders, 'that for this book a vocabulary of discussion had existed a few years ago and had then died? [. . .] [T]his book, once seductive in its vision of tragedy, now existed only as [. . .] the early symptom of a disease which was now a terrible reality [. . .] now it was known to be entirely reactionary because it cut off all hope of the future' (95). Maxim's article is clearly the offspring of this reactionary tragic pessimism. But Trilling implies that his own version of tragic thinking could befall the same fate as Spengler's, and soon appear as equally anachronistic.

In a recent essay on *The Middle of the Journey*, Katie Fitzpatrick concludes that, 'where his criticism clearly argues for the powerful ambivalence of literature', Trilling's 'fiction embodies that principle by demonstrating ambivalence about the literary imagination itself'.[89] Fitzpatrick argues that the novel is an exploration of how and to what extent a literary sensibility may or may not be useful in informing or indeed sustaining the institutions necessary to liberal politics. She evidences this claim in part by turning to an intriguing entry from Trilling's private journal, written while he was at work on the novel, which is partly a commentary on *Billy Budd*:

> Spirit. The modern feeling that spirit should find its complete expression immediately in the world of necessity and that all that falls short of the full expression of spirit is repulsive. I see this often in gifted students [. . .] who when they find that, say, a graduate school is not up to their standard and expectation, cannot endure staying and abandon their projects. They have, one might say, no irony – for irony, perhaps, is the awareness with acceptance of the breach between spirit and the world of necessity [. . .] They insist that spirit be wholly embodied in institutions [. . .] My students discussing *Billy Budd*, feel that there is really nothing to be said about the story. Vere is, to them, wholly culpable, Budd being good. Law does not express spirit – even kills it! [. . .] They do not understand the tragic choice [. . .] What they do not understand is that if Spirit exists in its purity, so does evil in the form of Claggett and that Claggett makes Vere necessary as an intermediate force between him and Budd. Something extensive could be written about this.[90]

Fitzpatrick suggests that the passage shows Trilling isn't the 'starkly anti-institutional thinker' he is sometimes assumed to be.[91] In its recognition that 'Law does not express Spirit', the passage indicates Trilling's 'commitment to some form of legal – and not only moral – judgment'.[92] This supports her broader reading of the novel as being about the 'irreconcilable tension' between laws and morals, and between legal and literary categories of judgement.[93] The novel demonstrates its ambivalence about how the literary imagination should mediate legal questions, Fitzpatrick suggests, by portraying 'moral judgment' as 'so tightly bound to Laskell's enlightened perspective [. . .] that it could never achieve a public or institutional form – precisely the forms that would be vital to any robust political response to the crisis of Nuremberg', which she reads as in the background of the novel's concern with judgement.[94] What the novel reveals, in Fitzpatrick's reading, is the 'political impracticality of individual moral judgment', in what amounts to 'a subtle critique of the political limitations of that same capacity'.[95] In my reading, by contrast, the novel's critique is aimed not only at personal moral judgement's lack of 'scalability', but also at the belief that a novel would be the place where one might find the kind of ideas that ever could translate into institutional politics. To conceive of the relation between literature and politics in this way is to expect too much of the novel, or to make it do 'more work and of a different kind than is proper', to recall Trilling's 1942 letter to Newton Alvin.

But it is perhaps worth considering the institution Trilling mentions in this journal entry, which isn't a legal institution, but the graduate school at Columbia. Never entirely settled at the university, Trilling seems to have been especially ill at ease teaching and supervising graduate students, which took up more of his time as he became better-known and as the graduate school itself grew in the postwar period. Writing of the graduate school in his journal in 1951, he expresses unease at the 'sense that I was part of an enterprise that I could in no way defend'. He goes on to admit to:

> the sensation of liberation I experienced when I arranged for my withdrawal from the graduate school [. . .] That involvement [. . .] has cost me much [. . .] For one thing I became a public character and always on view, having to live up to the demands made upon a public character, & finding that the role seemed to grow inward.[96]

He ends the entry by recording his 'ever-growing dislike of teaching & of the systematic study of literature – more and more it goes against the grain'.[97] Teaching and systematic study go together here with a loss of individuality, the institution demanding a public role that Trilling sees as a threat to the private self. A similar chain of connections is discernible in a letter, also from 1951, from Trilling to Norman Podhoretz, sent while the latter was in Cambridge. The pair had been discussing a renowned Cambridge fixture – not Forster this time, but F. R. Leavis. 'I now know how angry a man can get at an educational situation,' Trilling writes, apparently sympathising with Leavis's grumblings reported to him by Podhoretz, and perhaps with his own experience of the graduate school in mind. '[I]f I had two lives, I might give one of them, or half of one, to doing something here by way of opposition'. Instead, he uses the letter to set down what he calls, with mock-grandiosity, 'the last word on education I shall ever utter':

> Go punt, go develop a taste in sherry, go wear fine neck cloths, go play football, go bind your books in levant – go do anything that will remind you that man wasn't born to analyze texts or have right opinions, anything to remind you that man was born to be private – that you owe it to the public to be private (this is serious).[98]

We might agree with Fitzpatrick that Trilling acknowledges the necessity of institutions, but more insistently he wants to expose the limits of institutional thinking: there might be more to education than the study of texts, Trilling suggests, and there might be more to political life than the building of institutions. And the lesson of learning how to live with and within institutions might be learning how to resist them, or how not to over-identify with them, and this resistance might be for the good of the private self and, paradoxically, the public world of institutions ('you owe it to the public to be private').

Trilling's advocacy for a kind of vigilant ambivalence towards institutions would seem to be of a piece with the stance adopted by many postwar intellectuals. As Stephen Schryer explains, intellectuals developed a 'humanistic model of cultural education oriented toward the educated middle class', in which the cultivation of negative capability was imagined as 'the basis for a new kind of public service'.⁹⁹ In this model, 'critical intelligence has a mysterious, indirect impact on the society around it,' writes Schryer. 'Rather than building institutions, the intellectual improves the culture' by helping the expanding demographic of middle-class professional knowledge workers 'to adopt more complicated patterns of thinking associated with the practice of professionalism itself.'¹⁰⁰ But one intriguing aspect of Trilling's letter to Podhoretz is that the cultivation of the 'purely private aesthetic sensibility' described by Schryer doesn't happen through reading novels and it certainly doesn't happen in the classroom. His picture of education at Cambridge is one of acquiring taste, of experimenting with styles, of dressing up and trying out and trying on – of a kind of performance in the service of reminding oneself of the essential privacy of the individual (it also resembles a gentleman's education at Cambridge, the kind enjoyed before the establishment of the English Faculty). Trilling's worry about the professionalisation of literary study was that his students weren't so much trying out ideas as misappropriating important concepts and regurgitating information – turning everything into 'academic cliché', as he put it to Ransom.

The worst thing imaginable to Trilling is to have an opinion that isn't your own, and yet *The Middle of the Journey* is in part about the extent to which we cannot help but speak with a borrowed vocabulary – whether it's the Crooms, or Emily Caldwell, or the village pastor who presides over Susan's funeral and cribs his sermon verbatim from *The Pastor's Helpful Funeral Guide* (332). And this leaves even an evocative critical language like Trilling's vulnerable to becoming academic cliché, or to being abused, as when Laskell's tragic thinking morphs into Maxim's religious apocalypticism. Such a view of things is hardly conducive to the building of institutions, as Fitzpatrick rightly suggests. It is telling, then, that Trilling thinks through these issues by turning to a relation for which, as Trilling learnt from Forster, there can never really be an institutional framework, or a 'friendship office'. As well as reading the novel as about the failure of the literary imagination to translate into institutional politics, we might also read it as a book about a group of friends struggling to get along, a group of friends who find it difficult to hold a conversation because the language of politics and institutions keeps getting in the way, and because their public characters keep crowding out their private selves. Trilling focuses on this private failure between friends in the novel's closing scene, in which the Crooms are seeing Laskell off at the train station:

> [Laskell] said, 'I'm sorry that we seemed to get into so many disagreements.' Arthur began to brush this aside, but Nancy said, 'We did, didn't we? Why did we?' And she rose and stood facing him to make the question real.
> He wanted very much to be able to answer her. (360)

To read the novel as pitched at the scale of personal friendship rather than institutional politics might be to come closer to the account of it Trilling gave to Evelyn King Gilmore, rather than the more familiar account he provided to Devette Havez, the French school teacher; that is, as a novel of 'human touches' instead of 'a natural history of the intellectual liberal class'. Rather than a conventional novel of ideas, *The Middle of the Journey* dramatises Trilling's doubts, expressed throughout his critical work and private journals, about our investment in the novel form and our attachment to ideas. Modelled on the minor novels of Forster and James, Trilling's own minor novel is about the inadequacies of language, critical intelligence, and literary sensibility, and about the inability of the novel to offer anything more than a reflection of those limits. Echoing Forster's refusal to be great, Trilling's novel relinquishes any grander ambition than to recognise tragic limitations. While this reflects the broader climate of pessimistic or 'bleak' liberal thought, Trilling's Forsterian focus on friendship also suggests that if the novel were to give up on greatness, it might take up other things: those minor moments of connection between individuals, those small human touches, before the larger claims of the world of politics and ideas encroach.

The Novel Abandoned

Friendship becomes a way into thinking about institutional affiliations in Trilling's unfinished second novel, which he began drafting in the early 1940s. Trilling was keen that his new work of fiction would not be mistaken for a novel of ideas; the new book, he wrote to Richard Chase in 1947, would be 'richer, less shaped, less intellectualized, more open' than *The Middle of the Journey*.[101] It should have a 'sense of chronicle,' he writes in his commentary on the manuscript, satisfying his 'strong feeling (I have expressed it critically in my E. M. Forster) that a novel must have all the primitive elements of story and even of plot'.[102] The plot of *The Journey Abandoned* begins with the boyhood friendship of Vincent Hammell and Toss Dodge, who grow up together in a Midwestern city. When they reach college age, however, the friends drift apart. Toss goes to Yale, where he acquires a gentleman's taste for Hogarth and Fielding, and 'a political liberalism' of which he is 'rather proud' (the novel is set in the late 1930s and early 1940s).[103] Vincent goes to City University, loosely based on Columbia, where he falls in with an intellectual crowd, becoming an avid reader of 'Flaubert, Baudelaire and Joyce', and 'a close and careful student of poetry according to the methods of critics Toss never heard of' (13).[104] Vincent is a very well-read 'young man from the provinces' who knows 'the histories of Frederic Moreau, Rastignac and Julien Sorel' (20) and is, as Trilling writes in his preface to the novel, 'determined not to make their mistakes'.[105] In his early twenties, Vincent is already at work on an ambitious critical history of American literature reminiscent of *On Native Grounds* (1942), which made Alfred Kazin's name at the age of twenty-seven.

Vincent's first literary mentor is Kramer, his professor at City, who lectures 'on the literature of modern Europe [. . .] arranging into careful categories the lessons of rebellion to be found in Ibsen, Sudermann, Schnitzler' (28). But Vincent soon tires of Kramer's 'scrupulous intellectual honesty' which ensures he can 'bring no work to a satisfactory conclusion' (28). Kramer is both a figure of some ridicule in the novel and, like Vincent, a partial self-portrait of Trilling: the Jewish professor whose watchwords are 'integrity' and 'compromise' (29); who is a little in love with ideas of heroism and rebellion; and who is attracted to the notion of literary study as a retreat from 'material gain' and 'popular success' (29). There is also their shared history of unfinished projects.

Vincent courts another mentor, a former student of Kramer's who has betrayed his old teacher's dedication to intellectual integrity. Harold Outram's early reputation was launched on the strength of a series of essays and a 'startlingly good' novel. A short-lived conversion to radical politics followed, before Outram remerged as the doyen of 'magazine journalism', and, finally, as the 'director of the great new Peck Foundation' – loosely based on the Ford Foundation – 'with power to dispense at discretion those incalculable millions for the advancement of American culture' (16–17). Outram's apostasy recalls Maxim's renunciation of communism, but more crucial to the novel is his transition from writer to administrator. His function in the narrative is that of a glorified middleman: it is Outram who arranges for Vincent to become the biographer of Jorris Buxton. The young man recognises the name as belonging to an all-but-forgotten 'minor poet and novelist' who 'dropped from sight' (58) at the turn of the century: 'The novels were never popular, though every now and then someone discovers them and writes a little essay' (59). Outram invites Vincent up to his New England home, where the young man meets Buxton and enters a world of literary sophistication. Vincent is just beginning to get a sense of his enigmatic biographical subject and the group of admirers that surrounds him when Trilling's manuscript breaks off.

Trilling's unfinished novel, then, is about compromised ambition and underappreciated talent, a novel in which creative aspirations are renounced and early promise is betrayed or left unfulfilled. At City, Vincent and his friends watch over 'the integrity of certain heroes and demi-heroes whose fates', they believe, are 'a portent of their own. They had their martyrs; some cherished Scott Fitzgerald, some Hart Crane' (15). But while the tragic lives of these modernist writers are still an inspiration, they are no longer exactly an example to emulate. Vincent's own story is from the dawn of the Age of Criticism, when a young man makes his mark with a critical rather than creative work. 'Ah yes—your generation no longer worships the novel', Outram says when Vincent tells him of his critical project. 'In my time it was the novel or nothing':

> We spent our days getting ready for it [. . .] An *honest* novel it had to be [. . .] And always one novel was what we thought of. Only one, very big, enormous [. . .] you'd think we were constructing a bomb. We expected to blow everything to bits with our honesty [. . .] You're a cagier generation, you live—I suppose you think—in a tougher, narrower time, you play it safer and wiser. (54)

In his private journals, it sometimes seems that for Trilling, too, it was the novel or nothing, even as he was, like Vincent, making his mark with his criticism. But we have seen that he also shared some of Outram's scepticism about the idea of '*the* Great American Novel', and his sense of living – as the image of the bomb suggests – in the aftermath of modernism. *The Journey Abandoned* is the story of what happens to a young man of some literary talent and ambition in such a world as Outram describes, in which the novel is no longer available as a major cultural form – a world, that is, in which there are only minor novels, or abandoned ones.

Trilling took inspiration for the novel from the life of the Romantic poet Walter Savage Landor. In the preface he writes that he was drawn to the 'tragic simplicity' of Landor's biography and the notion that the poet lived by a code of honour that came to seem outmoded within the course of his long life, such that he represented to a younger generation of writers 'a bridge to the heroic time of poetry'.[106] Trilling aimed to write *The Journey Abandoned* in a deliberately 'old-fashioned way' (lii), and the novel plays with ideas of anachronism and obsolescence, exploring whether heroism and tragedy are still modes of thought evocative for the modern imagination and whether they still have a place in a novel.[107] Buxton is the Landor-esque figure of tragic nobility in the book, but Trilling also wants us to think of Vincent as a potential tragic hero in the mould of James's Hyacinth Robinson. Near the close of the manuscript, Philip Dyas, a headmaster and friend of Outram's, shares his opinion of Buxton's newly appointed biographer with Marion Cathcart, a young woman also part of Outram's circle. 'I like him, that young hero', Philip says of Vincent. 'Oh, that's just— *language*', Marion replies, assuming he is being 'ironical' (130). 'I meant only that Hammell is waiting for things to happen to him. That's really all I meant by heroism', Philip says, conceding, '[p]erhaps it's too big a word' (131). He goes on to say, however, that, 'if Hammell's a hero at all, he's—I'm afraid—a tragic hero', because '[h]e is demanding something happen to him. And that something may turn out to be tragic' (133):

> 'You use that word a great deal,' she said.
> 'What word?'

'Tragic. You use it as if it were the best thing you could say about anything.'
He looked confused for a moment, for a deep belief had been brought to light in a very casual way [. . .] He said, 'Yes, I think it is the best thing you could say about anything. And perhaps when you're my age you will think the same. You'll know as I do that the belief in [–]
[two blank lines in the original]
She listened to him attentively [. . .] (133)

In *The Middle of the Journey*, Trilling wonders whether tragedy might be just another critical term that risks becoming debased or outmoded. Here, there is a worry over whether heroism and tragedy are still vital concepts, or whether they are just 'language', as Marion dismissively suggests, echoing the scepticism towards intellectual discourse we saw in the earlier novel. Trilling asks whether an understanding of tragedy is something that comes with maturity, as Philip hopes, or if it is something that, in the passage from Philip's generation to Marion's, has already passed into obsolescence. But also at play in this unfinished scene is the larger question of what Trilling describes, in an essay written while he was at work on the novel, as 'the relation [. . .] between what we call creative literature and what we call ideas'; that is, of whether we should look to novels for ideas, and in what ways an idea encountered in a novel is different from one discussed in an essay.[108] It's tempting to think that the gap in the manuscript leaves these questions open, and that it gestures to Trilling's inability to find a satisfactory form in his fiction for addressing the preoccupations animating his criticism.

The narrative is structured as a series of mentorships, each implicating Vincent in an increasingly intricate network of institutional as well as personal relations. He transitions from a faintly archaic model of pedagogic patronage under Kramer to a murkier modern arrangement of philanthropic sponsorship with Outram and Buxton, Trilling updating the narrative structure of a Jamesian artist tale for his mid-twentieth-century moment. Though set in the late 1930s, the novel's portrayal of an emerging apparatus of cultural administration reflects debates regarding the shifting status of the academy, and of literary studies in particular, preoccupying Trilling and other intellectuals by the mid-1940s. Evan Kindley describes how a 'number of large and powerful institutions began to take a newfound interest in the development of American literature and literary criticism in the postwar period', inaugurating an era of what he calls 'Big Criticism'.[109] The funding of American literary scholarship formed one part of the broader project to institutionalise modernism at midcentury, described in the Introduction. At home, the institutionalisation of modernism became crucial to how intellectuals reconceived of their relation to mainstream US culture in general and to an expanding middle class of professional knowledge workers in particular.[110] Abroad, a 'defanged modernism', in Greg Barnhisel's phrase, was central to the 'cultural diplomacy' waged in Europe by government agencies and underwritten by private foundations.[111]

Trilling is closely associated with both 'fronts' of the project. His contribution to the 1952 *Partisan Review* symposium, 'Our Country and Our Culture' – in which he argues that US culture is at a stage when 'wealth' might 'submit itself to the rule of mind and imagination' (319), and a growing professional middle class might become 'supporters and consumers of high culture' (321–2) – is often cited as an example of the new consensus among intellectuals at midcentury.[112] Meanwhile, his editorship of an issue of *Perspectives USA*, a literary journal funded by the Ford Foundation and targeting European audiences with the aim, according to its founding proposal, of promoting peace 'by increasing respect for America's non-materialistic achievements among intellectuals abroad' is pointed to as evidence of his status as a Cold War warrior.[113] But the portrayal of institutionality in the unfinished novel speaks to the misgivings Trilling had about the changing place of intellectuals in American life, misgivings that, as Stephen Schryer points out, would resurface in his criticism by the 1960s.[114]

The novel pokes fun at the fastidious Kramer but also mourns the disappearance of his kind of humanist education. In *The Middle of the Journey*, Trilling portrays Arthur Croom as representative of a new class of professor plugged into the expanding bureaucracies of the federal state. In *The Journey Abandoned*, the picture of institutionality is complicated by the growth of new cultural centres that rival the university, and by the expansion of private foundations such as Outram's offering lucrative alternative funding opportunities; in this new ecosystem, the likes of Kramer are an endangered species. Trilling portrays the university as under threat from Meadowfield, the new 'center for the artistic life of the region', which will be supported by the Peck Foundation. While the university endures, 'alone in its grief' in the city, Meadowfield is expanding over 'three square miles of good ground' to include schools of painting, sculpture, and architecture, with workshops for 'ceramics and glassware' (39). Trilling has fun 'skewer[ing] Meadowfield and what it represents', Geraldine Murphy suggests – 'a complex of 1930s cultural trends associated with the Popular Front'.[115] But Meadowfield's success is also a harbinger of the broader trend in humanities funding by governmental and private foundations gathering pace in the postwar period, which saw, writes Kindley, a shift 'away from the accumulation of traditional scholarship and toward the democratic goal of wider public dissemination of culture'.[116] 'There were no two ways about it', Outram acknowledges, visiting the centre on Peck Foundation business: 'Meadowfield was a going concern, its endowment large and safe, its purposes sound and not only sound but *democratic*' (41).

Creative writing is one of the popular courses offered at Meadowfield. Vincent has written an essay for a little magazine on how 'literature is the most treacherous of all the artistic professions' because the young writer's 'is the art in which technique is least specific, least communicable, seems to depend largely on a condition of inner life' (48). But this doesn't stop him agreeing to teach 'Techniques of Creative Writing'. His class is comprised of nine middle-aged women all hungry for insider's tips on getting published in glossy magazines. Vincent isn't the first teacher to leave them disappointed. 'Each autumn the new man had been received with taut feminine expectancy, each spring he had been discarded, for he had not conveyed the precious, the inconceivable secret which the women had come in hopes to receive' (65). Trilling offers a familiar, and familiarly gendered, satire of middlebrow literary culture, and of the writers' workshop.[117] But the satire is complicated somewhat when, towards the end of his final class before he quits Meadowfield, Vincent decides to give up altogether trying to teach the class, and instead to simply read aloud from a short story he admires. In the 'musing silence' that follows, the women abandon their 'quest for the fierce and precious secret' and instead enter a mood of 'brooding relaxation' (71), the demands of technical instruction and the desire for publication giving way to a Forsterian enjoyment of a good story.

While Outram is in town to secure funding for Meadowfield, he also arranges to see Vincent to offer him the job of Buxton's biographer. The Peck Foundation 'only puts its money into institutions' (32), not individuals, so it isn't entirely clear in what capacity Outram makes his offer, what it consists of, or what its source is. After Vincent accepts, Outram sends him an 'elaborately wrapped' and 'extravagantly fine' Scotch whiskey, the enclosed card reading: 'To celebrate the beginning of your enterprise—and our friendship' (66). Those terms, 'enterprise' and 'friendship', continue to jostle one another when Vincent joins Outram at his New England home, where personal and institutional relations remain opaquely connected. Vincent is a bit dazzled by Outram's immaculate taste and by the group of writers, teachers, and intellectuals who gather to be near to Buxton. As he listens to the group passionately discuss school funding over dinner, it appears to Vincent that, whatever the moral compromises it involves, Outram's embrace of the riches of the foundation has allowed for the creation of something like the 'ultimate society' (115).

If in *The Middle of the Journey*, Trilling had been concerned to show how ideological commitments always get in the way of genuine conversation, then in *The Journey Abandoned* he seems intrigued as to whether a new set of institutional networks might allow for the disinterested expression of 'passionate differences of opinion' (115). But such an arrangement is perhaps not as 'democratic' as it first appears. Listening to the dinner debate intensify, Vincent wonders if the group are not engaging in it as a kind of performance for the benefit of Buxton, presiding at the head of the table, to whom they turn to pass judgment on the issue under discussion. His conclusion – 'I don't know whether you're right', he says to one of the group, 'but you're by no means wrong' – is not 'an equivocal answer' (115), but rather a finely balanced judgment, a quiet authority gently wielded, which affords Vincent 'a sense of deliverance so sudden and so sensual as to make him feel foolish':

> He had always thought it a failure in Greek tragedy when the god appeared high up on the tower to settle the disputes and resolve the action, thought it a failure in drama, but now he knew what dramatic possibilities there lay in the sudden voice that stilled the bickering of drama with irrefutable judgment. (116)

This is a version of tragedy that yields not only the poised 'equilibrium' Trilling prizes in James and seemingly models in Laskell, but also the finality of resolution, of judgment granted by a higher authority. Such an appeal in this instance rests on the nobility of Buxton's character, the sense that he is above the fray; indeed, this is how he is sometimes presented, as in a scene where he is said to embody the happiness derived from 'the intellectual activity of the soul' (104). But 'irrefutable judgment' is the opposite of negative capability, and so never entirely appealing to Trilling. At other times, Buxton is presented as all too fallible – as when he is childishly frightened by a storm, or when, near the end of the manuscript, there is an implication that he has been made a fool of by the conniving Mrs Post, who has designs on his fortune.

Seeing both sides of Buxton, Vincent isn't entirely sure what to make of him – and nor, one feels, at times, is Trilling; it is perhaps no coincidence that the novel trails off just as we are to learn more about the enigmatic writer. Murphy speculates that part of the problem may have been that Trilling began by basing Buxton on Landor but ended up modelling him on Henry James, as though Trilling was caught between the model of the minor poet and the Master.[118] At the end of the extant manuscript, Vincent, too, is poised between literary models, distrusting Outram and unable to pin down Buxton. And he is beginning to feel some ambivalence about his new literary life. He is only partly taken with the 'spade work' (141) of digging through letters that is the biographer's lot, and he is starting to wonder whether there might not be some nefarious reason that Outram has entrusted him, an untried young writer, with such a plumb commission.

In working out what he thinks about Buxton, and about his new career as a biographer, Vincent plans to write to Kramer, his old mentor and keeper of the flame of intellectual integrity. After his initial meeting with Buxton, Vincent is struck by the 'vital energy' (104) he perceives at play in the writer's eyes and records his first impressions in his journal. But these feel at once 'too private' and 'too pompous' to share, and so Vincent recounts the experience rather differently to Kramer. Vincent wants to find a way of 'continuing the connection between Kramer and Buxton' (106), and, in so doing, perhaps maintain a connection between his training in literary criticism and his role of biographer, and between the different kinds of literary vocation Kramer and Buxton represent.

The letter begins badly. Writing out of a feeling of 'generous insincerity', Vincent patronisingly tries to pitch his impressions of Buxton within Kramer's 'range' (107). But in the process of writing to his old mentor, he is struck by an illuminating 'recollection of his sophomore year':

> 'Do you remember', his letter continued, 'in that Wordsworth poem about the leech-gatherer of which you are so fond, how the very old man beside the stream seems to be a rock [. . .] and then the rock begins to seem like a great beast from the sea? A kind of metaphor within a metaphor? [. . .] And do you remember how what the old man says to the poet gets rid of the depression and the fear he experiences? [. . .] I understand how that could happen now and that it wasn't any particular thing that the old man said that cheered poor [Wordsworth] up, but just his existence in wonderful everlastingness.' That [. . .] came very close to the truth. The reduction of the incident that Vincent had made [. . .] led him to see it in a new fullness of meaning. (106–7)

Here, as in the *Billy Budd* scene in *The Middle of the Journey*, Trilling the novelist and Trilling the critic seem to merge. The letter makes the case for the particular kind of knowledge that literature can yield, and for the insights available through literary criticism, even as Vincent is leaving both behind for a different sort of literary career. In writing to Kramer, Vincent honours his old mentor and the humanist education he represents by putting into practice what he has learnt at the university. Vincent's bit about the leech-gatherers paraphrases Trilling's reading of the poem in 'Wordsworth and the Rabbis' (1950), but the letter also brings to mind Trilling's earlier essay on Wordsworth's 'Immortality Ode', included in *The Liberal Imagination* (1950). It is one of Trilling's more idiosyncratic close readings. The essay begins with a warning over the dangers of deterministic biographical readings of Wordsworth's poetry in general and, in particular, 'the common biographical interpretation of the Ode': it is not 'a dirge sung over departing powers,' Trilling argues, 'but actually a dedication to new powers' (151).[119] Rather than an elegy for 'the visionary gleam' that had inspired Wordsworth's earlier work, Trilling suggests that the poem is a resolute declaration of a 'shift in interest' in his writing and the affirmation of 'a new poetic subject'. To Trilling, the Ode is a poem of creative transition rather than decline. This interpretation largely rests on a speculative reading of the line referring to a 'timely utterance' that gives Wordsworth's speaker 'relief' from grief and restores their strength; Trilling suggests that this 'utterance' alludes to the words of the leech-gatherer in Wordsworth's 'Resolution and Independence'. Trilling therefore makes the Ode a poem about the conviction to follow through on a creative ambition, and about the resolve of the creative intelligence after a temporary crisis of confidence.

Despite his prohibition against biographical readings, we might say that Trilling's interpretation of the Ode reflects his own uncertainties about the transition he was attempting to make from criticism to fiction. Trilling seems sometimes to have felt himself stranded between 'the two categories, of the academic and the man of genius & real originality', as he writes in his journal in 1950, and it is as though his reading of Wordsworth's trajectory is conceived so as to make sense of his own.[120] In *The Journey Abandoned*, the Ode similarly speaks to Vincent's ambivalence, caught as he is between the life of the critic and that of the biographer, between mentors, and between the world of the university and that of the new foundations. For Trilling, the transition between criticism and fiction was complicated not only by his uncertainty about his role within the university, but also by his mixed feelings about the novel itself: about whether it should be a site for cultivating a sense of complexity and variousness, or whether it is a more 'primitive' contraption, made for the telling of a story; about whether the novel should aim for greatness, or settle for something humbler; about whether the novel was a major or minor form; about whether it should take as its subject institutional power and ideological commitment, or whether it should be about friendships, mentorships, and 'human touches'; and about whether the novel should countenance the 'irrefutable judgment' granted to the Gods in tragedy, or whether it should, like Forster's fiction, refuse 'to be conclusive' and focus instead on the tragic irresolution of ordinary life.[121] How does a novel reach an ending, Trilling asks in this unfinished novel, while leaving room for second thoughts?

Notes

1. Lionel Trilling, 'E. M. Forster', *Kenyon Review*, Vol. 4, No. 2 (Spring 1942), pp. 160–73 (160).
2. Lionel Trilling, 'Preface to the Second Edition', *E. M. Forster* [1943] (New York: New Directions, 1964), pp. 1–4 (3).
3. Ibid., 3–4.
4. Lionel Trilling, 'Reality in America', in *The Liberal Imagination: Essays on Literature and Society* [1950] (New York: New York Review Books Classics, 2008), pp. 3–21 (12); Trilling, *E. M. Forster*, 11–12.
5. Trilling, *E. M. Forster*, 13.
6. Ibid., 15, 12.
7. Trilling, 'Reality in America', 21.
8. Lionel Trilling, 'The Princess Casamassima', in *The Liberal Imagination*, pp. 58–92 (87).
9. Lionel Trilling, 'Manners, Morals, and the Novel', in *The Liberal Imagination*, pp. 205–22 (211).
10. Trilling, *E. M. Forster*, 23.
11. Trilling, 'Manners, Morals, and the Novel', 219.
12. Janice Ho argues that friendship is 'a trope of democratic citizenship' in Forster's fiction. *Nation and Citizenship in the Twentieth-Century British Novel* (Cambridge: Cambridge University Press, 2015), 27. On the 'failure of friendship' in Forster, see Sarah Cole, *Modernism, Male Friendship, and the First World War* (Cambridge: Cambridge University Press, 2003), 21–91 (74).
13. See Ho, *Nation and Citizenship in the Twentieth-Century British Novel*, 33–43.
14. '[Rickie] wished there was a society, a kind of friendship office, where the marriage of true minds could be registered'. E. M. Forster, *The Longest Journey* [1907] (London: Penguin, 2006), 64.
15. Trilling, 'Preface', in *The Liberal Imagination*, pp. xv–xxi (xx).

16. Trilling was an undergraduate and doctoral student at Columbia; he joined the faculty in 1939.
17. Lionel Trilling, Letter to John Crowe Ransom, 21 September 1948, in Adam Kirsch (ed.), *Life in Culture: Selected Letters of Lionel Trilling* (New York: Farrar, Straus and Giroux, 2018), pp. 171–5 (173).
18. Lionel Trilling, 'From the Notebooks of Lionel Trilling', *Partisan Review*, Vol. 51, No. 4/Vol. 52, No. 1 (Fall 1984/Winter 1985), pp. 495–515 (498–503).
19. Ibid., 511.
20. Lionel Trilling, Letter to Richard Chase, 11 February 1948, in *Life in Culture*, pp. 166–7 (166).
21. Quoted in Morris Dickstein, 'The Critics Who Made Us: Lionel Trilling and *The Liberal Imagination*', *Sewanee Review*, Vol. 94, No. 2 (Spring 1986), pp. 323–34 (325).
22. Ibid.
23. Lionel Trilling, Letter to Richard Chase, 11 February 1948, 166, 167. Emphasis original.
24. Trilling, *E. M. Forster*, 4.
25. Ibid., 9.
26. Ibid., 22.
27. Lionel Trilling, 'The Poet as Hero: Keats in His Letters', in *The Opposing Self: Nine Essays in Criticism* (New York: Viking, 1955), pp. 3–49 (31).
28. Irving Kristol, 'The Moral Critic' [April 1944], in John Rodden (ed.), *Lionel Trilling and the Critics: Opposing Selves* (Lincoln: University of Nebraska Press, 1999), pp. 92–7 (96).
29. E. M. Forster, *Aspects of the Novel* [1927] (London: Penguin, 2005), 40.
30. Trilling, *E. M. Forster*, 17, 10. Trilling describes Forster's 'tampering with the heroic' as 'a kind of mithridate against our being surprised by life' (17–18). He discusses 'the mithridatic function' of tragedy in 'Freud and Literature', in *The Liberal Imagination*, pp. 34–57 (56).
31. Trilling, *E. M. Forster*, 10.
32. Lubbock argues that 'the whole intricate question of method, in the craft of fiction, [is] governed by the question of the point of view'. *Craft of Fiction* [1921] (New York: Viking, 1957), 251. Forster quotes this sentence in *Aspects of the Novel*, and then suggests that, for him, 'the whole intricate question of method resolves itself not into a formulae but into the power of the writer to bounce the reader into accepting what he says' (81–2).
33. Kristol, 'The Moral Critic', 95.
34. Adam Kirsch, *Why Trilling Matters* (New Haven: Yale University Press, 2011), 16.
35. Lionel Trilling, 'From the Notebooks of Lionel Trilling, Part II', *Partisan Review*, Vol. 54, No.1 (Winter 1987), pp. 7–17 (13).
36. On Trilling's Jewishness, see Jonathan Freedman, *The Temple of Culture: Assimilation and Anti-Semitism in Literary Anglo-America* (Oxford: Oxford University Press, 2002), 193–9; Robert Benjamin, 'Lionel Trilling's Jewish "Reverberation" of February 1944', *Studies in American Jewish Literature*, Vol. 36, No. 2 (2017), pp. 205–28; Josh Lambert, *The Literary Mafia: Jews, Publishing, and Postwar American Literature* (New Haven: Yale University Press, 2022), 66–7.

37. Trilling, 'The Princess Casamassima', 83.
38. Trilling, 'From the Notebooks', 498.
39. Trilling, 'The Princess Casamassima', 80.
40. Adam Phillips, 'Lionel Trilling's Concentrated Rush', *Raritan*, Vol. 21, No. 4 (Spring 2002), pp. 164–74 (170).
41. Trilling, 'Art and Fortune', 278. Emphasis original.
42. Ibid., 276.
43. Amanda Anderson, *Bleak Liberalism* (Chicago: University of Chicago Press, 2016), 113.
44. Trilling, 'Preface', in *The Liberal Imagination*, xxi.
45. Trilling, 'Art and Fortune', 278.
46. Lionel Trilling, Letter to Newton Arvin, 10 May 1942, in *Life in Culture*, pp. 92–6 (94).
47. Trilling, 'Reality in America', 10; 'The Meaning of a Literary Idea', in *The Liberal Imagination*, pp. 281–303 (303); 'Reality in America', 9.
48. Trilling, 'Art and Fortune', 263; Letter to David Riesman, 24 August 1949, in *Life in Culture*, pp. 184–7 (185).
49. Trilling, 'Preface', in *The Liberal Imagination*, xxi.
50. Norman Podhoretz, 'The Arnoldian Function in American Criticism' (1952), in Rodden (ed.), *Lionel Trilling and the Critics*, pp. 175–81 (180).
51. In an essay on the midcentury reception of the novel, Michaela Bronstein notes that Trilling's essay helped transform *The Princess Casamassima*'s reputation: 'it was not just another minor James novel, but one of the key achievements of James's career'. My point is that Trilling is suggesting it is a key achievement because it is a minor novel. Bronstein, '*The Princess* Among the Polemicists: Aesthetics and Protest at Midcentury', *American Literary History*, Vol. 29, No. 1 (Spring 2017), pp. 26–49 (27).
52. Trilling, 'The Princess Casamassima', 89, 80, 85.
53. Ibid., 65–6, 64.
54. Trilling, 'Art and Fortune', 278.
55. Trilling, 'From the Notebooks, Part II', 11. Emphasis original.
56. Lionel Trilling, *The Middle of the Journey* [1947] (New York: New York Review Books Classics, 2002). Subsequent references are given in parentheses in the text.
57. Kirsch, *Why Trilling Matters*, 23. See, for example, Phillips, 'Lionel Trilling's Concentrated Rush'.
58. Lionel Trilling, 'Some Notes for an Autobiographical Lecture', in *The Last Decade: Essays and Reviews, 1965–75* (Oxford: Oxford University Press, 1982), pp. 226–41 (227).
59. Ibid., 228.
60. Edward Mendelson, *Moral Agents: Eight Twentieth-Century Writers* (New York: NYRB, 2015), 16. On Trilling's involvement with book clubs, see Arthur Krystal (ed.), *A Company of Readers: Uncollected Writings of W. H. Auden, Jacques Barzun, and Lionel Trilling from the Readers' Subscription and Mid-Century Book Clubs* (New York: Free Press, 2001).
61. Quoted in Mendelson, *Moral Agents*, 16.

62. Lionel Trilling, Letter to John Crowe Ransom, 21 September 1948, in *Life in Culture*, pp. 171–5 (174).
63. Mendelson, *Moral Agents*, 9.
64. Ibid., 6.
65. Lionel Trilling, Letter to Devette Havez, 29 May 1953, in *Life in Culture*, pp. 220–3 (222).
66. Lionel Trilling, Letter in Evelyn King Gilmore, 28 April 1952, in *Life in Culture*, pp. 203–4 (203, 204).
67. Anthony Hutchison, *Writing the Republic: Liberalism and Morality in American Political Fiction* (New York: Columbia University Press, 2007), 77. Emphasis original.
68. In his reading of the novel, Stephen Schryer notes that, 'In Kant's *Critique of Judgment*, flowers are the chief example of [. . .] objects that are utterly purposeless and thus elicit pure judgments of taste'. *Fantasies of the New Class: Ideologies of Professionalism in Post-World War II American Fiction* (New York: Columbia University Press, 2011), 4.
69. Lionel Trilling, Letter to Henry Rosenthal, July 1928, in *Life in Culture*, pp. 11–12 (12).
70. See, for example, Philip Rahv, 'Dostoevsky and Politics', *Partisan Review*, Vol. 5, No. 2 (July 1938), pp. 25–36.
71. Quoted in Hannelore Mundt, *Understanding Thomas Mann* (Columbia: University of South Carolina Press, 2004), 118. Mark Krupnick also makes the comparison to Mann; see *Lionel Trilling and the Fate of Cultural Criticism* (Evanston: Northwestern University Press, 1986), 91.
72. Geraldine Murphy, 'The Politics of Reading *Billy Budd*', *American Literary History*, Vol. 1, No. 2 (Summer 1989), pp. 361–82 (368).
73. Katie Fitzpatrick, 'Between Law and Justice: Legal Authority, Liberal Democracy, and Postwar Fiction', PhD thesis, Brown University, 2017, 48, 43; Katie Fitzpatrick, '"A Not-Exactly-Good Man": Lionel Trilling on Law and Judgment', *Twentieth-Century Literature*, Vol. 64, No. 2 (June 2018), pp. 129–60 (130).
74. Robert Warshow, 'The Legacy of the 30's: Middle-Class Mass Culture and the Intellectual's Problem', *Commentary*, December 1947, pp. 538–45 (544).
75. Krupnick, *Lionel Trilling and the Fate of Cultural Criticism*, 95.
76. Anderson, *Bleak Liberalism*, 99, 108.
77. Ibid., 109.
78. Ibid.
79. Hutchison, *Writing the Republic*, 78.
80. Anderson, *Bleak Liberalism*, 109.
81. See Munro Leaf, *The Story of Ferdinand* (New York: Viking, 1936).
82. 'We have forgotten that there are such people in the world, growing right out of their soil', says Nancy. 'Not that I think much of socialists as such, but it does mean something, doesn't it, for a farmer to have come even so far?' (68–9).
83. Murphy, 'The Politics of Reading *Billy Budd*', 362. On the importance of *Billy Budd* to *The Middle of the Journey*, see Hutchison, *Writing the Republic*, 84–92; Fitzpatrick, '"A Not-Exactly-Good Man"', 146–51.

84. Hutchison, *Writing the Republic*, 91.
85. Murphy, 'The Politics of Reading *Billy Budd*', 369.
86. Anderson, *Bleak Liberalism*, 112.
87. Deborah Nelson, *Tough Enough: Arbus, Arendt, Didion, McCarthy, Sontag, Weil* (Chicago: University of Chicago Press, 2017), 24.
88. Lionel Trilling, Letter to R. W. Flint, 17 June 1946, in *Life in Culture*, pp. 137–9 (137).
89. Fitzpatrick, '"A Not-Exactly-Good Man"', 154–6.
90. Trilling, 'From the Notebooks', 508. The entry is dated 1946–7. Emphasis original.
91. Fitzpatrick, 'Between Law and Justice', 63.
92. Ibid.
93. Fitzpatrick, '"A Not-Exactly-Good Man"', 145–6.
94. Fitzpatrick, 'Between Law and Justice', 50.
95. Ibid.
96. Trilling, 'From the Notebooks', 515.
97. Ibid.
98. Lionel Trilling, Letter to Norman Podhoretz, 8 May 1951, in *Life in Culture*, pp. 192–5 (194, 195).
99. Schryer, *Fantasies of the New Class*, 6, 5.
100. Ibid., 6.
101. Lionel Trilling, Letter to Richard Chase, 1 June 1947, quoted in Geraldine Murphy, 'Introduction', in *The Journey Abandoned*, pp. xi–xlii (xii).
102. Lionel Trilling, 'Commentary', in *The Journey Abandoned: The Unfinished Novel*, ed. by Geraldine Murphy (New York: Columbia University Press, 2008), pp. 155–61 (156); 'Preface', xlviii–xlix.
103. Lionel Trilling, *The Journey Abandoned*, 12. Subsequent references are given in parentheses in the text.
104. City University also resembles City College of New York, whose alumni of the late 1930s and early 1940s included Alfred Kazin, Irving Howe, Irving Kristol, and Daniel Bell. See Richard M. Cook, *Alfred Kazin: A Biography* (New Haven: Yale University Press, 2008), 23–9.
105. Lionel Trilling, 'Preface', in *The Journey Abandoned*, pp. xlv–lii (li).
106. Ibid., xlv, xlvi.
107. Ibid., lii.
108. Trilling, 'The Meaning of a Literary Idea', 281.
109. Evan Kindley, 'Big Criticism', *Critical Inquiry*, Vol. 38, No. 1 (Autumn 2011), pp. 71–95 (73).
110. See Schryer, *Fantasies of the New Class*, 1–28.
111. Greg Barnhisel, *Cold War Modernists: Art, Literature, and American Cultural Diplomacy* (New York: Columbia University Press, 2015), 184.
112. Lionel Trilling, contribution to 'Our Country and Our Culture: A Symposium', *Partisan Review*, Vol. 19, No. 3 (May 1952), pp. 318–26 (319, 321–2).
113. Quoted in Barnhisel, *Cold War Modernists*, 186.
114. See Schryer, *Fantasies of the New Class*, 206, fn 5.
115. Murphy, 'Introduction', xx.

116. Kindley, 'Big Criticism', 72.
117. The chapter set in Vincent's class at Meadowfield is based on Trilling's short story, 'The Lesson and the Secret', originally published in 1945 in *Harper's Bazaar*.
118. Murphy, 'Introduction', xxi–xxxi.
119. Lionel Trilling, 'The Immortality Ode', in *The Liberal Imagination*, pp. 129–59 (151).
120. Quoted in Louis Menand, 'Regrets Only', *The New Yorker*, 29 September 2008.
121. Trilling, *E. M. Forster*, 16.

CHAPTER 2

Breaking Into Laughter: Anticommunism, Late Modernism, and Eleanor Clark's *The Bitter Box*

On 6 April 1946, Lionel Trilling wrote to Eleanor Clark to congratulate her on the publication of her debut novel, *The Bitter Box*. 'I have not had a chance till now to tell you what a very beautiful book it is,' Trilling wrote, 'and how often it is really wonderfully witty and funny.'[1] The novel had, Trilling knew, been long in the making; since the late 1930s, Clark had been sending him drafts, asking his opinion. When she had worked in publishing earlier in her career, Clark had been the first reader at Norton to recommend Trilling's *Matthew Arnold* (1939).[2] They got to know one another through *Partisan Review*, attending the same parties and sometimes appearing in the same issue of the magazine.[3] Trilling sought her advice over which essays to include in *The Liberal Imagination* (what 'most troubles me,' he confided, is the 'delicate [. . .] matter of tone'); in the 1950s, Trilling and his wife Diana would, for three consecutive summers, rent a Connecticut farmhouse belonging to Clark and her husband, Robert Penn Warren.[4] Both Trilling and Clark were frustrated novelists who became known for their work in other genres – Trilling for his criticism, Clark for her travel writing.[5] Both were also uncertain about the future of the novel. 'I have taken a great dislike to the word "novel" at all, for current use,' Clark wrote to Trilling, the same month that *The Bitter Box* appeared.[6]

In the 1930s, Trilling and Clark had been involved in radical politics. Looking back in 1966, Trilling reflected that 'the radical movement of the Thirties [. . .] may be said to have created the American intellectual class as we now know it [. . .] [F]rom that radicalism came the moral urgency, the sense of crisis, and the concern with personal salvation that mark the existence of American intellectuals'.[7] The Trillings had for a time belonged to the National Committee for the Defense of Political Prisoners (NCDPP), a Communist front, had moved in radical circles, and been on friendly terms with Sidney Hook, Herbert Solow, and Whittaker Chambers, the last of whom became the model for *The Middle of the Journey*'s Gifford Maxim.[8] In his book reviews of the early 1930s, Trilling 'flirted with Soviet-style revolution', though he was always ambivalent about the Party and sceptical of socialist realism (he 'never could believe that a communist book was a good book,' he wrote in a 1946 letter).[9] Trilling had broken from radical politics long before the Moscow trials of 1937, but his brief involvement with the revolutionary left became, he reflected in later life, his 'indispensable' point of orientation for understanding modern American culture.[10] It left him with 'a deep fear of Stalinism at my heart,' he wrote in 1946. 'I think of my intellectual life as a struggle [. . .] against all the blindness and malign obfuscations of the Stalinoid mind of our time.'[11]

For Clark, too, the 1930s were 'a trembly time,' she later said, a period of 'great searching and soul-searching' which 'took the form of a certain involvement in what can be called the Trotskyite periphery'.[12] She had been politically aware since college. As a student at Vassar, Clark had, together with her sister Eunice and classmates Mary McCarthy and Elizabeth Bishop, set up a short-lived 'rebel' literary magazine, *Con Spirito*, in 1933.[13] The 'clandestine' publication was intended to be a 'counter-establishment blast', featuring high modernist writing: 'We demand nothing but fresh conception,' its manifesto declared.[14] Some of *Con Spirito*'s contributors were discovering radical politics under the tutelage of English professor Helen Lockwood, who has a small role in McCarthy's *The Group* (1963), and to whom *The Bitter Box* is dedicated. Clark was among the more politically engaged Vassar students, 'outspoken' in her defence of workers' rights.[15] She became more active after she graduated in 1934 and moved to New York, where she met Herbert Solow, who was to be 'a catalyst in leading an important layer of intellectuals away from Stalinism'.[16] In his journalism, Solow shone a light on the violent reality of the Communist underground; his reporting likely influenced Trilling's portrayal of Maxim and

Clark's depiction of the Party in *The Bitter Box*, in which a dissident called Brand is 'liquidated'.[17] As Trilling suggests in an essay from the 1960s reflecting on their relationship, Solow's 'most notable achievement was the organization of the Trotsky Commission in 1937', an attempt by American Trotskyists to clear Trotsky's name after the Moscow trials.[18] Clark got involved in the Commission, travelling with Solow's entourage to Mexico City, where Trotsky was exiled, to work as a translator, and marrying Jan Frankel, one of Trotsky's top secretaries, to help him secure a visa to the US.[19] They divorced in 1938, by which time Clark had 'drifted away' from Trotskyism; but, as they did for Trilling, the 1930s left their mark on her political outlook.[20] 'Whatever the errors may turn out to have been,' she said in a 1977 interview, 'there was a great personal integrity to be found in the anti-Stalinist left.'[21]

By the end of the decade, both Trilling and Clark were trying to find a way to fictionalise their formative experience of political disillusion. They weren't alone in doing so; the anti-communist novel was a 'genre coming into its own' by the 1940s.[22] An early example was *The Unpossessed* (1934) by Tess Slesinger, who was married to Solow; later examples include Saul Bellow's *Dangling Man* (1944) and Ralph Ellison's *Invisible Man* (1952), the latter of which bears a certain resemblance to *The Bitter Box*, a similarity I return to near the end of the chapter. For Trilling and Clark, fictionalising the 1930s would entail grappling with their mixed feelings not only about the left but also the novel form itself, and with their uncertainties as to the relationship between politics and aesthetics. What form, they wondered, might an anti-communist novel take, and what might constitute an anti-Stalinist aesthetics? For Trilling, as we've seen, the preferred option was a revised, reflexive version of the Forsterian novel of manners, one in which our attachment to ideas is scrutinised and our belief in the novel itself queried (a novel of ideas wearied by and wary of the work and talk of intellectuals). Clark, by contrast, would try to write a novel more overtly engaged with the tastes and preoccupations of the *Partisan* crowd, which were shaped at midcentury by the existentialism of Kierkegaard and Sartre and the fiction of Dostoevsky and Kafka, and invested in a defence of high modernist difficulty and experimentation. As we will see, Clark had been, as Alan Wald observes, 'intimately involved' with the magazine since its relaunch in 1937 as the house journal of the New York Intellectuals; most of her stories of the late 1930s and early 1940s appeared in its pages.[23] In her first novel, Clark explores what one might make of *Partisan*'s influential brand of anti-Stalinist aesthetics without being beholden to it; and in so doing, she writes a novel at once of a piece with and yet critical of the midcentury intellectual milieu from which it emerges.

Partisan Style

Looking back in later life to the beginning of her career, Clark offered a sense of what she had perceived to be the difficulties facing her. 'When I got out of college and started writing,' she told her interviewer in 1978:

> I was very discombobulated by the influence of two people, Joyce and Kafka. Kafka and Joyce brought realistic fiction to an end as far as I was concerned. I lost a lot of time – I don't know whether it was lost, really – pushing around to find a tone, to find a way in [. . .] Narrative had become [. . .] unnatural, technically. It was hard to find a tone to say what you wanted to say, and at the same time avoid being old hat, out of tune. It wasn't so much that anyone was striving for anything radically innovative, but certain kinds of approach had been made untrue by Joyce, Kafka, and others.[24]

Clark echoes the common perception, held by writers and intellectuals alike, of the situation confronting novelists in the 1940s. Midcentury critics had canonised a version of high modernism but also suggested that the movement had come to a close, leaving contemporary writers with a sense of arriving 'at the end of the tradition', a tradition that was now the object of literary criticism rather than a source of imaginative inspiration.[25] At the same time, modernism had made an older tradition of realism appear anachronistic, or 'old hat', as Clark puts it. She also articulates a sense of the attenuated ambition of the midcentury writer compared to their modernist forbears in regard to formal experimentation, echoing a common criticism of 1940s fiction; critic John Aldridge, for instance, bemoaned the 'technical conservatism' of midcentury writing compared to the innovations of the Lost Generation.[26] The dilemma confronting the midcentury novelist, Clark suggests, was not so much how to continue experimenting with new forms but how to 'find a tone' for a feeling of aesthetic belatedness or suspension; or how to write a novel after modernism.

Clark's allusion to Kafka points more specifically to the influence of *Partisan Review* and its particular version of high modernism. Affiliated with the CPUSA-backed John Reed Club in the early 1930s, the magazine broke with the Party in 1937. Under the editorship of Williams Phillips and Philip Rahv, the relaunched *Partisan* 'intended from the first to create a radical opposition to Communist and Poplar Front influence in American culture', soon establishing itself as a 'center for anti-Stalinist intellectuals'.[27] Phillips and Rahv advocated for a 'Europeanization' of American literature as a rebuttal to Popular Front socialist realism, and throughout its heyday in the 1940s and early 1950s the magazine became home to a rich variety of writing on and by European writers and philosophers, many associated with – or soon recruited into – a modernist tradition.[28] These included Kafka, whose work the new *Partisan* took up as 'one its central discoveries and a centerpiece of its worldview'.[29] From the late 1930s onwards, the magazine published Kafka's short stories, passages from his diaries, and extracts from Max Brod's biography, alongside articles on his work, including Hannah Arendt's 1944 'Revaluation'.[30] For the 'generation of the forties', and especially those who lived 'under the most terrible regime history has so far produced,' writes Arendt – who had escaped from Europe to America as a refugee three years earlier – the 'terror of Kafka is adequate to the true nature of the thing called bureaucracy – the replacing of government by administration and of laws by arbitrary decrees. We know that Kafka's construction was not a mere nightmare.'[31] Arendt's feeling that Kafka's work spoke to the political catastrophes of 1940s was widely shared, and his 'understanding of the limitation of human freedom', as Isaac Rosenfeld put it in 1947, chimed with *Partisan*'s chastened radicalism.[32] In the Introduction, we saw that, for Deleuze and Guattari, Kafka's work is a model for a 'minor literature', in which, through a 'deterritorialization' of language, Kafka explores the idea of becoming 'a stranger *within* his own language'; in America at midcentury, Kafka's work was felt to capture what Arendt called 'the modern feeling of homelessness in the world'.[33]

Describing the protagonists of Kafka's fiction, Arendt writes, 'They certainly are not persons whom we could meet in a real world, for they lack all the many superfluous detailed characteristics which together make a real individual.' Rather, stripped of 'human possibility' by the 'senseless automatism' of the bureaucratic state, they are reduced to only their 'function'.[34] Arendt calls Kafka's heroes 'small people'; we might call them minor characters. At midcentury, these diminutive figures were compared to the 'little men' familiar from nineteenth-century Russian literature, Morris Dickstein explains – the 'clerks, bureaucrats, and minor functionaries' of Gogol and Dostoevsky's stories, 'who lived pinched lives, hounded by their superiors and their creditors, tormented even by their families'.[35] The influence of Russian fiction, combined with 'the Kafka vogue', led to a flurry of 'Little Man' stories by American writers after the war.[36] In the pages of *Partisan*, a Dostoevsky revival was also well under way by 1938. In his revisionary reading of *The Possessed* (1873) – the novel John Laskell fails to finish in *The Middle of the Journey*, and to which the title of Slesinger's *The Unpossessed* alludes – Philip Rahv recruits Dostoevsky as an important writer for anti-Stalinist thought by reading the Russian as an 'analyst of contradictions, who was ever vibrating between faith and heresy'.[37] In this regard, Dostoevsky was made to resemble another European writer also undergoing a 'major revival' in the late 1930s – Kierkegaard, and especially the Kierkegaard of *Repetition* (1843), in which the narrator exclaims, 'My whole being screams in self-contradiction'.[38]

Kierkegaard's work was understood to be a 'wellspring of modern existentialism', which in the 1940s enjoyed a surge in popularity among American intellectuals, fuelled partly by *Partisan*; when the magazine published the pamphlet *What is Existentialism?*, by editor William Barrett, in 1947, it became an influential primer.[39] Existentialism was something of a 'fad' in America, to be sure, bolstered by the celebrity of Sartre and Simone de Beauvoir, and declining in importance fairly rapidly.[40] But for a time, Sartre was an important interlocutor for the anti-Stalinists, another connection to European thought. Sartre was framed as a theorist of 'disappointed rationalism', which could well describe the outlook of some of the *Partisan* crowd.[41] He was read in much the same way as Kafka was by Arendt and Dostoevsky by Rahv: not as a prophet of absurdism per se, but as a critic of the hidden irrationalism at the heart of bourgeois society.[42] Sartre's focus on the anxiety elicited by the individual's recognition of the conditions and limitations of their freedom struck a chord with American midcentury thought, for which anxiety had become a conceptual touchstone (the midcentury imagined itself, in Auden's famous phrase from 1947, as the 'Age of Anxiety').[43] Kierkegaard had argued that 'anxiety is freedom's possibility, and only such anxiety is through faith absolutely educative, because it consumes all finite ends and discovers all their deceptiveness' (Whittaker Chambers ended up a Kierkegaardian).[44] But in the atheistic existentialism of Sartre, this religious *angst* was replaced by 'an authentic confrontation with the recognition that there is no prior supra-personal constraint on individual freedom, a recognition that is both dreadful and liberating'.[45] Sartrean existentialism offered a compelling image of man as 'emptied out, unprotected, in extremis, but, therefore, purely human', a universalist image that Louis Menand argues we see in the midcentury paintings of Jean Dubuffet and the sculptures of Alberto Giacometti.[46] It was also the image that *Partisan* critics found in the work of Kafka and Dostoevsky: the harried, frightened K.; the disillusioned, ironic protagonist of *Notes from Underground* (1864) and his American incarnations – Bellow's dangling man, and the underground men of Richard Wright and Ralph Ellison, to whom we shall return. At the same time, Gregory Ariail suggests, Kafka's 'assemblage' stories, featuring odd 'hybrids' of man and animal or machine, offered readers a picture of the modern subject as less than 'purely' human, but rather alloyed with the non-human in ways that queried the categories of action and agency to which midcentury thought repeatedly turned.[47]

Clark's *Partisan* short stories of the 1930s and 1940s show the degree to which her work belongs to this intellectual milieu. 'Asleep a King' (1938) – which appears in the magazine immediately after an extract from Brod's biography – shares something of the nightmare quality of Kafka's work.[48] The story focuses on a working-class family in a modest town: a mother who takes in laundry; a son, David, whose ambition to be a musician has 'petered out'; his brother, Mark, who has been in hospital with an unspecified illness and fallen in love with his nurse. The shadow of the Depression hangs over the story and the family's money troubles are never forgotten, but Mark's depression is of a different order, his struggles more existential than economic – 'It seemed to him that at some point he must have had a dream for himself but he could not remember it'. Everyone but Mark appears to have 'some secret understanding with the month of June', the town lit in summer sun while he is engulfed in darkness.[49] Gradually, it becomes clear that Mark is not of this world at all: we learn that he shot himself a year or so after leaving hospital having apparently recovered. The story thus takes place after a sickness for which there is no cause or remedy, in some dark region between life and death.

'The Heart of the Afternoon' (1948) seems similarly marked by the feeling of anxious suspension – 'the sense of being between beginnings and endings, lapsed certainties and new potentialities, recent horrors and strange, often opaque futures' – that Claire Seiler describes as 'a principal imaginative construct of the midcentury'.[50] The narrative centres on 'a boy of nine or ten' and is told in a jagged present tense, in a style recalling Gertrude Stein as well as Kafka: 'It is the very heart of the afternoon, the point when the day goes dead and nothing matters and it seems that nothing will ever change'.[51] The story seems to be one of arrested development, and yet also to hinge on a dramatic 'change' witnessed by the boy – a motorcycle accident in which the rider crashes 'over on his head. The machine twitches and shakes upside down on him.'[52] But the heart of the afternoon and the heart of the story is not this sudden accident but a slower, stranger disaster, more trivial and more disturbing, unfolding repeatedly throughout the narrative: the boy's grandmother, in the grip of something unidentified, throwing a 'headless doll' from her third-storey apartment for the 'twentieth time' that day, and the boy fetching and returning it to her before she grows too distressed. We are told that 'the head came off a long time ago from so much falling to the ground every day'.[53] The doll doesn't twitch like the motorbike but nonetheless has a life of its own; the narrative has the quality of one of Kafka's parables or assemblage stories, its style as well as its theme one of dislocation. The odd routine with the grandmother resembles an intergenerational game of fort/da, a staging and restaging of a traumatic loss in a kind of suspended present tense.

These stories suggest Clark's familiarity with *Partisan*'s modernist aesthetics. Yet the magazine also proclaimed that the European modernist tradition it championed, and to which Clark's stories pay their dues, was at an end, and that the contemporary American novel paled in comparison; indeed, the revival of writers like Dostoevsky and Kafka was taken to be indicative of the paucity of good contemporary fiction. In *The Bitter Box*, Clark works within and against the tastes and commitments of *Partisan* in an attempt to 'find a tone', as she puts it in the 1978 interview, that might acknowledge the complex legacy of high modernism. Her novel is engaged with existentialism, pervaded by anxiety, wedded to an anti-Stalinist political perspective, and indebted to the influence of modernists feted in the magazine, especially Kafka. And yet, at the same time, *The Bitter Box* also internalises something of the magazine's dim view of contemporary fiction, acceding to the idea that the midcentury novelist could no longer straightforwardly emulate their modernist forbears nor return to an older tradition of realism. Clark dramatises this aesthetic impasse in a manner I suggest is typical of the midcentury minor novel, making a virtue of what were taken to be the novel's reduced capacities.

The Bitter Box is the story of Mr Temple, a conscientious bank clerk who one day unexpectedly abandons his post and joins a revolutionary political movement resembling the CPUSA of the late 1930s. In a memo written while working on the book, Clark reminds herself that she is 'not writing a combination of the *Divine Comedy*, *War and Peace* and *Das Kapital*. I am writing about Mr. T who is a little man, and what he needs and I need is a little book'.[54] Rather than the broad social canvas of Tolstoy – of nineteenth-century realism and the tradition of the historical novel – Clark suggests she will restrict herself to telling a smaller story with something of the quality of one of Kafka's allegories ('Mr. T's own crime [. . .] stands for all crimes,' she writes in the memo. 'Leave it at that'), about a particular kind of minor character: a Kafkaesque little man, who, as we've seen, was all the rage in midcentury fiction. Littleness will be part of the project of the novel, Clark suggests; *The Bitter Box* will be an experiment in writing small.

Laughter, Anxiety, Nightmare

Soon after he had written to Clark congratulating her on the publication of *The Bitter Box*, Trilling accepted an invitation from John Crowe Ransom, the editor of *Kenyon Review*, to write a piece on it. 'The Life of the Novel' appeared in the Autumn 1946 issue; although not well-known, it is one of the most substantial and intriguing of Trilling's uncollected essays.[55] Much as he had, by his own admission, 'recruited' Forster into a 'quarrel' he was having in the early 1940s 'with American literature as at that time it was established', in 'The Life of the Novel' Trilling recruits Clark into his long-running quarrel with *Partisan*-style modernism.[56] Although closely associated with the magazine throughout his career, Trilling was always circumspect in his endorsement of some of the European modernist writing celebrated in *Partisan*. The 'stock of Henry James [had] gone up in the same market as that of Kafka' in the early 1940s, Edmund Wilson said, but Trilling was always more taken with the former than the latter. 'I like stories of realistic moral situations, expressed more or less in realistic action and have an eye on Henry James and Dostoievsky [sic] as the outside limits,' he wrote in a March 1939 letter to Clark.[57] In 'The Life of the Novel', *The Bitter Box* becomes the occasion for Trilling to mark the critical distance between his idea of anti-Stalinist aesthetics and *Partisan*'s.

Trilling opens the essay by framing the novel within the broader discourse of the death of the novel that we have seen was so prevalent at midcentury. Dismissive of the notion that the novel has reached 'a last stage in its autonomous life-cycle', he instead argues that the 'present bad condition of the novel' is a 'result of a present condition of our minds'. In keeping with the tenor of his more famous essays of the mid-1940s, Trilling suggests that the novel is 'based in an interest in morals and manners and we have shut our minds to that interest, no doubt because we do not like to look at ourselves'. The dominance of rationalism – upheld and defended in different ways by Marxists and liberals alike – means that 'we can think about morality only when it is contained in a solution of science, calling it sociology, psychology, or anthropology – that is, we can think about it only without joy and without reference to personal action'.[58] I'll return to this slightly unexpected invocation of joy shortly.

Trilling finds evidence of our inability to 'look at ourselves' in the fact that, 'although the Communist Party has been in existence in this country for more than a quarter-century, it has not appeared in our novels except as a figment'. This is telling, because the Communist Party would seem to be the perfect novelistic subject – or at least, perfect for the kind of revised novel of manners Trilling had in mind and was himself trying to write. The Party's 'relative intimacy' of 'organizational apparatus brought ultimate matters wonderfully close', while 'the fierce tensions of doubt and belief [. . .] of ideal by necessity [. . .] have comprised, in concentrated form, the moral drama that we of our time best understand'. 'As if this were not enough to tempt the novelist', there is the 'great richness in the matter of manners, for the Communist Party creates a culture within a culture and has generated in its adherents a characteristic habit of mind [. . .]'.[59]

Praising Clark for addressing the role of the Communist Party in American culture, Trilling reads the novel as a 'fable of the moral life' on the great Miltonic theme of 'freedom and salvation'; with Milton, Clark recognises that 'salvation is more painful than judgment'.[60] The 'great statement' in 'modern times' of this theme comes from Dostoevsky, Trilling writes – though not the Dostoevsky of *Notes from Underground* preferred by the *Partisan* crowd, but of the poem of the Grand Inquisitor from *The Brothers Karamazov* (1880).[61] Elsewhere, Trilling writes that this passage dramatises a 'confrontation' between 'the two great concepts that preoccupy the modern mind, freedom on the one hand, happiness and security on the other'.[62] In 'The Life of the Novel', he describes this confrontation in more pointedly political terms as being between 'the bland "security" of the projected totalitarian social-service State' and 'the wilderness dangers of the liberty which is a pre-condition of salvation or of being wholly human'. In *The Bitter Box*, we see Temple attached first to the 'bland security' of the bank and its bureaucracy, and then enamoured by the sense of purpose and structure afforded by being part of a political organisation. 'His long unrealized protest is, as we say, "channeled",' writes Trilling, 'his native gifts of loyalty and generosity are given "a definite object".[63] Only at the end of the novel, thrown out into the swirl of a snowstorm having lost both his job and his faith in the Party, does Temple find himself confronting the wilderness of his liberty.

Trilling admires the theme and the 'moral realism' of the novel, then, but he takes issue with its 'method'. Expressing scepticism at the idea that 'only a new and extreme infusion of method will save' the novel from decay, Trilling describes novels written in the style of Joyce or Kafka – the writers Clark identifies as exerting such an influence on her early work – as belonging to 'the art of nightmare', a nightmare he hears echoed in the writing of Sartre. 'I cannot help feeling that the interesting nightmares of the Existentialist writers are very much more simple than they pretend,' he writes, amounting to the 'sentimentality of frustrated expectation'.[64] Lacking the dialectical modulation of moral realism, the art of nightmare is ultimately 'submissive' – much as he suggests elsewhere that contemporary American literature is too 'passive'[65] – born of the sense that, 'since we can learn little new and nothing good, we should now devote ourselves only to an intenser perception of what sad knowledge we have'.[66] As a Freudian, Trilling understands this position as not simply nihilistic but traumatised, comparing 'our compulsive recapitulation of nightmare' to 'the soldier's compulsive recapitulation of the trauma that caused his war-neurosis' (bringing to mind the compulsive repetition in 'The Heart of the Afternoon').[67] That the novel might be interested in trauma after the war is no surprise; 'we all observe with baffled wonder and shame,' Trilling writes a couple of years later, 'that there is no possible way of responding to Belsen and Buchenwald'.[68] But aesthetically, he argues, trauma has already gotten old, and he worries that anxiety – the 'collective mood' of the midcentury – has already become a 'modern cliché'.[69] Whatever the contemporary novel was to be, Trilling felt, it couldn't be the stuff of modernist nightmare. Although he acknowledges that *The Bitter Box*'s 'anxious, claustrophobic quality' appears to resemble 'that which we have discovered and applauded in Kafka', Trilling warns that 'even anxiety can have its academicism'.[70]

Trilling tries hard to separate the novel's anti-communism and moral realism from its Kafkaesque, Sartrean, *Partisan*-ready method, and he does so by way of an interesting redescription of naturalism.

As Thomas Hill Schaub explains, both the New York Intellectuals' high modernist aesthetics and the New Critics' formalism defined themselves against literary naturalism. Early twentieth-century naturalism came to be disparaged for its 'naive rationalism' and 'certainty in human affairs,' Schaub writes, and for what Trilling in 'Reality in America' (1946) calls its 'informing idea of the economic and social determination of thought'.[71] But although Schaub is right to say that midcentury critics associated naturalism with the 'dangerous optimism' of the 1930s, they also tended to trace a naturalistic tradition back to nineteenth-century French literature, and to Zola in particular.[72] In *The American Novel and its Tradition* (1957), for example, Richard Chase writes of the 'attempt of Zola' to 'write a new kind of scientific fiction' in which one places 'one's character in a certain environment, as one places specimens in a laboratory experiment [. . .] report[ing] without fear or favor how they acted according to natural laws'.[73] Like 'nineteenth-century science', Chase suggests, 'the naturalistic novel took a bleakly pessimistic view when considering the ability of the individual to control his fate'. Although critics like Chase could admire naturalism's attempt at 'reviving a genuine tragic art by evoking fate in terms of heredity and environment', they took issue with its limited conception of the individual, and its low regard for agency and contingency, for private judgement and personal folly.[74]

In 'The Life of the Novel', Trilling draws a distinction between 'the programmatic naturalism we associate with Zola' and a 'larger naturalism [. . .] characterized not by a "scientific" view of the world but rather by a social tradition – it is marked by men talking to each other about themselves and the universe and being able to understand each other'.[75] He suggests an unlikely affinity between the modernist 'art of nightmare' and 'the program of Zola which holds that art must reproduce the immediate reality of the world'.[76] Trilling acknowledges that modernist writing has 'much more complex notions of what it means to "reproduce" or "represent" reality' – not 'the obvious one of economic or social circumstance' but the 'intenser reality of the mind of the bizarre totality of man's condition'. But, he maintains, 'the essence' of naturalism's 'doctrine is at its root', and so there is 'no such great distance between Zola and Kafka as at first appears'.[77] This diverges markedly from how naturalism's relation to modernism tended to be conceived of in *Partisan*; in his contribution to the magazine's 1948 symposium on 'The State of American Writing', for example, Leslie Fiedler articulated the more commonly held view that 'Kafka pre-eminently conditions the revolt against naturalism' underway in contemporary fiction.[78] For his own, 'larger naturalism', Trilling wants to claim a more capacious conception of, and complex relation to, reality. This includes the ability to actively 'project' a 'potentiality of states of being'; that is, to imagine a future different from the present, one emerging out of the social world of morals and manners, from interactions and conversations – or what he called, in reference to his own anti-communist novel, 'human touches'.[79]

Trilling's redescription of naturalism in his review of *The Bitter Box* is prefigured in his correspondence with Clark. In a June 1939 letter, Trilling writes that 'what modern writers need' is to 'recapture the love of telling a story, of wonder and suspense [. . .] We've turned too scientific. Agree?'[80] By 'scientific', Trilling has in mind 'the program of Zola'; his celebration of wonder and suspense, then, is a riposte to what Chase describes as the 'laboratory' conditions of naturalistic writing and its commitment to rationalism. In his April 1946 letter congratulating Clark on *The Bitter Box*'s publication, Trilling suggests that her book 'is written from a "theory" of the novel that is not mine, and this makes its capture of me that much more significant'. He continues:

> I know that you will insist that there is no theory at all, and I know that you don't like to be made conscious of having worked within one, but sometime soon, when we meet, I would like to talk to you about it at length. One thing that struck me about the book was how very fluid it was [. . .] by fluid, I mean narrative and social. I think that the things I liked most of all were the moments of meeting between people when they talked together or quarrelled [. . .] You see what I am trying to do is to drag you into my own more naturalistic theory of the novel, which in part shows how much I liked yours.[81]

Here, Trilling has in mind the 'larger naturalism' he sketches more fully in 'The Life of the Novel'. In the letter, he writes of wishing to 'drag' Clark towards his own conception of the novel, and, in the review, he tries, more elaborately, to do the same.[82] He does so by suggesting that, in fact, *The Bitter Box* is not as committed to its *Partisan* method as it might at first appear, and that Clark herself 'is not wholly in love with the elements of anxiety in her book'. This becomes evident, Trilling suggests, when the novel 'breaks into laughter and liberates its characters and its readers from its [. . .] claustral matrix of anxiety'.[83] For Trilling, the art of nightmare is an aesthetic as well as political dead-end because, like a trauma, it can only instantiate a reductive reality which it cannot see beyond, narrowing the repertoire of human possibility; like more conventional forms of naturalism, it forecloses the prospect of surprising ourselves. 'It is very difficult to believe, in such a world as ours,' writes Trilling, 'that forms of free being can be projected, and very difficult to remember that it is one of the things art can and should do.'[84] It is these forms of free being that are projected when *The Bitter Box* breaks into laughter.

Trilling's emphasis on laughter might at first seem surprising; he was after all not well-known for being a barrel of laughs ('noble sadness' was more his critical style, R. W. B. Lewis once said).[85] But in *E. M. Forster* (1943), Trilling 'weighs, considers, and earnestly defends the rights of laughter,' Michael Levenson notes.[86] In his championing of Forster's 'serious whim', Trilling was drawn to the idea that humour, comedy and a certain lightness of touch might be an antidote to liberal progressivism and rationalism (remember Laskell laughing at Alwin Folger talking nonsense to his dogs); his interest in laughter represents, paradoxically, an extension of his thinking about tragedy. Indeed, joy, wonder and humour feature in Trilling's midcentury critical vocabulary just as prominently as, and often in tandem with, tragedy, complexity, and morality. In 'The Life of the Novel', Trilling has in mind a particular kind of laughter – not 'that desperate social smile which Kafka perhaps in part derived from the seminarist's ironic deprecation of his own cleverness that is so boring in Kierkegaard, but actual laughter':

> When the laughter comes we remember why Stendhal loved Mozart, and why Nietzsche loved Stendhal and the Mediterranean air. For the laughter breaks the obsessive, submissive circle of recapitulation; it constitutes a demand, for it is the representation of a form of free being in which normative mind is frankly and naturalistically at work.[87]

Trilling is thinking here, partly, of Nietzsche's remark in *Ecce Homo* (1908) that Stendhal 'robbed me of the best atheist joke, which was just made for me to tell: "God's only excuse is that he doesn't exist"'.[88] But he is also thinking of their shared conception of laughter as a response to suffering. For Stendhal, Harriet Murphy explains, laughter is 'knowing the pain of pursuing happiness'.[89] Nietzsche similarly 'recommends a special kind of joy and laughter as the only alternative to a pessimistic denial of existence, or to an optimistic fantasy that negation and limits can somehow be resolved'.[90] Zarathustra describes himself as 'the laughing prophet', replacing Jesus' crown of thorns with a 'laugher's crown'.[91] His ability to laugh even in the face of tragedy emerges from an insight into the nature of history. 'Eternal recurrence' is Nietzsche's term for the idea that, within the infinitude of time, the affairs of man are finite and so will recur. 'Everything that happens has happened before and will happen again, time after time', though 'not always and only with the precise detail in which it once occurred'.[92] To affirm the idea of eternal recurrence is to conceive of a relation to time that allows for a future, as opposed to a traumatised or nihilistic relation to the past which is perpetually caught in a nightmare of history; recurrence, then, as an alternative to repetition. As Elizabeth Grosz explains, Nietzsche argues that 'to be mired in the past is to be unable to think and act the future; conversely, to be unanchored in the past [. . .] is to have no place from which a future can be made that is different from the present'. The affirmation of eternal recurrence recognises the 'possibility of being untimely, of placing ourselves outside the constraints [. . .] of the present', thereby preserving the open-endedness of the future.[93] Laughter in Nietzsche is the sound of the affirmation of this insight into the nature of history, of human possibility born of the knowledge of the tragic boundedness of our agency. For Trilling, breaking into Nietzschean laughter breaks the spell of existentialist nightmare and modernist anxiety.

Trilling's engagement with Nietzsche belongs to a broader 'revival of interest among American intellectuals' at midcentury in the German philosopher's work.[94] As Benjamin Mangrum explains, this revival of interest 'gathered around what Nietzsche in *The*

Gay Science calls "gaiety," or life-affirmation'. For Nietzsche, writes Mangrum, 'the consequence of the "death of God" is that the value of our world resides in the here and now, in the lives we live independently of those forces (God, popular morality, nationalism) that would determine the shape and meaning of life on our behalf. The 'only way to take life seriously,' Nietzsche insists, 'is through "gaiety," the pleasure we find in existence itself'.[95] Having been associated with political tyranny and the rise of European fascism, the postwar reception of Nietzsche in America was remarkable for the way in which it 'rebranded his work as a critical ally within the literature opposed to totalitarianism'. 'Not unlike Arendt's theory of action,' Mangrum observes, 'the postwar American interpretation of Nietzsche found an alternative to political tyranny by extoling the virtues of being an independent soul.'[96] Nietzsche was often framed within the context of 'European existentialism,' Jennifer Ratner-Rosenhagen notes, perhaps most influentially so in Walter Kaufmann's popular *Portable Nietzsche* (1954).[97] But Nietzsche's work also offered a project of individuation different in emphasis and style from Sartre's existentialism, a difference Trilling makes much of in his opposing of Nietzschean laughter to Sartrean nihilism.[98]

In his effort to 'drag' *The Bitter Box* in line with his own theory of the novel, however, Trilling perhaps fails to hear other timbres of laughter echoing in Clark's text; for laughter might not always be the sound of Nietzschean gaiety, or 'life-affirmation'. For instance, laughter plays a prominent role in Tyrus Miller's influential account of interwar 'late modernism'.[99] Late modernism 'makes self-conscious' the limits of high modernist fiction's emphasis on 'formal cohesion' and 'discursive mastery,' Miller writes. It does so through a 'variety of satiric and parodic strategies' that work to 'deflate' the modernist novel's 'symbolic resources' and 'unsettle' its 'signs of formal craft', exposing 'the comic fragility of modernist attempts to contain contingency and violence aesthetically'.[100] In particular, the late modernist fiction of Wyndham Lewis and Samuel Beckett 'loosens the modernist dominance of form' through conjuring 'the disruptive, deforming spell of laughter'. 'Within the late modernist novel,' Miller suggests, formal breaks and lapses 'bound to laughter' allow 'expression of those negative forces of the age that could not be coaxed into any admirable design of words: its violence, madness, absurd contingencies, and sudden deaths'.[101] Miller draws on Henri Bergson's 'notion of the comedic aspects of mechanized bodies' in his conception of late modernist laughter.[102] For Bergson, Sara Crangle explains, 'rigidity is comic and laughter is its corrective'; we laugh, Bergson writes, 'at something mechanical encrusted on the living', at the incongruity when some aspect of another's behaviour or manner seems automated.[103] Laughter, in this account, marks the moment when the human and mechanical combine and, at the same, when the self is salvaged from automatism; laughter as the precarious recovery of a 'subjectivity at risk of dissolution', as Miller puts it.[104] Late modernism is full of these expressions of the subject's 'minimum self-confirmation' amidst the 'negative forces' of modernity, and late modernist texts are full of subjects in extremis or in collapse, figures – like Lewis's puppets or Beckett's clowns – clinging to some vestigial, unstable sense of self.[105] In these works, Miller writes, 'laughter, itself a kind of spasmodic automatism [. . .] can help serve to convince us that a self, however minimal, is still there [. . .] The self confirms itself in laughter, persists in the interval between automatism and its comic reflex.'[106] Late modernism tends not towards the 'projection of forms of free being', to return to Trilling's phrase, but to a 'close of the horizon of the future', a dwindling of possibility. Late modernism is 'permeated with a foreboding of decline and fall,' Miller argues.[107] Rather than expressing Nietzschean gaiety, late modernist laughter belongs to 'a kind of bitter comedy' of barely surviving; 'I laugh therefore I (still) am'.[108]

The bitter comedy of late modernist laughter suggests there might be something unnerving about laughter in *The Bitter Box*. The line between laughter on the one hand and anxiety on the other might be less clear than Trilling suggests: laughter in Clark's novel might at times be 'the laughter of unease', in Freud's phrase. Anxiety, according to Freud, has a 'quality of indefiniteness and lack of object'.[109] While fear 'compels a subject's action', anxiety lacks 'a singular point of origin' and so defers the subject's actions and forestalls their decisions.[110] Anxiety can also 'become self-referential,' Claire Seiler notes, 'perpetuated by the experience of being anxious'.[111] Laughter, too, can be difficult to locate, a strange physiological contortion of body and voice issuing from no fixed point, and often with no identifiable object. It can sometimes be hard to say why we're laughing, and even harder to make ourselves stop. Just as anxiety 'suspends' the subject, leaving them incapable of decision or action, laughter can overwhelm us, or make us lose control. In *Laughter: Notes on a Passion* (2010), Anca Parvulescu explores the idea that laughter sometimes manifests a modality of action somewhere between the usual binary of active and passive. Parvulescu draws on Émile Benveniste's work examining how Indo-European languages have 'historically known a triple distinction between active, middle, and passive'. The 'middle position,' Parvulescu writes, suggests 'only a certain relationship of the action with the subject, or an "interest" of the subject in the action'.[112] Laughter, that is to say, might signal not an affirmation of the soul but rather an anxious, Bergsonian ambiguation of the subject's agency, or only 'the minimal condition of subjectivity', as Miller puts it.[113]

Trilling and Miller's contrasting pictures of the laughing self shape their divergent aesthetic projects. Both agree that laughter marks the limits of a certain version of high modernism, but their sense of what lies beyond those limits is different: for Trilling, the promise of a 'larger naturalism'; for Miller, the enervated aesthetics of late modernism, which 'strongly anticipate' later postmodernist fiction.[114] Clark's novel explores these different resonances of laughter, shifting between the contrasting aesthetic possibilities they suggest. *The Bitter Box* is not quite 'parodic' in the way Miller argues is characteristic of late modernism, nor are its formal 'lapses' from *Partisan*-modernist 'method' as stark as those he analyses in the work of Lewis and Beckett; but sometimes laughter in her novel does seem to stage the sorts of crises of agency or ambiguation of subjectivity he describes, even as, at other times, as Trilling suggests, laughter in the novel seems to 'project forms of free being', to gesture more joyously to the future. In its curious admixture of laughter, *The Bitter Box* arrives at the kind of aesthetic impasse that characterises the midcentury minor novel's project. To put it another way, when the novel breaks into laughter, it's hard to distinguish whether we're listening to an aesthetic breakthrough or a breakdown; whether the novel is breaking free or only breaking apart.

Caged Laughter: *The Bitter Box*

'Pale and small-boned' with 'pinched' features, Temple resembles the Kafkaesque 'little men' who proliferated in midcentury American fiction, and perhaps also the late modernist subjects *in extremis* described by Miller.[115] He is neurotic, sexually repressed, and fastidiously cautious, 'apt to suffer from constipation and insomnia' (24). This careful vigilance makes him an excellent employee at the bank where he works as a teller, renowned for his efficiency and instant recall of the most trifling details of the smallest accounts – a 'recognizing machine' (9). He feels so 'marvellously safe' at work 'that sometimes he cut[s] short his lunch hour just for the pleasure of going back into the cage', where he is 'protected by all sorts of devices, including an electric button to be pushed in case of an emergency' (15). In his imprisonment, Temple resembles not only the protagonists of Kafka's stories as described by Arendt – a functionary of a bureaucracy – but also the laughable automaton described by Bergson.[116] He is in thrall to the bank's hierarchy, willingly subjugating himself to the 'second vice-president' in much the way that Arendt or Erich Fromm, in his influential study of fascism, *Escape from Freedom* (1941), suggest is symptomatic of what happens under totalitarian rule: the individual 'escape[s] from the burden of his freedom into new dependencies and submission'.[117] Throughout the novel, Clark connects the bureaucracy of the bank with the bureaucracy of the revolutionary political party Temple will later join, suggesting that both require a relinquishment of personal autonomy that diminishes the individual, and that this relinquishment is often freely made.

The novel is set in a faintly hallucinatory New York, Temple finding himself turning 'interminable grey corners' as he walks 'through miles of concrete tunnels', and in a room 'far larger than would have seemed possible from the geography of the building' (191, 25). There's a Mitteleuropean air to the novel familiar from other American anti-communist fictions of the period. Temple lives in a thin-walled boarding house reminiscent of the setting of *Dangling Man*, and, like Bellow's protagonist, he is often bothered by an elderly neighbour, a hoarder who tries to press on him religious pamphlets telling 'all about the new world that's coming' (14);

Temple will soon find himself walking the streets handing out political propaganda promising another kind of salvation.[118] When he leaves his cage one afternoon, he does so without thinking. It is less a 'decision' (10) than a compulsion; he does not seize his 'emancipation' (16) but remains 'as passive as a tuning fork' (190). In this state, he ends up in a restaurant, where he is dazzled by the waitresses who blithely approach the automatic doors leading to the kitchen with what the cautious Temple sees as thrilling abandon: 'It pleased him to remain ever so slightly in suspense [. . .] what was remarkable was not the electric beam but the act of faith that kept [the waitresses] from backing up at the last moment' (17).

Temple's break for freedom is characterised by this feeling of 'suspense' and by the ambiguous mediation of the mechanical or non-human. This is emphasised by the recurring image of manikins which Temple starts to notice in shop windows; like the broken doll and twitching motorbike of Clark's earlier short stories, these manikins figure a disturbing confusion of autonomy and automation. Leaving the restaurant, Temple is troubled by the sight of a shopkeeper 'calmly dismembering a naked manikin' (19), and it is during this dismemberment that we hear the first laugh of the novel. It belongs to a man whom Temple recognises as a customer at the bank, called Brand – an allusion, perhaps, to Hawthorne's tale, 'Ethan Brand', and to Hawthorne's interest in untimely laughter ('Laughter, when out of place, mistimed or bursting forth from a disordered state of feeling, may be the most terrible modulation of the human voice').[119] Resting 'casually back on his heels' as he stands beside Temple at the shop window, Brand laughs 'the kind of deep and easy laugh that generally gives confidence, as being associated with a clear conscience' (20). But it is a little ambiguous as to what Brand is finding so funny, and it unnerves Temple. Later in the novel, Brand lets out another 'burst of laughter' at the sight of a caged monkey, 'a broken chain dragging from its neck' (103). There might, then, be something merciless in Brand's laughter at the dismemberment of the manikin, a cruelty which fails to distinguish between the creaturely and the inanimate (or between a monkey in its cage and a bank teller in his).

When Temple at first resists his efforts to recruit him into the Party, Brand is 'as carefree in his laughter as he had been before the dismembered manikin', which leaves the teller 'confused' (29). After Brand launches into another 'gleeful tirade against capitalism', Temple is left in a trance, wandering home 'like a sleepwalker' before discovering he has begun to laugh: 'He was not used to laughing and it sounded more as if a medical instrument had been pushed down his throat' (35). Here, in a sort of internalised version of the mechanical encrusted on the living, it is unclear from where the laughter emanates or what its object is; whether it is 'actual laughter', to use Trilling's term, or an imitation (like a manikin), or perhaps belongs to the nightmare through which Temple is still 'sleepwalking'. When, back at the bank, he fantasises about absconding again, Temple imagines how he will 'roll [. . .] on his heels with laughter' (imitating Brand, perhaps), only to discover that he is 'laughing a little already' at the very thought of it, 'to the astonishment of the teller on his left, who had never before heard a non-professional sound from that cage' (41–2). Temple's involuntary laughter seems provoked by his giddy sense of his expanding freedom, but there continues to be something nightmarish in his vision of the world. On the streets he sees 'manikins by the dozen on the verge of life', and later dreams of the vice-president's secretary 'writing shorthand with her legs removed' (49, 56).

When Brand 'snatche[s] him back' from an oncoming bus, Temple has the 'fantastic notion' that his companion is in fact 'trying to push him under it'. Something about the incident provokes 'a giggling fit' which Temple attempts to 'throttle', managing 'to hide his condition' except for 'a hoot of untimely laughter' (57). The nature of Temple's 'condition' is opaque, as is the cause of his out-of-place laughter; it might be brought on by his brush with death, or by his suspicion that Brand means him harm. A bout of laughter overcomes him again when he suggests to a fellow comrade that 'sooner or later' he will end up in prison as a result of his revolutionary activities (151). And he feels another 'one of his giggling fits coming on' when he learns of a rumour circulating in the Party that he is an 'agent provocateur' (162). In these instances, Temple's laughter carries a certain awareness of the absurdity and possible danger of his situation; but rather than ironic or self-reflexive, his laughter seems born of his violent detachment – or dismemberment, we might say – from his own experience. In these moments, Temple's laughter resonates with a set of anxieties – around agency, totalitarianism, automatism, and bureaucracy – familiar from the pages from *Partisan*, and, at the same time, to register the kind of minimal affirmation of subjectivity characteristic of late modernism.

But Trilling is right that laughter sometimes also seems to sound the possibility of freedom in the novel. Brand's wife and comrade, Hilda, has a creative energy that cannot be 'channelled' by the Party. She spends her spare time making paper and wire mobiles depicting animal and plant life – assemblages that revise the novel's troubling portrayal of the mechanical and non-human, and recall the work of Alexander Calder.[120] Temple sees one mobile consisting of 'some cloth fish suspended upside down over a polished metal plate' and another resembling a 'white mouse [hanging] from a slender wire stem like a fading lily's' (26). Now zealously committed to the Party, Temple cannot 'imagine a purpose' for Hilda's mobiles and urges her to 'be serious' (27). But he is unexpectedly moved by another mobile, depicting a crimson bird, leading him to let out an 'involuntary exclamation of pleasure' which is met by Hilda's 'embarrassed little laugh' (110). The mobiles seem to figure a playfulness that is anathema to the rigidity of the Party line; like laughter, in their lightness the mobiles are a kind of counterweight to the 'heavy, oppressive seriousness' of ideology.[121] They enact a form of suspension that isn't an anxious 'paralysis', to recall Thomas Hill Schaub's description of 1940s fiction, but a kind of poised, dynamic free-floating.[122]

Then there is Mr Schonfeldt, Temple's colleague at the bank. Central to their relationship is Schonfeldt's passion for imitating bird calls, connecting him to Hilda and her 'crimson bird' mobile. Hearing Schonfeldt's beautiful rendition of a bird song, Temple enjoys 'a few seconds of pure lucidity, unrelated to anything but itself' (126) – a sense of suspension akin to that offered by Hilda's artwork, and that also brings to mind Laskell's affair with the flower in *The Middle of the Journey*. Near the novel's conclusion, Schonfeldt gives his final, greatest performance on the floor of the bank:

> So for the length of a breath Mr. Schonfeldt stood tuning up his soul, and [. . .] everyone in the place heard the pure cascade of sound that he appeared not to be producing but only passing on from wherever it

was his mind had travelled a minute before. He did it three times [. . .] pouring forth at the end a ridiculous burble of mounting clarity, that at what seemed its topmost limit took on a whole new range of life and plunged higher still, as if that were only the beginning; after the last of which incredible flights he whipped out his handkerchief, ostensibly to mop up his saliva but really to hide his smile, while the counterman and the two other customers there, relaxing from the sudden strain, burst into a medley of laughs and exclamations of astonishment. (260–1)

Schonfeldt's song brings briefly into being a small community of laughers, a picture of sociability quite different from the Party's rallies or the usual transactions conducted at the bank. In her description, Clark extends the interlude the song marks, stretching a moment of charged suspension and working towards a climax composed of a collective collapse into laughter. In this moment – in which, to borrow a phrase from Anne Dufourmantelle, 'drollery forges a community' – the novel seems to 'break free' in the way Trilling suggests, released from the world of bureaucracy and the art of nightmare; notably, Clark's prose style also seems to take on a certain Jamesian dilation, or Forsterian relaxation.[123]

But the bitter laughter of Brand and the anxious giggling of Temple also belong to the 'medley of laughs' audible in the novel. As such, laughter is never only affirmative in the way Trilling wants it to be, but is also Bergsonian in the manner Miller describes as characteristic of late modernism; it never only 'projects forms of free being', as Trilling suggests, but also forms of impaired or illusory freedom. To put it another way, it's sometimes hard to distinguish in the novel between intimations and imitations of freedom, or between a joke and a nightmare. The different timbres of laughter suggest how the novel dramatises an uncertainty as to what extent modernist aesthetics can be moved on from (or laughed away), and an uncertainty as to what kind of political future, if any, is imaginable after the betrayals of the 1930s and horrors of the 1940s, brought vividly into focus by Brand's violent murder near the novel's close. In its laughter, the novel therefore gestures to but does not pursue aesthetic and political possibilities beyond the coordinates of its midcentury moment. Instead, it elaborates something like the 'middle' modality of action –

neither passive nor active but between the two – that Parvulescu suggests captures something of laughter's ambiguous relation to agency, and which also captures something of the minor novel's always-transitional aesthetic project. It is precisely this unsettled 'middle' modality that Trilling obscures by trying a little too hard to separate modernist nightmare from Nietzschean laughter. He misses how it is the novel's very equivocation between the two that represents its innovation (like Hilda's mobiles it never stays still, or settles on a final form); that it is in its failure to wholly adhere to either his tastes or those of *Partisan* that marks the novel's minor achievement.

Ellison's American Joke

In this final section of the chapter, I want to pursue a seemingly unlikely affinity between *The Bitter Box* and Ralph Ellison's *Invisible Man* (1952). As for Clark, laughter plays an important role in Ellison's efforts to situate his work in relation to the modernist aesthetics of *Partisan*. I want to argue that the different kinds of laughter that can be heard in Clark and Ellison's novels suggest how they ultimately represent two divergent forms of midcentury writing: the minor novel and the high cultural pluralist novel.

Clark and Ellison knew one another through Clark's husband, Robert Penn Warren, with whom Ellison had a close friendship; Warren's *All the King's Men* (1946) is sometimes cited as an influence on Ellison's novel.[124] Ellison began work on *Invisible Man* in 1945, and the book emerges from the same intellectual milieu as *The Bitter Box*. Ellison himself often flagged the importance of Dostoevsky to the 'philosophical dimension' of his work, suggesting that the narrator of *Invisible Man* was 'inspired' by the protagonist of *Notes from Underground*.[125] He was less forthcoming in acknowledging the influence of Kafka. In February 1952, shortly after the Prologue to *Invisible Man* had been published in *Partisan*, Ellison wrote to Albert Murray that the piece had 'caused some comments, but I don't think Rahv has decided what he thinks about the book as a whole. He does know that it isn't Kafka as others mistakenly believe. I tell them, I told Langston Hughes in fact, that it's the blues, but nobody seems to understand what I mean.'[126]

Ellison was similarly circumspect in recognising the influence of existentialism on his work. In 1983, responding to a researcher asking about his reading of Sartre, Ellison emphasises that 'I was well under way with my novel before Sartre made his American debut'. But he is happy enough to acknowledge that 'I became consciously aware of existentialism (lower case) during the summer of 1936 when I read Malraux [. . .] for the first time', and that this 'put me on the trail of Kierkegaard'. He then qualifies his disavowal of Sartre's influence: 'This is not to say that I didn't read anything of Sartre that I could get my hands on [. . .] but as far as I am aware his influence upon my writing was limited to the general intellectual excitement which marked the post-war years'.[127] A similar two-step of acknowledgement and disavowal of influence characterises Ellison's account of the part played by Richard Wright in his development as a writer. Wright was his guide to the radical political and literary world of Harlem after Ellison came to New York in 1938. But while he continued to acknowledge his debt to Wright, Ellison increasingly defined his own work against that of his one-time mentor. After the publication of *Invisible Man*, he was especially keen to disabuse readers of the idea that his basement-dwelling protagonist was at all inspired by the central character of Wright's novella, 'The Man Who Lived Underground' (1942). 'Wright's work suffers from an esthetic over-simplification,' Ellison wrote in November 1945 to Kenneth Burke, who was to replace Wright as his intellectual sparring partner. 'I am aiming at something I believe to be broader, more psychological, and employing, let us say, a scale of twelve tones rather than one of five [. . .] I should like an esthetic that restores to man his full complexity.'[128] 'Complexity' became Ellison's 'favorite term,' Barbara Foley writes, signifying 'the binary opposite of reductionism, whether leftism in politics, naturalism in writing, or sociology in the study of human beings'.[129]

Ellison's disaffiliation from Wright's work is often read as part of his disaffiliation from leftist politics more broadly. Ellison moved in radical circles throughout the late 1930s and early 1940s, long after the Moscow trials. But even as he hewed to the Party line on some issues, Ellison was (like the *Partisan* intellectuals and, indeed, like Wright) frustrated by the narrow limits of a Marxist literary aesthetics at odds with the work of modernist authors he had come to admire, among them Joyce. In its portrayal of the Brotherhood, a stand-in for the Communist Party, *Invisible Man* offers a 'mordant satire on Marxist politics' in which the nameless narrator is dehumanised and exploited by the revolutionary movement in ways that are shown to ironically parallel his treatment in the Jim Crow South.[130] The novel is thus usually interpreted as marking Ellison's 'withdrawal' from collective politics towards liberal individualism, in keeping with the drift of many anti-Stalinist intellectuals.[131]

'Complexity' was not only a 'favorite term' for Ellison, of course, but also, Amanda Anderson notes, a 'key Trilling term'.[132] The two writers often spoke of the novel in similar ways. Ellison emphasised 'the moral seriousness of the form', suggesting that its 'primary social function' is to 'project the shiftings of society' and make sense of 'social change'.[133] Like Trilling, he ultimately hung his hat on the example of nineteenth-century novelists, rather than the modernists, as the one for the contemporary writer to follow. They also shared a sense that, at midcentury, 'the iron-weight of tragic awareness has descended upon us', in Ellison's words, and that 'progress now insistently asserts its tragic side' (in the same essay Ellison writes that 'the Age of Anxiety is truly more than a poetic conceit').[134] As with his caveated recognition of the influence of Sartre and Wright, however, Ellison always made sure to highlight his differences with Trilling. In 'Society, Morality, and the Novel' (1957) – the title of which alludes to Trilling's 1948 essay, 'Manners, Morals, and the Novel' – Ellison notes that 'some of our most important critics [are] handing the death sentence of the form' while 'boasting of their loss of interest in contemporary novels'.[135] But it is only 'the nineteenth-century European novel of manners' which is dead, Ellison argues, suggesting that the misdiagnosis made by the death-of-novel critics reveals their limited conception of American history.[136] To Ellison, the Civil War always figured as the 'historical watershed' in the life of the nation, the core 'contradiction' from which issued the animating conflict of American democratic experience: the question of racial identity.[137] It was the 1860s, rather than the 1930s, that were always the crucial decade for Ellison.

It was this longer historical perspective that Ellison argued midcentury critics (aside from Southerners like Warren) lacked. Taking aim at Trilling's 'theory of the novel of manners', Ellison notes that Trilling in his essay paraphrases Henry James's 'catalogue of those items of civilization which were missing from Hawthorne's America', a catalogue based on a well-known entry from Hawthorne's notebooks: 'no state; barely a specific national name; no sovereign; no court; no aristocracy'.[138] But Trilling crucially omits the conclusion of James's comments, Ellison observes: that despite the absence of these European institutions and social structures, 'the American knows that a good deal remains; what it is that remains – that is his secret, his joke, as one may say'.[139] As John Wright explains, James was arguing that the fact that 'American society appeared void of the time-worn European manners, morals, and institutions was a sign not of deficiency but of new novelistic possibilities'.[140] 'The most surprising aspect of Mr. Trilling's paraphrase,' writes Ellison, 'is that he says nothing at all about what James calls the "American joke" – a matter which, as a novelist, intrigues me no end.' And he wonders 'what the state of novel criticism would be today if Mr. Trilling had turned his critical talent to an examination of the American joke'.[141]

Ellison turned his own critical talent to an examination of the American joke, and joking and laughing became key terms in his critical idiom – from 'Change the Joke and Slip the Yoke' (1958) to his 1985 essay 'An Extravagance of Laughter'.[142] What Ellison calls 'the joke at the center of American identity' emerges from the nation's origins and the social construction of racial difference and hierarchy. In Ellison's telling, it's a joke played on African Americans but which they also 'get' in a way no one else can: 'On his side of the joke, the Negro looks at the white man and finds it difficult to believe that [he] can be so absurdly self-deluded over the true interrelatedness of whiteness and blackness'.[143] As 'intimates' to the great American joke, African Americans have a 'special perspective on the national ideals and the national conduct,' Ellison writes elsewhere, which provides them 'a tragicomic attitude toward the universe'.[144] For Ellison, the blues is the distillation of this distinctly African-American attitude. 'Negroes express the joke [. . .] in the blues,' he writes, because 'the blues speak to us simultaneously of the tragic and comic aspects of the human condition'.[145] This is what Ellison meant when he told Langston Hughes that *Invisible Man* wasn't Kafka, but the blues.

In his Introduction to the thirtieth anniversary edition of *Invisible Man*, Ellison writes that he started working on the novel when he began to hear 'an ironic, down-home voice' speaking to him, 'persuasive with echoes of blues-toned laughter' – a voice that got the joke.[146] Listening to it, Ellison began to reflect that, 'given the persistence of racial violence and the unavailability of legal protection', what else do black Americans have 'to sustain our will to persevere but laughter?' And he started to wonder whether there was a 'subtle triumph hidden in the laughter', a 'secret, hard-earned wisdom', and whether the laughter was therefore 'more affirmative than raw anger'. The 'blues-toned laugher-at-wounds' whom Ellison hears laughs with the knowledge that 'what is commonly assumed to be past history is actually as much a part of the living present as William Faulkner insisted'.[147] This knowledge, bestowed upon Faulkner and Ellison alike, is the inheritance of Southern history; but it might also be a version of Nietzsche's 'eternal recurrence', knowledge of which brings Zarathustra to a 'higher laughter' that could well be described as 'blues-toned' and 'more affirmative than raw anger'.[148] Ellison places a Nietzschean emphasis on the idea of recurrence when he argues that 'the primary social function of the novel [. . .] is that of seizing from the flux and flow of our daily lives those abiding patterns of experience which [. . .] help to form our sense of reality'.[149] In doing so, he argues, the novel can be a 'raft of hope', a crucial form for realising America's 'project of democracy'.[150]

Ellison thus conceives of black laughter as resonant with the paradoxes of American democracy, such that what might appear a minoritarian discourse is recast as a national one; in turn, he suggests that the novel might once again be a major cultural form in the US through its examination of the racial joke at the centre of American identity, the joke that death-of-the-novel critics like Trilling failed to get. In racialising laughter, then, Ellison gestures to a more complex politics and history of laughter than that which Trilling develops in his reading of *The Bitter Box*. Trilling suggests that laughter in Clark's novel reminds us that a core function of the novel is to project 'forms of free being'; laughter in Ellison's novel will remind us that such projections of freedom are always implicated in and must contend with a particular history of oppression.

Ellison described *Invisible Man* as 'one long, loud rant, howl, and laugh', and throughout the novel he explores black laughter's ambiguous resonances.[151] Soon after his recruitment, the narrator attends a Brotherhood gathering at which he is accosted by a drunken comrade who asks him to sing a 'spiritual', or 'one of those real good ole Negro work songs'.[152] The comrade is quickly escorted from the room and in the 'enormous silence' that follows, the narrator begins 'laughing hysterically', 'bending double, roaring' in an 'eruption of laughter':

> 'Three sheets in the wind,' I laughed, getting my breath now, and discovering that the silent tension of the others was ebbing into a ripple of laughter that sounded throughout the room, growing swiftly to a roar, a laugh of all dimensions, intensities and intonations. Everyone was joining in [. . .] as I calmed I saw them looking at me with a sort of embarrassed gratitude. (301)

'Is it an act of assertion or submission?' Jason Baskin asks of this outburst, noting that the narrator's 'precarious situation in this scene, placed in a position from which both clear opposition and mute acceptance seem to be equally impossible responses, speaks to the fundamental questions about race and political agency raised in Ellison's work'.[153] Laughter in this scene seems to bring to the surface the issue of race, yet whether it does so to undermine or only assuage the status quo is uncertain. Laughter unexpectedly (and uncontrollably) crosses the colour line in this exchange, bringing into being unlikely forms of sociability, an idea Ellison also explores in 'The Extravagance of Laughter'; but whether this is a community of laughers of the kind imagined in *The Bitter Box* remains unclear. We are left to wonder who is in on the joke, and who is the object of ridicule. A collaboration has occurred, but of what kind?

Similar questions are raised by another scene of laughter near the end of the novel. By this time, the narrator has risen in the Brotherhood but become increasingly disillusioned with the movement. Returning to Harlem, he comes across a crowd gathered around a street seller hawking 'some kind of toy', a 'grinning doll of orange-and-black tissue paper', its head and feet moving by 'some mysterious mechanism'. The Sambo doll is a kind of perversion of

Hilda's Calder-like wire and paper mobiles, a disturbing assemblage of the human and mechanical. The seller's spiel promises that Sambo will '*make you laugh, he'll make you sigh* [. . .] *He'll make you weep sweet – Tears from laughing*' (415). The seller turns out to be Clifton, formerly an inspiring youth leader in the Brotherhood. As Ellison explains in a 1969 letter, by selling the dolls, Clifton 'acts out a decision to punish himself by embracing the negative stereotypes as a means of cleansing himself of any shreds of hope in the promises of Brotherhoodism [. . .] He ha[s], in other words, learned irony; a bitter, masochistic irony'.[154] Forging the progressive history of radical politics, Clifton has fallen 'outside of *history*', the narrator recognises – not into a Nietzschean untimeliness from which a future might be imagined, but into a despairing nihilism. Or, as Anne Anlin Cheng suggests, we might think of Clifton as performing a kind of racial melancholy, 'dramatizing and exposing the role that had been assigned to him':

> In taking up the Sambo doll [. . .] he is melancholically acting out what the Brotherhood has made him. The idea of a healthy progressive history, in which events can be successfully mourned and left behind, echoes far too closely the kind of blind, corrective, historical logic that undersigns [. . .] the Brotherhood's idea of progressive history.[155]

Watching the performance, the narrator is caught 'between the desire to join in the laughter' of the crowd, or 'leap upon' the doll 'with both feet' (415). The crowd seem at first to laugh at the racist caricature of the doll, and then, as they notice the narrator among them, at Clifton's suggestion that the 'brotherly' Sambo and the narrator are alike in their lack of autonomy – that both are mere puppets. 'I saw a short pot-bellied man look down, then up at me with amazement and explode with laughter, pointing from me to the doll' (416). This Bergsonian laughter ridicules the narrator's ideological rigidity while enforcing a racialised social order. And yet Sambo is also said to provoke a kind of blues-toned ambivalence – '*tears from laughing*' – that the novel and Ellison's essays elsewhere seem to celebrate. If, as Cheng suggests, Clifton and Sambo dramatise a traumatic racial history that cannot be mourned, then the scene not only problematises the Brotherhood's idea of progressive history, but also complicates Ellison's own investment in the 'hard-earned wisdom' of black laughter and its democratic potential.

If black laughter is ultimately 'more affirmative than raw anger', as Ellison suggests, it is never straightforwardly cathartic or redemptive. Rather than sounding a break from social and historical realities, when black laughter erupts it brings to the surface the tragic ironies of American racial politics. At the same time, laughter – difficult to locate, control or contain – sometimes opens up in Ellison's writing, however briefly, unpredictable lines of affiliation, unsettling the social order so as to, if not instantiate, then make conceivable, new social arrangements, grounded (or embodied) in an expanded racial awareness. As such, black laughter represents an important facet of Ellison's project of elaborating an aesthetics for the novel distinct from the *Partisan* milieu, and, Jason Baskin writes, of imagining 'the social role of African American artistic production beyond high modernist vanguardism'.[156] Unlike the minor novelists considered in this book, Ellison never doubted that the novel was a major form, and he never bought the midcentury critics' critique that the novel was dying, or that it had never existed in America ('Fuck Trilling and his gang', as Ellison concisely put it in a 1957 letter to Albert Murray).[157]

Ellison's project in his novel was to discover how national histories and universal themes might emerge from an account of the particularities of black experience, and how the abstract political-philosophical concerns he shared with the anti-Stalinist left – around agency, autonomy, consciousness, and individual freedom – might be refracted through the prism of the specific history of race in America ('I find that I am forced to arrive at that universe through the racial grain of sand', Ellison wrote in a 1945 letter to Burke).[158] Such a project required a new kind of minor character – not a Kafkaesque 'little man', but a minoritarian character of psychological and intellectual complexity, for part of Ellison's response to Richard Wright's fiction was an effort to portray an African-American protagonist more capable of 'philosophical articulation' than Bigger Thomas or Wright's own underground man.[159]

For many critics, including Thomas Hill Schaub, Ellison's effort to 'make the experience of his central character resonate universally for all readers had the effect of mediating historical and political urgencies within the ahistoricism of mythic form and tragic vision so typical of postwar critical thought'.[160] But if we listen to the novel's laughter, the protagonist's experience seems to 'resonate' more complexly than Schaub suggests. 'Rather than appeal to individual experience as an aesthetic realm free from social conditions,' Jason Baskin argues, 'Ellison articulates an account of embodied subjectivity as intertwined with society and history, including the history of racism' in America.[161] For Ellison, black laughter is social in origin and so always already implicated in, freighted with and expressive of African-American culture.[162] Laughter in the novel is thus also indicative of *Invisible Man*'s status as an early example of 'high cultural pluralist fiction', Mark McGurl's term to describe 'a body of fiction that joins the high literary values of modernism with a fascination with the experience of cultural difference and the authenticity of the ethnic voice', a category which includes a swathe of widely read and taught Jewish-, Native-, Asian-, and African-American novels that have shaped the post-1945 canon.[163] High cultural pluralism, in McGurl's account, was the road minority writers took to 'literary distinction in the postwar period'.[164]

Breaking into laughter in Ellison's novel is therefore a harbinger of the 'breakthrough' to come, a clue as to how the postwar novel would go about going on from the aesthetic and political impasses of the midcentury moment: by cultivating difference and privileging diversity, and by encompassing the plural histories and experiences of a greater range of literary voices from ethnic and cultural minorities (even if Ellison remains more committed than most high cultural pluralist writers to the universalism of midcentury political thought).[165] This is the by-now familiar story of the postwar literary field and the postwar academy (and McGurl shows us how closely these stories are related). But to listen to and compare the different timbres of laughter resonating in Clark and Ellison's anti-communist fictions is to tell this story slightly differently; to return, as it were, to a prehistory of this moment of high cultural pluralist breakthrough, and to recover another kind of minor writing emerging at midcentury. For Ellison, laughter resonates with a history of African-American struggle that has national and even universal reverberations, in keeping with his conception of the novel as a major form wedded to the project of American democracy, and befitting his own 'ambition to take African American literature to unprecedented heights', and his 'highly self-conscious efforts to position himself in relation to both American literary tradition and modernist world literature'.[166] Clark's ambitions, by contrast, were more modest: to write a 'little book' about a 'little man'. Laughter in *The Bitter Box* sounds her uncertainty as to what form the novel should take in the wake of Joyce and Kafka, and her ambivalence about both the modernist aesthetics of *Partisan* and the 'naturalistic' alternative offered by Trilling – and indeed, as she put in a letter to Trilling, whether 'the word "novel" at all' was fit 'for current use'.[167]

Notes

1. Lionel Trilling, Letter to Eleanor Clark, 6 April 1946, Box 33, Folder 486, Eleanor Clark Papers, Beinecke Rare Book and Manuscript Library, Yale University.
2. Natalie Robins, *The Untold Journey: The Life of Diana Trilling* (New York: Columbia University Press, 2017), 86.
3. See, for example, the December 1948 issue of the magazine, featuring Trilling's essay 'Art and Fortune' and Clark's story 'The Heart of the Afternoon', discussed later.
4. Lionel Trilling, Letter to Eleanor Clark, 18 August 1942, Box 33, Folder 486, Eleanor Clark Papers; Robins, *The Untold Journey*, 158.
5. Clark is best-known for *Rome and a Villa* (1952) and *The Oysters of Locmariaquer* (1964). Clark's second novel, *Baldur's Gate*, appeared in 1974.
6. Eleanor Clark, Letter to Lionel Trilling, 25 April 1946, Box 12, Folder 3, Lionel Trilling Papers, Rare Book & Manuscript Library, Columbia University.
7. Lionel Trilling, 'A Novel of the Thirties', in *The Last Decade: Essays and Reviews, 1965–75* (Oxford: Oxford University Press, 1982), pp. 3–24 (15–16).
8. See Michael Kimmage, *The Conservative Turn: Lionel Trilling, Whittaker Chambers, and the Lessons of Anti-Communism* (Cambridge, MA: Harvard University Press, 2009), 62. Trilling discusses his relationship with Chambers in 'Whitaker Chambers' Journey', in *The Last Decade*, pp. 185–203.
9. Kimmage, *The Conservative Turn*, 57; Trilling, Letter to Eric Bentley, 13 February 1946, quoted in Kimmage, *The Conservative Turn*, 55.
10. Trilling, 'A Novel of the Thirties', 4.
11. Lionel Trilling, Letter to Eric Bentley, 7 March 1946, in Adam Kirsch (ed.), *Life in Culture: Selected Letters of Lionel Trilling* (New York: Farrar, Straus and Giroux, 2018), pp. 131–4 (133).
12. Eleanor Clark, 'Talk with Eleanor Clark', interview by R. W. B. Lewis, *New York Times*, 16 October 1977, 251.
13. See '*Con Spirito*', Vassar Encyclopedia. Available at: https://vcencyclopedia.vassar.edu/student-organizations-and-activities/student-publications/con-spirito/.

14. Quoted in Bethany Hicok, *Degrees of Freedom: American Women Poets and the Women's College* (Pennsylvania: Bucknell University Press, 2008), 110.
15. 'Eleanor Clark', Vassar Encyclopedia. Available at: https://vcencyclopedia.vassar.edu/distinguished-alumni/eleanor-clark/.
16. Alan Wald, 'Herbert Solow: Portrait of a New York Intellectual', *Prospects*, Vol. 3 (October 1978), pp. 419–60 (421).
17. Alan Wald suggests that the Chambers episode in 1938 'provided important background' to *The Bitter Box*. *The New York Intellectuals: The Rise and Decline of the Anti-Stalinist Left From the 1930s to the 1980s* [1987], 30th Anniversary edition (Chapel Hill: North Carolina University Press, 2017), 249.
18. Trilling, 'A Novel of the Thirties', 8. Trilling and Solow knew one another through the *Menorah Journal*, a liberal journal of Jewish thought and culture edited by Elliot Cohen.
19. See Wald, *The New York Intellectuals*, 133.
20. Joseph Blotner, *Robert Penn Warren: A Biography* (New York: Random House, 1997), 276.
21. Clark, 'Talk with Eleanor Clark', 251.
22. Kimmage, *The Conservative Turn*, 174.
23. Alan Wald, *American Night: The Literary Left in the Era of the Cold War* (Chapel Hill: University of North Carolina Press, 2012), 175.
24. Eleanor Clark, 'Interview with Eleanor Clark and Robert Penn Warren', interview by Jay Parini, *New England Review*, Vol. 1, No. 1 (Autumn 1978), pp. 49–70 (69).
25. John Aldridge, *After the Lost Generation: A Critical Study of the Writers of Two Wars* (New York: McGraw-Hill, 1951), 90.
26. Ibid., 88.
27. Terry Cooney, *The Rise of the New York Intellectuals:* Partisan Review *and Its Circle* (Madison: University of Wisconsin Press, 1986), 121, 144.
28. Ibid., 92.
29. Mark Greif, *The Age of the Crisis of Man: Thought and Fiction in America, 1933–1973* (Princeton: Princeton University Press, 2015), 136.
30. Hannah Arendt, 'Franz Kafka: A Revaluation, *Partisan Review*, Vol. 11, No. 4 (Fall 1944), pp. 412–22.
31. Ibid., 416.
32. Isaac Rosenfeld, 'Kafka and His Critics' [1947], in Mark Shechner (ed.), *Preserving the Hunger: An Isaac Rosenfeld Reader* (Detroit: Wayne State University, 1988), pp. 166–74 (174).
33. Gilles Deleuze and Félix Guattari, *Kafka: Toward a Minor Literature* [French, 1977], trans. Dana Polan (Minneapolis: University of Minnesota Press, 1986), 25; Hannah Arendt, 'What is Existenz Philosophy?', *Partisan Review*, Vol. 13, No. 1 (Winter 1946), pp. 34–56 (35).
34. Arendt, 'Franz Kafka: A Revaluation', 414.
35. Morris Dickstein, *Leopards in the Temple: The Transformation of American Fiction, 1945–1970* (Cambridge, MA: Harvard University Press, 2002), 63.
36. Ibid.

37. Philip Rahv, 'Dostoevsky and Politics', *Partisan Review*, Vol. 5, No. 2 (July 1938), pp. 25–36 (27). On Slesinger's allusion to Dostoevsky, see Ian Afflerbach, 'On the Use and Abuse of Dostoevsky's *The Possessed* for Reading Tess Slesinger's *The Unpossessed*', *Notes and Queries*, Vol. 259, No. 1 (March 2014), pp. 135–6.
38. Greif, *The Age of the Crisis of Man*, 72; Søren Kierkegaard, *Repetition* [1843], trans. Howard and Edna Hong (Princeton: Princeton University Press, 1983), 200. On the Kierkegaard revival, see George Cotkin, *Existential America* (Baltimore: Johns Hopkins University Press, 2003), 54–91.
39. Ann Fulton, *Apostles of Sartre: Existentialism in America, 1945–1963* (Evanston: Northwestern University Press, 1999), 5.
40. Ibid., 8.
41. Ibid., 40.
42. See Cooney, *The Rise of the New York Intellectuals*, 215.
43. W. H. Auden, *The Age of Anxiety: A Baroque Eclogue* [1947] (Princeton: Princeton University Press, 2011). See Claire Seiler, *Midcentury Suspension: Literature and Feeling in the Wake of World War II* (New York: Columbia University Press, 2020), 83–135.
44. Søren Kierkegaard, *The Concept of Anxiety* [1844], trans. Reidar Thomte (Princeton: Princeton University Press, 1980), 155, quoted in Louis Menand, 'Freud, Anxiety, and the Cold War', in John Burnham (ed.), *After Freud Left: A Century of Psychoanalysis in America* (Chicago: University of Chicago Press, 2012), pp. 189–208 (194). On Chambers and Kierkegaard, see Cotkin, *Existential America*, 75–9.
45. Menand, 'Freud, Anxiety, and the Cold War', 95.
46. Louis Menand, *The Free World: Art and Thought in the Cold War* (New York: Farrar, Straus and Giroux, 2021), 91.
47. Gregory Ariail, 'Kafka's Copycats: Imitation, Fabulism, and Late Modernism', PhD thesis, University of Michigan, 2018, 10.
48. Eleanor Clark, 'Asleep a King', *Partisan Review*, Vol. 4, No. 6 (May 1938), pp. 30–42.
49. Ibid., 34, 33.
50. Eleanor Clark, 'The Heart of the Afternoon', *Partisan Review*, Vol. 15, No. 12 (December 1948), pp. 1332–6; Seiler, *Midcentury Suspension*, 5, 84.
51. Clark describes engaging in a 'terrific struggle' with the influence of Stein, who 'contributed to the end of a certain kind of natural narrative'. 'Interview with Eleanor Clark and Robert Penn Warren', 69.
52. Clark, 'The Heart of the Afternoon', 1332–3.
53. Ibid., 1333.
54. Eleanor Clark, untitled memo, undated, Box 4, Folder 31, Eleanor Clark Papers.
55. Lionel Trilling, 'The Life of the Novel', Vol. 8, No. 4 (Autumn 1946), pp. 658–67.
56. Lionel Trilling, 'Preface to the Second Edition', *E. M. Forster* [1943] (New York: New Directions, 1964), pp. 1–4 (3–4).

57. Edmund Wilson, *The Triple Thinkers: Twelve Essays on Literary Subjects* (New York: Farrar, Straus and Giroux, 1948), 130; Lionel Trilling, Letter to Eleanor Clark, 16 March 1939, Box 33, Folder 486, Eleanor Clark Papers.
58. Trilling, 'The Life of the Novel', 658.
59. Ibid., 659.
60. Ibid., 658.
61. Ibid., 659, 660.
62. Lionel Trilling, 'Commentary on "The Grand Inquisitor" by Fëdor Dostoevski', in *The Experience of Literature* (New York: Holt, Rinehart and Winston, 1967), pp. 482–5 (482).
63. Trilling, 'The Life of the Novel', 660.
64. Ibid., 664.
65. Lionel Trilling, 'The Meaning of a Literary Idea', in *The Liberal Imagination: Essays on Literature and Society* [1950] (New York: New York Review Books Classics, 2008), pp. 281–303 (292).
66. Trilling, 'The Life of the Novel', 666.
67. Ibid., 664, 666.
68. Lionel Trilling, 'Art and Fortune', in *The Liberal Imagination*, pp. 255–80 (265).
69. Seiler, *Midcentury Suspension*, 100; Trilling, 'The Life of the Novel', 662.
70. Trilling, 'The Life of the Novel', 664.
71. Thomas Hill Schaub, *American Fiction in the Cold War* (Madison: University of Wisconsin Press, 1991), 42; Lionel Trilling, 'Reality in America', in *The Liberal Imagination*, pp. 3–21 (3).
72. Schaub, *American Fiction in the Cold War*, 42.
73. Richard Chase, *The American Novel and its Tradition* (Baltimore: Johns Hopkins University Press, 1957), 186.
74. Ibid., 220.
75. Trilling, 'The Life of the Novel', 663.
76. Ibid., 665.
77. Ibid.
78. Leslie Fiedler, 'The State of American Writing, 1948: A Symposium', *Partisan Review*, Vol. 15, No. 8 (August 1948), pp. 855–93 (873).
79. Trilling, 'The Life of the Novel', 667; Trilling, Letter in Evelyn King Gilmore, 28 April 1952, in *Life in Culture*, pp. 203–4 (204).
80. Lionel Trilling, Letter to Eleanor Clark, 5 June 1939, Box 33, Folder 486, Eleanor Clark Papers.
81. Lionel Trilling, Letter to Eleanor Clark, 6 April 1946.
82. In her reply, Clark writes that she doesn't 'too much like thinking' in terms of 'theories of the novel', because she has found it feeds a 'kind of atrophy'. She cannot accept Trilling's 'invitation to naturalism,' she continues, because it would 'impose an arbitrary limitation on the novel as distinguished from poetry, and I don't accept that'. Letter to Lionel Trilling, 25 April 1946.
83. Trilling, 'The Life of the Novel', 666.
84. Ibid., 666–7.
85. R. W. B. Lewis, 'Lionel Trilling and the New Stoicism', *Hudson Review*, Vol. 3, No. 2 (Summer 1950), pp. 313–17 (316).

86. Michael Levenson, 'Earnest Ironies: Trilling's Forster', in John Rodden (ed.), *Lionel Trilling and the Critics: Opposing Selves* (Lincoln: University of Nebraska Press, 1999), pp. 104–9 (109).
87. Trilling, 'The Life of the Novel', 666.
88. Friedrich Nietzsche, *Ecce Homo: How To Become What You Are* [1908], trans. Duncan Large (Oxford: Oxford University Press, 2007), 25.
89. Harriet Murphy, *Canetti and Nietzsche: Theories of Humor in Die Blendung* (Albany: State University of New York Press, 1997), 88.
90. Lawrence Hatab, 'Laughter in Nietzsche's Thought: A Philosophical Tragicomedy', *International Studies in Philosophy*, Vol. 20, No. 2 (1998), pp. 67–79 (68).
91. Friedrich Nietzsche, *Thus Spoke Zarathustra* [1883], trans. R. J. Hollingdale (Harmondsworth: Penguin, 1969), 303.
92. John Lippitt, 'Nietzsche, Zarathustra and the Status of Laughter', *British Journal of Aesthetics*, Vol. 32, No. 1 (January 1992), pp. 39–49 (40); Elizabeth Grosz, *The Nick of Time: Politics, Evolution, and the Untimely* (Durham, NC: Duke University Press, 2004), 140.
93. Grosz, *The Nick of Time*, 116, 117.
94. Benjamin Mangrum, *Land of Tomorrow: Postwar Fiction and the Crisis of American Liberalism* (Oxford: Oxford University Press, 2018), 43.
95. Ibid.
96. Ibid., 44.
97. Jennifer Ratner-Rosenhagen, *American Nietzsche: A History of an Icon and His Ideas* (Chicago: University of Chicago Press, 2011), 221. Mangrum also discusses the influence of Kaufmann's work (43–5).
98. Mangrum notes that 'Nietzsche's rising stock' and 'Trilling's opposition to bureaucratic liberalism' both belong to a 'cultural and intellectual milieu that turned [. . .] against organizational and institutional politics' (44).
99. Tyrus Miller, *Late Modernism: Politics, Fiction, and the Arts Between the World Wars* (Berkeley: University of California Press, 1999).
100. Ibid., 19, 20.
101. Ibid., 20.
102. Rachel Potter, *Obscene Modernism: Literary Censorship and Experiment 1900–1940* (Oxford: Oxford University Press, 2013), 191.
103. Sara Crangle, *Prosaic Desires: Modernist Knowledge, Boredom, Laughter, and Anticipation* (Edinburgh: Edinburgh University Press, 2010), 112; Henri Bergson, *Laughter: An Essay on the Meaning of the Comic* [1900], trans. Cloudesley Brereton and Fred Rothwell (Mineola, NY: Dover, 2005), 31.
104. Miller, *Late Modernism*, 63.
105. Ibid., 49.
106. Ibid., 48.
107. Ibid., 13.
108. Ibid., 49.
109. Sigmund Freud, *Inhibitions, Symptoms and Anxiety* [1926], trans. Alix Strachey (London: Norton, 1989), 100.
110. Seiler, *Midcentury Suspension*, 83.
111. Ibid.

112. Anca Parvulescu, *Laughter: Notes on a Passion* (Cambridge, MA: MIT Press, 2010), 14.
113. Miller, *Late Modernism*, 62.
114. Ibid., 7.
115. Eleanor Clark, *The Bitter Box* [1946] (London: Michael Joseph, 1947), 9. Subsequent references are given in parentheses in the text.
116. Temple also resembles the telegraphist in Henry James's 'In the Cage' (1898), who spends her time 'in framed and wired confinement'. The narrative perspective stays limited to the telegraphist's misguided notion of her role in an affair being carried on by telegram by some of her well-to-do customers, James developing a dramatic irony in the gap between her self-delusion and the grubby reality of the scandal. There is a similar irony to Temple's naïve unawareness of the violent underside of the revolutionary movement. James, 'In the Cage' [1898], in *Complete Stories, 1892–1898*, ed. David Bromwich and John Hollander (New York: Library of America, 1996), pp. 835–924 (835).
117. Erich Fromm, *Escape from Freedom* [1941] (New York: Holt, 1994), x.
118. Mark Greif notes the 'deliberate accents of mid-European rooming-house/ boarding-house misery' (151) in *Dangling Man*.
119. Nathaniel Hawthorne, 'Ethan Brand', in *Young Goodman Brown and Other Tales* (Oxford: Oxford University Press, 1998), pp. 316–32 (320).
120. Calder gave Sartre a mobile resembling 'a bird of paradise with wings of iron'. In an essay written for a Paris exhibition of Calder's work, Sartre describes the mobile as 'a little local festival; an object which exists only in, and which is defined by motion; a flower which dies as soon as motion stops [. . .] These mobiles have been made neither wholly living nor wholly mechanical, they fly apart at every instant.' Jean-Paul Sartre, 'Existentialist as Mobilist', *Art News*, No. 46, December 1947, pp. 22–3 (22, 23).
121. 'If laughter could be called a project, it would a project against deep, heavy, oppressive seriousness.' Parvulescu, *Laughter*, 5. Anne Dufourmantelle describes laughter as a 'light and communicable convulsion'. *In Praise of Risk*, trans. Steven Miller (New York: Fordham University Press, 2019), 95.
122. See Schaub, *American Fiction in the Cold War*, 50.
123. Dufourmantelle, *In Praise of Risk*, 95.
124. On the Warren-Ellison friendship, see Timothy Parrish, *Ralph Ellison and the Genius of America* (Amherst: University of Massachusetts Press, 2008), 128–40; on the influence of *All the King's Men* on Ellison, see Arnold Rampersad, *Ralph Ellison: A Biography* (New York: Knopf, 2007), 250–1.
125. Ellison, Letter to Stanley Hyman, 29 May 1970, in John Callahan and Marc Conner (eds), *The Selected Letters of Ralph Ellison* (New York: Random House, 2019), pp. 676–84 (680).
126. Ralph Ellison, Letter to Albert Murray, 4 February 1952, in *Selected Letters*, pp. 297–301 (301).
127. Ralph Ellison, Letter to Miss Messenger, 7 March 1983, in *Selected Letters*, pp. 789–90.
128. Ralph Ellison, Letter to Kenneth Burke, 23 November 1945, in *Selected Letters*, pp. 203–8 (206).

129. Barbara Foley, *Wrestling with the Left: The Making of Ralph Ellison's Invisible Man* (Durham, NC: Duke University Press, 2010), 6.
130. John Callahan, 'Letters from the Fifties', in *Selected Letters*, pp. 265–83 (273).
131. See Jason Baskin, *Modernism Beyond the Avant-Garde: Embodying Experience* (Cambridge: Cambridge University Press, 2018), 109–10.
132. Amanda Anderson, *Bleak Liberalism* (Chicago: University of Chicago Press, 2016), 119.
133. Ralph Ellison, 'Hidden Name and Complex Fate', in John Callahan (ed.), *The Collected Essays of Ralph Ellison* (New York: Modern Library Classics, 2003), pp. 189–209 (207); 'The Novel as a Function of Democracy', in *Collected Essays*, pp. 759–69 (759).
134. Ralph Ellison, 'Society, Morality, and the Novel', in *Collected Essays*, pp. 698–729 (714, 728, 727).
135. Ibid., 699.
136. Ibid., 713.
137. Anderson, *Bleak Liberalism*, 118; 'Society, Morality, and the Novel', 708.
138. Ellison, 'Society, Morality, and the Novel', 719. See Henry James, *Hawthorne* (New York, Doubleday, 1900), 43.
139. James, *Hawthorne*, 43.
140. John Wright, *Shadowing Ralph Ellison* (Jackson: University Press of Mississippi, 2006), 178.
141. Ellison, 'Society, Morality, and the Novel', 722.
142. My reading draws on discussions of laughter in Ellison's work in Parvulescu, *Laughter*, 59–78; David Bromwich, 'Ellison and the Visibility of Laughter', *Literary Imagination*, Vol. 23, No. 2, pp. 202–15; Patrick Giamario, *Laughter as Politics: Critical Theory in an Age of Hilarity* (Edinburgh: Edinburgh University Press, 2022), pp. 95–122; Robert O'Meally, *Antagonistic Cooperation: Jazz, Collage, Fiction, and the Shaping of African American Culture* (New York: Columbia University Press, 2022), 117–67.
143. Ralph Ellison, 'Change the Joke and Slip the Yoke', in *Collected Essays*, pp. 100–12 (109).
144. Ralph Ellison, 'The Word and the Jug', in *Collected Essays*, pp. 155–88 (178).
145. Ellison, 'Change the Joke and Slip the Yoke', 107; 'Blues People', in *Collected Essays*, pp. 278–87 (286).
146. Ralph Ellison, 'Introduction to the Thirtieth Anniversary Edition of *Invisible Man*', in *Collected Essays*, pp. 473–89 (481, 482).
147. Ibid., 483.
148. My reading is indebted to Michael Germana's discussion of the influence of Nietzsche on Ellison's work in *Ralph Ellison, Temporal Technologist* (Oxford: Oxford University Press, 2017), 57–69. Germana calls the prologue to the novel 'a riff on *Zarathustra*' (65).
149. Ellison, 'Society, Morality, and the Novel', 702.
150. Ellison, 'Introduction to the Thirtieth Anniversary Edition of *Invisible Man*', 487.
151. Ellison, 'Change the Joke and Slip the Yoke', 111.
152. Ralph Ellison, *Invisible Man* [1952] (Harmondsworth: Penguin, 2016), 338. Subsequent references are given in parentheses in the text.

153. Baskin, *Modernism Beyond the Avant-Garde*, 108.
154. Ralph Ellison, Letter to John Lucas, 29 July 1969, in *Selected Letters*, pp. 646–50 (647).
155. Anne Anlin Cheng, 'Ralph Ellison and the Politics of Melancholia', in Ross Posnock (ed.), *The Cambridge Companion to Ralph Ellison* (Cambridge: Cambridge University Press, 2005), pp. 121–36 (130–1).
156. Baskin, *Modernism Beyond the Avant-Garde*, 111.
157. Ralph Ellison, Letter to Albert Murray, 4 April 1957, in *Selected Letters*, pp. 477–80 (477). Ellison's faith in the flexibility and capaciousness of the American novel may well have thwarted his attempts to complete the follow-up to *Invisible Man*. On the composition of his unfinished second novel, see Adam Bradley, *Ralph Ellison in Progress: The Making and Unmaking of One Writer's Great American Novel* (New Haven: Yale University Press, 2010).
158. Ralph Ellison, Letter to Kenneth Burke, 23 November 1945, in *Selected Letters*, 204.
159. Ralph Ellison, Letter to Stanley Hyman, 27 May 1957, in *Selected Letters*, pp. 486–8 (487).
160. Schaub, *American Fiction in the Cold War*, 92.
161. Baskin, *Modernism Beyond the Avant-Garde*, 111.
162. Ibid., 113.
163. Mark McGurl, *The Program Era: Postwar Fiction and the Rise of Creative Writing* (Cambridge, MA: Harvard University Press, 2009), 32.
164. Ibid., 57.
165. I return to the metaphor of 'breakthrough' in relation to post-1945 Jewish-American literature in Chapter 4.
166. Michael Nowlin, *Literary Ambition and the African American Novel* (Cambridge: Cambridge University Press, 2019), 179; Marc Conner, 'Ellison's Agon with the Fathers in *Three Days Before the Shooting. . .*', in Marc Conner and Lucas Morel (eds), *The New Territory: Ralph Ellison and the Twenty-First Century* (Jackson: University Press of Mississippi, 2016), pp. 167–93 (168), quoted in Nowlin, *Literary Ambition and the African American Novel*, 179.
167. Clark, Letter to Lionel Trilling, 25 April 1946.

CHAPTER 3

Changing Form: Jean Stafford and the Limits of New Criticism

In a foreword to her *Collected Stories* (1969), Jean Stafford reflected that she 'might have been expected to become a regional writer'.[1] Her father, after all, had written 'Western stories under the *nom de plume* Jack Wonder' and 'published a novel called *When Cattle Kingdom Fell*', while a cousin had penned a 'reminiscence of her girlhood in frontier days in Kansas'.[2] But Stafford always had a more uncertain sense of where she was from and where she belonged. Born in California but raised mostly in Colorado, she 'could not wait to quit my tamed-down native grounds', travelling to Europe in her youth and later living across the United States. While her 'roots remain' in Colorado, she writes, 'the rest of me may abide in the South or the Midwest or New England or New York'. In this, she has an affinity with 'Mark Twain and Henry James', two of her 'favorite American writers' to 'whose sense of dislocation and whose sense of place I feel allied'.[3] These unlikely alliances are suggestive of how Stafford's fiction has often seemed to many critics difficult to place. At midcentury, Twain and James would have been understood to be representative of 'the two polar types' of American writer identified by Philip Rahv in his 1939 essay 'Paleface and Redskin'. The paleface writer is the Jamesian sophisticate for whom American identity is 'a source of endless ambiguities', the cosmopolite drawn to the 'distillations of symbolism' who, at his best, 'moves in an exquisite moral atmosphere'.[4] The redskin writer is the Whitmanian democrat who 'glories in his Americanism' and inclines to a 'riotous naturalism' (among the redskins Rahv includes the 'boisterous' Twain). Fatally torn between these two types, Rahv concludes that American literature 'suffers from the ills of a split personality', and that 'the typical American writer has so far shown himself incapable of escaping the blight of one-sidedness'.[5] As we saw in the Introduction, such a view of the divided nature of American literature – and the sense that the nation had never quite succeeded in producing a mature, cohesive work – was widely shared at midcentury. In her allusion to James and Twain, then, Stafford signals the influence on her work not only of these two writers, but also of midcentury literary critical discourse. In particular, Stafford seems in the foreword to be querying the role of the regional writer in the national literary history that midcentury critics were constructing. Raising and then dismissing the idea of thinking of her as a Western writer, and claiming allegiance to the two divergent tendencies within American literature, Stafford presents herself as a kind of literary orphan, a regional writer from nowhere.[6]

As Mark McGurl notes, 'the most important form of literary regionalism in the twentieth century has been the Southern variant'.[7] In midcentury criticism, Southern short stories were often highlighted as an exception to the general malaise of contemporary fiction. We find an echo of this view in the 1978 interview with Eleanor Clark and her husband Robert Penn Warren quoted in the previous chapter. There, Clark, looking back to the start of her career in the late 1930s and early 1940s, reflects on how the powerful influence of high modernist writers like Joyce and Kafka had 'brought realistic fiction to an end', their writing making realist narrative seem 'unnatural, technically'. But Clark then wonders whether 'the marvellous story-telling sense that seems to be innate in the south' was a 'saving grace for fiction writers there. Think of Katherine Anne [Porter], Eudora [Welty], Flannery O'Connor – along with their own great gifts, you feel you're hearing a thousand voices telling stories that they grew up with'.[8] The idea that Southern writers maintained a connection to a living tradition and historical sensibility was influentially disseminated by the Southern New Critics (including Warren). Below, I follow Stafford's lead in suggesting that her work 'abides' at least some of the time in the South as well as the West, arguing that her second and final novels, *The Mountain Lion* (1947) and *The Catherine Wheel* (1952), reveal a deep engagement with the work of the New Critics, some of whom she came to know personally at an important juncture in her career. The New Critics' formalism emerged from a strong 'sense of place', to adopt Stafford's phrase, their emphasis on self-contained form, unity, and proportion reflecting their commitment to a regional identity rooted in an agrarianism that stressed the importance of religion, tradition, and local ways of life. In keeping with the tenor of bleak liberal thought, the New Critics emphasised the tragic limits of human knowledge and rationalism. They translated this into a literary aesthetics prizing containment, constraint, and order, and into in a method of literary analysis that had at its heart the idea that a critic's insight into the meaning of a literary work was always only partial. In her fiction, Stafford appears to adhere to the strictures of New Criticism, sharing its investment in symbolism, Catholicism, and tragedy, and keeping within the parameters of its limited conception of literary form. But, as she suggests in her foreword, Stafford was never entirely at home anywhere, and this includes among the New Critics. While some of her celebrated short stories would not be out of place in one of the influential anthologies the New Critics edited and through which generations of students became familiar with their literary aesthetics, her lesser-known novels offer a revision of midcentury formalism. Something of this ambivalence is suggested in Stafford's choice of the faintly archaic and religious word 'abide'. For 'abide', the OED has 'to stay habitually in a place; to remain in residence; to reside, dwell', but also 'to wait before proceeding further'; 'to await submissively or patiently', but also 'to await defiantly', 'to endure, suffer, bear'.[9] To abide might be to belong somewhere or to anticipate leaving; it might be an act of acquiescence or quiet resistance. If Stafford didn't quite become a regional writer in the mould of her father, or Twain, I suggest she became instead a minor writer, fashioning a distinctive aesthetic freedom within and against the limits of New Criticism.

In Baton Rouge

Stafford got to know some of the New Critics and their work when, in the summer of 1940, she moved to Baton Rouge with the poet Robert Lowell, whom she had married in April that year. By then,

Lowell was already under the New Critics' sway. He had just graduated 'top of his class' from Kenyon College, where he was taught by John Crowe Ransom, one of the architects of the New Criticism (two of Lowell's undergraduate poems appeared in the first issue of the *Kenyon Review*, edited by Ransom).[10] Also formative for Lowell was his relationship with Allen Tate, a former student of Ransom's and 'the wittiest and most pungent' of the New Critics.[11] In 1937, aged twenty, Lowell – one of the Lowells of Boston, of impeccable Brahmin stock – had dropped out of Harvard and travelled to Clarksville, Tennessee to visit Tate and his wife, the novelist Caroline Gordon. Lowell wished to submit himself to Tate's authority and seek his mentorship. He recalled driving up to their house unannounced and accidentally 'mashing' the Tates's 'frail agrarian mail box post' with his car: 'I had crashed the civilization of the South'.[12] Undeterred, Lowell pitched a tent on their front lawn and stayed three months – although, as he recollected in 1959, in a piece marking Tate's sixtieth birthday, 'in a sense I have never left'.[13] In Clarksville, Lowell received a crash course in Southern culture and personal instruction in the rigorous literary formalism that Tate would help define in essays such as 'Tension in Poetry' (1938). As Langdon Hammer writes, 'The poems Tate taught Lowell to write exemplify the formalist, New Critical poetics that came to prominence in the decade after the war'.[14]

It was Tate who arranged a fellowship for Lowell at Louisiana State University, where two other New Critics, Cleanth Brooks and Warren – both of them also former students of Ransom's – were on the English faculty. Part of the package was that Stafford would be given a secretarial job at the *Southern Review*, the quarterly Brooks and Warren edited out of LSU.[15] Together with *Kenyon* and the *Sewanee Review*, the *Southern Review* was one of the three literary journals that 'were instrumental in the ascendancy of New Criticism during the 1940s'.[16] In their pages, the New Critics challenged the orthodoxies of historical scholarship and philology which still dominated English departments. In 'The Function of the Critical Quarterly', published in the *Southern Review* in 1935, Tate outlined his vision for a journal based upon a 'concentrated editorship functioning through a small group of regular contributors' who would articulate a 'sound critical program' allowing 'the reader no choice in the standards of judgment'.[17] This is what the *Southern Review* offered. Unlike the more ecumenical *Kenyon*, which published essays by the New York Intellectuals (including, as we've seen, Trilling), the *Southern Review* was something of a closed shop. It tended to publish essays by Southern New Critics, or sometimes formalists from further afield; in poetry, it championed modernist experimentation alongside works by Southern poets; in fiction, Brooks and Warren published the short story writers Clark mentions in her interview, with Welty a particular favourite.[18]

An editor should stick to their critical principles and personal aesthetic tastes, Tate argues, because these will reflect the editor's 'sense of the moral and intellectual order upon which society should rest'.[19] Tate indicates here how the New Critics' literary aesthetics were an extension of a shared political agenda and intellectual heritage. While never exactly 'a coterie or even a school', a core group of New Critics did have in common a set of cultural preoccupations derived from a shared sense of history.[20] In the 1920s, Ransom, Warren and Tate had all been members of the Fugitives, a group of poets based at Vanderbilt University who sought to redefine Southern literature and who became central to the 'Southern Renaissance' of the early twentieth century.[21] They were brought together by 'a collective hostility toward the Romantic stereotypes of Southern identity' and by their shared embarrassment at the sentimentality of the picturesque local colour writing that dominated Southern literary culture.[22] In their work, the Fugitives attempted a more complex engagement with regional identity informed by a modernist aesthetics originating partly in T. S. Eliot's early literary criticism. The Fugitives' preoccupation with regionalism was folded into a broader critique of modern society after the group disbanded in the late 1920s and reformed as the more overtly political Southern Agrarians. Their analysis echoed the tenor of midcentury bleak liberalism in its emphasis on the dangers of positivism, the limits of rationalism, and the dehumanising effect of technocracy. But the solution to these modern ills offered in *I'll Take My Stand*, the group's 1930 manifesto, was peculiarly Southern: a return to an agrarian way of life defined by local customs, myths, crafts, and traditions and firmly rooted in religion.

The Symbolic Imagination: Catholicism and Criticism

Tate concluded that 'only Catholicism could sustain an agrarian culture'.[23] Although he only converted in 1950, Tate had been a 'Catholic fellow-traveler almost from the beginning of his career'.[24] In his essay on Southern religion in *I'll Take My Stand*, he argued that the fall of the old South had been due to the fact that it had 'failed to produce a religion' that could counter the challenge of Northern industrial capitalism and scientific rationalism; its 'adherence to Protestantism rather than Catholicism had cost it dear'.[25] Southerners had had 'a religious life,' Tate acknowledges, 'but it was not enough organized with a right mythology [. . .] their rational life was not powerfully united to the religious experience, as it was in medieval society'.[26] Tate's turn to Catholicism and the broader religious character of the Agrarian project reflected a number of influences. 'If the Fugitive poetics were strongly influenced by Eliot and his ideas regarding tradition and individual talent', it was 'Eliot's social criticism' that inspired the Agrarians.[27] Their description of modern man as 'increasingly divided [. . .] as industrialization and secularism progressed' clearly echoed 'Eliot's pessimistic reading of modernity', especially as it emerged in essays written after his conversion to Anglo-Catholicism in 1927.[28] Like Eliot, the Agrarians thought of themselves as fighting 'a rear-guard action to preserve a community that they [saw] slipping away'.[29] Both Eliot and Tate's conversions belong to a broader Catholic revival in the early twentieth century, which permeated American culture through the neo-Thomism of the French theologian Jacques Maritain, whom Eliot cited as an influence, and who became Tate's godparent following his conversion.[30] Maritain traced the problems facing modern society back to the hubris of Cartesian rationalism – of thinking one could separate spirit from body, mind from matter. As Paul Giles explains, in a commentary on Maritain's *The Dream of Descartes* (1932), 'In Maritain's eyes, the "cultural significance" of Cartesian idealism was that "it carries along with it a sort of anthropocentric optimism of thought" that ignores the fact that human reason can never achieve perfect autonomy but needs always to be informed by divine grace.'[31]

Maritain's emphasis upon man's fallibility chimes with other strains of counter-Enlightenment thought emerging at midcentury, and helps explain what William Barrett called, in 1949, 'the rather strange religious revival' emerging within American cultural thought at this time.[32] 'The mid-century years may go down in history as the years of conversion and return,' a *Partisan* editorial the following year suggested, introducing a special symposium on 'Religion and the Intellectuals'.[33] In the same magazine in 1943, Sidney Hook had already diagnosed a 'new failure of nerve' among American intellectuals.[34] Borrowing his title from the classicist Gilbert Murray's account of 'the rise of asceticism', 'mysticism', and 'pessimism' during the Hellenistic period, Hook suggests that both the ancient and the modern failures of nerve were marked by the same 'flight from responsibility, both on the plane of action and on the plane of belief'.[35] You could see it, Hook writes, in the 'recrudescence of beliefs in the original depravity of human nature', the 'refurbishing of theological and metaphysical dogmas', and in a more general pessimism about the possibility of social reform.[36]

Hook had Eliot and the Southern critics in his sights, but also, more immediately, the Protestant theologian Reinhold Niebuhr.[37] In *The Nature and Destiny of Man* (1939/43), Niebuhr condemns Enlightenment thought for its assumption that 'all development means the advancement of the good. It does not recognize that every heightened potency of human existence may also represent a possibility of evil.'[38] 'Niebuhr meant to restore limit and prophetic religion to the center of human nature', putting forward 'a view of Christian man that intended to steer between the twin evils of unrestrained human freedom and power, on the one hand, and the equally dangerous nihilism and anarchy that arose out of a lack of meaning, on the other'.[39] As George Cotkin explains, 'Niebuhrian man acted freely within the paradoxical and ironic confines of history and his own limitations'.[40] A point of commonality between Maritain's and Niebuhr's critiques, Mark Greif notes, is their framing of the medieval period as 'the last safe place before the modern undermining had begun in the Renaissance' and intensified in the Enlightenment – a historicisation also at work in Tate's Agrarianism and important to Eliot's cultural criticism. Across their work, the medieval period was imagined 'as a time of the whole, undivided, organic – the integrated, when the present era was said to be disintegrating'.[41]

Over the course of the 1930s, Ransom, Warren and Tate returned more concertedly to aesthetics. As the Agrarians became the New Critics, they increasingly came to invest literature, and poetry in particular, with a special importance, imagining it as 'the only remaining counterweight to the triumph of technical rationality', and as 'capable of reasserting the limits of positivism'.[42] The New Critics' conception of the literary text as a key site of non-instrumental experience tallies, to an extent, with Trilling's aesthetics. But while the novel for Trilling ultimately reflected, mediated, and helped constitute a social reality – a world made up of manners, conversation, and 'human touches' – for the New Critics the poem was a kind of 'metaphysical bridge' between human reality (or nature) and a higher realm of experience (or the divine).[43] They conceived of the poem as an 'organic unity', an 'integrated whole in which form and content could not be separated'; in this, the poem was made to resemble the imagined communities of the medieval period and agrarian past.[44] The poem was resistant to mere summary or explanation. 'If the poem is a real creation,' Tate writes in 'Narcissus as Narcissus' (1938), 'it is a kind of knowledge that we did not possess before. It is not knowledge "about" something else; the poem is the fullness of that knowledge.'[45] Hence the New Critics' famous injunction against 'the heresy of paraphrase'; a poem is a form not of communication, Tate argued, but of 'communion'.[46] The job of the critic is not to extract meaning from the poem, but to attend to the ways in which it struggles to achieve its unity.[47] Because they held that the meaning of the poem was always beyond critical explication, the New Critics' formalism dramatised the limits of reason and knowledge in a way that spoke to their broader resistance to the technocratic optimism of modern society; every act of critique was inevitably an act of failed or only partial critique. The New Critics sought to make the poem 'a quasi-religious, ontological sanctuary from all secularizing discourses that would situate literature in history'.[48] As John Sykes puts it, they 'created room for what might be called linguistic mystery, a sacred dimension'.[49]

At the centre of their aesthetics was a special attention to the role of symbolism in poetry.[50] In a 1952 essay, Tate describes how Dante's poetry works through allegory and analogy to embody divine 'essence' in concrete images, rather than the intellectual abstractions that most modern poetry tends towards.[51] For the 'symbolic poet,' Tate writes, 'nature offers clearly denotable objects in depth and in the round, which yield the analogies to the higher syntheses'.[52] The symbolic imagination 'takes rise from a definite limitation of human rationality which was recognized in the West until the 17th Century,' he continues; 'in this view the intellect cannot have direct knowledge of essences'.[53] 'For Tate,' Mark Jancovich explains, 'Dante's thought predates the division between intellect and experience which emerges with modern society, and as a result, these essences are presented as forms to be experienced not facts to be transmitted.'[54] Tate is careful to point out that 'the gift of analogy was not Dante's alone', as 'every medievalist knows', but rather belonged to his Catholic sensibility, a sensibility from which most modern poets are disassociated but to which Tate, following Eliot's lead, hopes to reconnect.[55] In so doing, Tate, like Eliot, seeks something akin to what Michael Trask calls 'the spiritualization of the modernist canon'.[56]

Given the curious intellectual heritage of the New Criticism, and its apparent hostility towards modern forms of institutionality and professionalisation, it might seem surprising, and indeed ironic, that it caught on in quite the way it did, shaping the practice of literary criticism in and out of the academy through the midcentury and well beyond. But, as John Paul Russo argues, 'in important ways New Criticism can be seen to have accommodated itself to technological society'.[57] In their relative neglect of wider literary and historical context in favour of a focus on the words on the page, and in their stress upon questions of form and technique in contrast to the 'impressionism' of earlier literary scholarship, the New Critics 'fostered the straightforward, roll-up-your-sleeves attitude to criticism that mirrored technocratic expertise [and] bureaucratized efficiency'.[58] Close reading was also eminently teachable, well suited to the demands of the larger classes of the post-GI Bill university. Nowhere is this clearer than in the textbooks and anthologies that

Brooks and Warren and others produced in the late 1930s and early 1940s, which 'did more to establish the New Criticism within the departments of English than any other activity'.[59] In particular, Brooks and Warren's *Understanding Poetry* (1938) was 'responsible for redefining the object of literary study' and introducing generations of students to the tenets of New Criticism and its distinctive key terms – among them, ambiguity, tension, paradox, and unity.[60]

Fiction and Formalism

Stafford had arrived at one of the centres of New Criticism just as it was in the ascendancy, and when its ideas of literary form and aesthetic experience were making their way from quarterlies to classrooms and beyond. Not for the last time in her life, Stafford found herself a prose writer among poets, for it was the poem rather than the novel that was the prestige literary genre in Baton Rouge in 1940.[61] Fiction would always place second to poetry for the New Critics, and they remained uneasy about what to make of the novel in particular, uncertain as to whether it could yield the kind of concentrated aesthetic experience offered by poetry. In 'Techniques of Fiction' (1944), Tate suggests that 'it has been through Flaubert that the novel has at last caught up poetry', but he seems a little baffled as to how he was supposed to go about analysing one.[62] 'Who can remember well enough to pronounce upon it critically, all of *War and Peace*, or *The Wings of a Dove*,' Tate asks. 'For the life of me I could not pretend to know them as wholes, and without that knowledge I lack the materials of criticism.'[63] And yet Tate's essay also testifies to the fact that the New Critics were slowly turning their attention to fiction – and indeed trying to write the stuff themselves: Tate's only novel, *The Fathers*, appeared in 1938, while Warren's *Night Rider* was published the following year.[64] In their essays, the New Critics reappraised fiction writers in the terms they had developed for the study of poetry and in relation to the preoccupations of their cultural criticism. Thus Faulkner was celebrated for both his formal experimentation and deep investment in Southern history and mythology, his writing said to reflect what Tate called a 'regional consciousness'.[65] Warren similarly draws attention to the 'vividness of the natural background' in Faulkner's novels, the importance of which isn't merely as scene setting: 'it's the atmosphere which counts, the poetry [...] the symbolic weight'.[66] In an essay on Welty's short stories, meanwhile, Warren describes her fiction as 'a tissue of symbols which emerge from, and disappear into, a world of scene and action', a method that is at once 'similar [...] to that of much modern fiction' and 'at the same time [...] as old as fable, myth, and parable'.[67] As Warren describes it, the basic pattern of her stories fits neatly with the New Critics' religious and bleak liberal outlook: a 'dream must be carried to, submitted to, the world, innocence to experience, love to knowledge, knowledge to fact, individuality to communion'.[68]

New Critical close reading lent itself especially to the study of short fiction, exemplified in Brooks and Warren's *Understanding Fiction* (1943). In their introduction, the editors announce their intention to place a new 'emphasis on formal considerations in the evaluation of fiction'.[69] As in the earlier poetry textbook, they stress that literary criticism is not a process of 'moral message-hunting or sociological documentation', but a practice of attending to the 'set of organic relationships' that constitute the work's 'total structure'.[70] They provide a critical vocabulary for doing so that partly overlaps with that used in the poetry anthology – most importantly irony, unity, conflict, symbolism – but which also extends to include terms meant to capture the particular formal qualities of fiction. These include, for example, 'scale', and the concept of an epiphanic 'key moment', which should contain the 'total meaning of the story' and without which 'the structure of the story will be loose and vague' (a 'story', in Brooks and Warren's definition, is 'a movement through complexity to unity, through complication to simplicity, through confusion to order').[71] In their critical commentaries, Brooks and Warren restrict themselves 'almost entirely to those issues that came to dominate the formal study of fiction at mid-century,' Michael Levenson writes: 'tone, pace, focus, scale, distance, denouement'.[72]

In his own anthology, *The House of Fiction* (1950), edited with Gordon, Tate similarly stresses the importance of 'tonal unity', 'proportion' and 'symbolism'.[73] Of the latter Tate tells the would-be writer that, 'since the end of the eighteenth century, the social and historical symbol has more and more been cut off from an even deeper source of symbolic insight: the religious source'.[74] He highlights works of fiction mostly by nineteenth-century European writers and a handful of modernist masters said to have 'achieved something of the self-contained objectivity of certain forms of poetry'.[75] As the collection's title suggests, Tate was taking up Henry James's idea of the novel as 'a living thing, all one and continuous, like any other organism', as well as James's directive that a work of fiction should be a 'direct impression of life', an aesthetics influentially repackaged in Percy Lubbock's *The Craft of Fiction* (1921).[76] *Understanding Fiction* similarly synthesises New Critical terminology with a 'Jamesian lexicon' which, Michael Levenson writes, 'offers Brooks and Warren a way to extend their concern with organic form from lyric poetry to prose fiction'.[77] Not that James was above critique. In a 1950 commentary on 'The Beast in the Jungle' (1903), Tate praises how the 'revelation' at the centre of the story 'forces Marcher into a tragic and ironic awareness' (always a good thing for New York Intellectuals and New Critics alike), but argues that 'the structure suffers' from a certain 'disproportion', and that there is not enough 'naturalist detail' to 'give the situation reality' (as there is in Dante and Faulkner), and that therefore 'the symbolism tends to allegory'.[78] James, in other words, sometimes wasn't sufficiently Jamesian to meet New Critical standards of symbolism and proportion.

Considering the New Criticism in the round, Mark McGurl notes the 'striking' attraction of this 'close-knit group of Southern intellectuals to the idea – indeed to the very term, which peppers their writing – of "limitation"'.[79] It's there most overtly in their commitment to regionalism, to a conception of identity and culture rooted in the history and customs of a particular place – what Tate calls a feeling for 'locality in the sense of local continuity in tradition and belief'.[80] It's there, too, in their emphasis upon the limits of human reason and progress, an emphasis also found in the wider midcentury religious revival. In their literary criticism, meanwhile, the New Critics translated the idea of limitation into aesthetic terms: in their stress upon scale and unity; in their preference for controlled verse forms and for short stories, usually told in the 'Jamesian third person limited'.[81] Similarly, their critical method demanded a constricted attention to the words of the text and held that a critic's access to the poem is itself limited. In different ways, both Lowell and Stafford tested the limits of New Critical formalism, exploring whether and how their work could be shaped to fit the critics' precepts. For Lowell, in the early part of his career, limits were there to be submitted to. In the summer of 1937 he had, as he put it, 'converted to formalism' and by 1941 he had also converted to Catholicism, remarrying Stafford under the auspices of the Church.[82] Catholicism gave him not a 'subject' for his poetry, he said, but a 'form', shaping his first two collections and infusing them with religious imagery and themes.[83] In the story Lowell liked to tell about the progress of his career, his development depended initially upon 'appropriating the rigorous verse forms and cultural pessimism in Tate's work, writing poems that satisfied his mentor's demand for symbolic art' and steeping himself in Catholic teaching and Southern culture – including picking up an 'Agrarian-Eliotic accent' that he 'never wore out'.[84] The next stage was to throw off the shackles of formalism to write from 'his own experience' in *Life Studies* (1959).[85] By contrast, Stafford's relation to New Criticism and Catholicism doesn't lend itself so readily to such mythmaking. While Lowell was ready to renounce his Boston background and embrace Southern culture, Stafford had, as we've seen, a more complex sense of where she was from, and so responded differently to the New Critics' celebration of 'locality'. Stafford had herself converted to Catholicism at college but was already 'growing cool' towards the Church by the time Lowell found faith; she was 'deeply ambivalent' about the fervour of his religious commitment.[86] For Lowell – uncompromising and 'rigidly devout' – conversion was supposed to be a process of total transformation.[87] But Stafford was always more sceptical about the promise of, and her capacity for, such radical change. Rather than embrace and then renounce New Criticism and Catholicism, as Lowell had by the late 1940s, Stafford's relationship with each was more nuanced. In her work, we find her engaging with and revising the terms and values of the formalist aesthetics she encountered in Baton Rouge, pushing at its limits and querying its investment in symbolism, proportion, and unity.

Conversion Narratives: from Catholicism to Psychoanalysis

Lowell had begun studying Catholic theology and philosophy as soon as he reached LSU. In her biography, Ann Hulbert suggests Stafford found at least one text among her husband's heavy reading that appealed to her: *The Interior Castle*, an account by St Teresa of Ávila of her teachings and mystical experiences. Stafford was drawn to St Teresa's refreshingly intimate and witty style, Hulbert writes, and by her core teaching that 'to suffer is to learn'.[88] The text gave Stafford the title of one of her best short stories ('The Interior Castle' appeared in *Partisan Review* in 1946), but also, more importantly, the inspiration for her first novel, *Boston Adventure* (1944), her most commercially successful work.[89] 'Stafford's novel was not religious in the same sense that Lowell's contemporaneous poems were,' Hulbert acknowledges. 'She was not working with explicitly Christian symbolism [. . .] as he was [. . .] But her basic inclination, like that of her teachers Tate and Ransom [. . .] was to see [. . .] mankind as fallen and art as a kind of redemptive witness to that plight.'[90] *Boston Adventure* is a story of 'social, but also of spiritual, exile', structured around the contrast of Catholicism and Brahmin Boston. Stafford had signed the contract for the book at Tate's desk, and he and Caroline Gordon had read and commented on an earlier draft.[91]

But if the novel's broad themes reflect Stafford time in the South, her debut was far from adhering to the formalist approach with which she had become familiar. Rather than a tightly structured work of carefully patterned design and keen sense of scale, working through conflict and complication towards a 'key moment' and built around an organising symbol, the novel was, Stafford later judged, 'filled with digressions', overly 'leisurely' and 'embroidered'.[92] Rather than a Jamesian narrator set at an ironic distance from the action, the novel is told in the first person (like St Teresa's text); and indeed, Stafford's primary model wasn't James but Proust, as many reviewers spotted (or at least 'Moncrieff's Proust', as Lowell put it).[93] The novel was imitative and 'old-fashioned', Stafford later said, both in what one critic called its 'baroque' style and its theme of social manners.[94] In her review in *Partisan*, Elizabeth Hardwick noted that, in the character of Hopestill Mather, the novel included the kind of 'pampered, fast living, rebellious girl who became a literary convention in the novels of the twenties'; Mather is no less an outdated cliché, Hardwick writes, because of her à la mode 'vague interest in psychoanalysis'.[95]

Stafford had 'read Freud sympathetically since college', but her interest in psychoanalysis gained more definitive shape in the years immediately following *Boston Adventure*'s publication.[96] Her Catholicism, meanwhile, started to wane as her marriage to Lowell began to break down (they separated in late 1946). In 1945, they were living in Maine in a house bought with money from Stafford's book. Here, she wrote *The Mountain Lion* in an intense nine-month spell between summer 1945 and spring 1946, a contrast to the drawn-out process of revising her first book. Stafford describes this period in 'An Influx of Poets' (1978), a posthumously published short story drawn from her unfinished autobiographical novel.[97] The story is set during the 'summer after the war', a summer when it seems that 'every poet in America' has come to visit the narrator Cora, a stand-in for Stafford, and the poet Theron Maybank, a thinly veiled version of Lowell.[98] 'I admit they were brilliant poets, if you happen to be interested in that sort of thing,' Cora writes, but she soon tires of the poets' 'conceit', resenting their demands that their poems be retyped 'if they changed an "a" to a "the"' (466). Like Lowell, Theron has undergone an apprenticeship at the feet of an esteemed poet ('the famous and reclusive' Fitzhugh Burr (465)), and his literary tastes are also shaped by the New Critical canon; he repudiates as 'soulless' 'everything that had been [. . .] written (except for certain poetry and the prose of certain contemporary English divines) after 1850' (486). Theron 'had found Catholicism shortly after he found me' (476) Cora writes, chronicling her husband's humourless piety and her own misgivings about his 'old-time religion' (478). As Theron becomes increasingly preoccupied with the Church (and with Minnie, another poet's ex-wife with whom he has an affair), Cora turns to psychoanalysis – which Theron dismisses as 'Viennese chicanery' (469) – to understand the 'genesis' of her 'brutish headaches' and 'lurching nausea' (469).

Stafford, too, looked for help in this period, as she sought to address various long-running psychological issues. She first consulted Gregory Zilboorg, a respected psychoanalyst and historian of psychology, and himself later a convert to Catholicism, who was eager to read her fiction for symptoms of her condition. According to Stafford, Zilboorg told her that *'Boston Adventure* was "the product of one of the most tormented minds in a woman of my age" that he had ever seen'.[99] When Zilboorg refused to see her again, she began what would prove to be a long therapeutic relationship with Mary Jane Sherfey (Stafford was her client until the late 1950s).[100] Sherfey is now remembered for her contributions to the feminist critique of orthodox Freudian psychoanalysis; her work centres on the relation of female sexuality to male dominance, a topic about which Stafford knew a thing or two from her marriage to Lowell.[101] From their correspondence, it seems as though Sherfey did not try to convert Stafford to psychoanalysis, nor did she demand the kind of discipleship so much in evidence in New Critical (and psychoanalytic) circles. She didn't look to Stafford's work for symptoms, either; instead, she tried to support Stafford enough to keep her writing. There would be no conversion but an ongoing conversation. 'Remember,' Sherfey once wrote to Stafford, 'transference works both ways'.[102]

Stafford and Sherfey's analytic relationship began as psychoanalysis's influence on American intellectual and popular culture reached a high watermark, and as 'the psychological mapping of ordinary life became part of the common American vocabulary'.[103] Dorothy Ross describes how an 'Apollonian' version of Freudianism underpinned midcentury literary intellectuals' conception and canonisation of high modernism, while the bleak tenor of liberal thought chimed with what Trilling praised as psychoanalysis's 'tragic courage in its acquiescence to fate'.[104] More generally, Mary Esteve notes, Freud's 'highly literary' method of dream interpretation – based in the 'operations of symbolic condensation, displacement, and secondary elaboration' – ratified midcentury critics' sense of 'literature's special status as the medium through which humanity most forcefully expresses its psycho-existential truths' ('Freudian psychology,' Trilling writes, 'makes poetry indigenous to the very constitution of the mind').[105] For their part, the New Critics shared with psychoanalysis an interest in mythology and symbolism, and they largely subscribed to the 'tragic' Freud described by Trilling and others. A 1940 editorial in *Kenyon* on Freud's legacy, for example, acknowledges that his work represents 'a major revolution in man's knowledge of himself', suggesting that 'not the least of his achievements was to bring some ground for renewed faith in the potential dignity of man'.[106] But the New Critics were generally wary of the influence of psychoanalysis on literary studies. In *Understanding Fiction*, Brooks and Warren warn student-writers against creating characters too 'eccentric' or 'perverse': 'Fiction at this point passes off imperceptibly into the psychiatrist's case study'.[107] Like Trilling, the New Critics worried that in the wrong hands psychoanalysis risked turning close reading into a form of diagnosis, with texts understood to be evidence of an author's neurosis rather than autonomous aesthetic objects. As Brooks put it, 'speculation on the mental processes of the author takes the critic away from the work into biography and psychology [. . .] which should not be confused with an account of the work'.[108]

Stafford was wary too. In 'An Influx of Poets', she describes 'the fashion to use Freud's works as a recipe book and to add garniture from Henry James and Proust' (475), which captures something of the flavour of *Boston Adventure*, and echoes the *Kenyon* editors' worries about fiction's 'faddish and half-baked' engagement with psychoanalysis.[109] In 'The Psychological Novel' – a rare lecture, delivered in 1947 at Bard College – Stafford began by wondering whether her title might strike her audience as both a cliché and a tautology:

> A cliché because for so long now there has been so much talk about Freud and his fellows and their literary uses [. . .] and a tautology because the novel does not exist that is not psychological, is not concerned with motivations and their intellectual resolutions, with instincts and impulses and conflicts and behaviours, with the convulsions and complexities of human relationships, with the crucifixions and the solaces of being alive.[110]

Most striking here perhaps is 'crucifixions', suggestive of the connections Stafford was now making, in her life and in her work, between Catholicism and psychoanalysis; as though she were looking for a way to draw together – or hold in 'tension', to borrow a New Critical watchword – these two evocative and seemingly irreconcilable vocabularies, and the very different pictures of human potential they describe. She poses a similar juxtaposition of psychological and religious language in 'An Influx of Poets', when Cora describes her fear of snakes and water. Her phobia of the former has nothing to do with their venom or size, she claims, but the 'especial *essence* of the creature' (471, emphasis original), bringing to mind Tate's discussion of Dante's symbolic figuration of divine 'essences'. Her fear of water, meanwhile, is, she realises, 'irrational', and so not assuaged by Minnie's logical reassurances: 'The more she tried to persuade me, the more stubbornly I resisted, until finally I was angry, protective of this neurosis – which, in point of fact, had been [. . .] an impediment to me all my life and one I would have given anything to be delivered from' (471). To be 'delivered' from a neurosis is to imagine a kind of salvation not quite promised by psychoanalysis. Cora turns to therapy to find the 'genesis' (471) of her headaches, and, in this symbolically overdetermined moment in the story, we see Stafford counterposing the very different origin stories – the story of where we begin and belong – offered by Catholicism and psychoanalysis.

Lean Simplicity: *The Mountain Lion*

Critics quickly realised that *The Mountain Lion* was a very different kind of book to *Boston Adventure*. Orville Prescott praised the new work's 'restricted scope', judging it to be '[s]horter, simpler, with none of the lush extravagance' of Stafford's debut, which he had found 'overwrought and overstuffed'.[111] Howard Mumford Jones similarly noted that 'the book is shorter than its predecessor and gains from being better shaped', while *The Washington Post*'s reviewer praised *The Mountain Lion*'s 'lean simplicity'.[112] Phillip Rahv wrote to Stafford congratulating her on the new novel which, though 'narrower in scope and invention' than its predecessor, he thought 'more unified [. . .] as a work of art', praising how 'the symbolic meanings come through [. . .] without strain or distortion'.[113] The novel was recognised as a 'model of New Critical tautness', the reviews' stress upon its compact, circumscribed form – 'lean', 'restricted', 'narrower', 'simpler' – suggestive of how Stafford was explicitly engaging with the 'limitations' imposed by midcentury formalism in a manner quite distinct from her first book.[114] Most reviews framed the novel as a coming-of-age story in which siblings Ralph and Molly Fawcett, ten and eight when the narrative begins, face the travails of growing up, Ralph gradually accepting the demands of adulthood and Molly refusing to do so. Most reviewers also noted that as well as the contrast between the two siblings, the novel is structured around the often-comic contrast between the genteel Californian home in which they are raised and the wilder life they encounter on their Uncle Claude's Coloradoan ranch, the narrative oscillating between a satire of manners and kind of 'western' story – or between the divergent paleface and redskin influences of James and Twain.[115] Almost all reviewers praised the novel's closing sequence, set high up in the Colorado mountains, in which Ralph accidentally kills Molly, mistaking her for the rare mountain lion he and his uncle have been hunting (nearby, the lion also lies dead, killed by Claude) – very much the ironic, tragic clinching 'key moment' that Brooks and Warren describe in their textbook. The ending 'achieves the verisimilitude of inevitable tragedy,' the *Washington Post*'s reviewer wrote, while Prescott also thought it 'a tragic conclusion, which is surprising and yet somehow inevitable', and Rahv told Stafford that 'the ending is wonderful, and not only for its dramatic power – it integrates plot and meaning'.[116] In these readings, the ending is powerfully symbolic in just the way that the New Critics outline, with the mountain lion interpreted as a symbol of lost innocence and natural order, and the tragic deaths of the lion and Molly symbolic of what happens to innocence when it comes into contact with the violent reality of the world of men.[117]

But I want to suggest that the novel in fact problematises and exceeds the New Critical limits to which is appears to 'abide', and in so doing elaborates a minor aesthetics all of its own. In unpacking this a little, two dissenting reviews are instructive. Mark Schorer's review in *Kenyon* was part of a roundup of recent American novels, which he criticises en masse for their 'desperate aimlessness', bemoaning the 'deadly competence which now prevails in American fiction'.[118] In terms similar to those he would employ in his influential essay 'Technique as Discovery' (1948), published a few months later, Schorer judges all the books under review to be to a greater or lesser extent 'technically innocent'.[119] The piece is in fact typical of Schorer's and the New Critics' low estimation of the novel in general and of contemporary fiction in particular. Stafford's is the best of the bunch, Schorer writes, but is still blighted by problems of 'structure' and a sense of 'aesthetic aimlessness': 'The novel seems to be written only for the sake of the final chapter, where the *whole* really is'. Schorer suggests that this chapter is 'so evocative of the entire relationship [between Molly and Ralph] and its history' that it 'could be detached from the novel and read as a short story with no loss whatever in force or meaning'. While the finale would work well in a New Critical anthology of short fiction, as a novel there seems to Schorer to be 'some deficiency [. . .] in the formal analysis of the limits of the material'.[120] In his *Sewanee* review, meanwhile, Robert Heilman was less strident but reached a similar conclusion. He praises *The Mountain Lion* for its 'sensitively-observed detail' of 'Colorado scenery' and life on the ranch.[121] But he too feels the novel suffers from 'structural inadequacies' and a lack of 'unity of action'. At the heart of this is the mountain lion itself, which seems to Heilman no more that 'an afterthought, never enlarged into a symbol that compellingly subordinates the personalities to it, and the catastrophe of which it is the center is simply rigged – as it would seem less to be if the lion were effectually managed as symbol'.[122] Part of the problem, Heilman suggests, is that 'one is never sure about the structural center of *The Mountain Lion*', and so the novel lacks 'a single line of action which might give the story a continuous forward impetus [. . .] the story stops rather than reaches a conclusion, just as it has stepped from point to point rather than grown as an organism'.[123]

In these reviews, the novel's ending either overwhelms the rest of the narrative, or else is insufficient to it; the problem, in New Critical terms, is one of scale and proportion. Both reviewers take the mountain lion to be operating as an organising symbol in the way outlined by the New Critics, but they feel that the lion is either too big, or too small, but in any case, is not the right size for the role. There is, these reviews suggest, something 'deficient' about how the novel develops, unnatural, even, in how it 'grows'. Writing in two of the leading New Critical journals, Schorer and Heilman judge the novel to be trying and failing to fulfil the New Critical criteria of unity and organic structural order. But we might instead argue that the novel appears to invest in these New Critical ideas only to query and depart from them; the novel does indeed fail to keep to New Critical 'limits', but Stafford is not quite the technical 'innocent' Schorer assumes her to be. As Heilman himself notes, the novel indicates that it might pursue something other than the familiar coming-of-age narrative by the way in which it disrupts one of the conventions of the bildungsroman, focusing on not one but two tales of adolescence. The narrative gradually shifts its focus from Ralph's story of masculine initiation on the ranch to Molly's altogether less certain developmental plot; to return for a moment to Deleuze and Guattari's terms, we might say that Ralph's is the story of a majoritarian identity in formation, and Molly's the story of a minoritarian 'becoming'. That Heilman can't find the structural centre of the novel is therefore instructive, because one of the things the novel explores is how Molly doesn't fit the *bildung* narrative in which she appears to be emplotted. And Molly's not fitting might be taken as one facet of the novel's broader questioning of New Critical ideas of narrative form and unity.

Ralph and Molly are both examples of a kind of minor character that, like the Kafkaesque 'little man' discussed in the previous chapter, was much in vogue at midcentury: the adolescent. For Morris Dickstein, the adolescent protagonists of Stafford, Carson McCullers, Truman Capote, and J. D. Salinger are harbingers of the youth culture that would sweep America in subsequent decades.[124] At midcentury, however, critics were uncertain what to make of the trend for what one reviewer called 'juvenile fiction', and of the prevalence of adolescent characters in 'classic' American literature.[125] Trilling suggested that part of the 'greatness' of *Huckleberry Finn* was that it succeeded first and foremost as a 'boys' book'. 'No one,' he writes, 'sets a higher value on truth than a boy', and Twain's tale has 'the truth of moral passion'.[126] Unexpectedly linking Twain to Eliot's 'The Dry Salvages', Trilling gestures to the religious revival afoot in midcentury intellectual culture, claiming that the complex morality of the story lies in the fact that 'Huck is at odds [. . .] with the only form of established religion he knows'; Huck's relationship with Jim, Trilling suggests, resembles a 'community of saints'.[127] But the predominance of adolescent characters in both contemporary fiction and American literacy history was also taken to be indicative of the immaturity and sentimentality of American culture, an argument that found its most strident elaboration in Leslie Fiedler's claim that 'the great works of American fiction are notoriously at home in the children's section of the library'.[128] Stafford's portrayal of adolescence is freighted with something of this critical ambivalence. Molly's failure to grow up figures the broadly held view that American fiction was oddly arrested in its development, while also echoing the New Critics' uneasiness about the novel itself, a literary form they sometimes treated as too unwieldy for proper analysis, or suspected of being only a kind of overgrown short story.

The Mountain Lion takes up some of these concerns in the siblings' divergent conceptions of scale. Ralph has a clear sense of the difference in scale between the insular world of the Fawcetts' bourgeois Californian home where he is raised and the open expanse of Uncle Claude's Colorado ranch. He contrasts 'the house in Covina with all its flurry of little objects, little vases and boxes on little gilt tables' to the 'big, bare rooms of the ranch', and reflects that in Colorado he feels as though he is 'living within the present time and on a large scale'.[129] This perception of scalar expansion is of a piece with Ralph's narrative of growth and development – the *bildung* plot as one of widening horizons and initiation into 'national time', even as it also adheres to a New Critical emphasis on 'locality'.[130] By contrast, Molly's sense of scale is attuned to qualities and dynamics other than straightforward enlargement. One of her pastimes in Colorado is studying a mass of 'hibernating ladybugs' (204) she discovers near the summit of one of the mountains surrounding the ranch, carefully packing specimens into matchboxes to send to the local agricultural college for further observation. From this vantage, she can also use her uncle's field glasses to look at 'the cattle moving down from the summer range', noting that at such a distance they 'appeared to be hundreds of small red blocks [. . .] as small as her ladybugs' (206). Rather than simple expansion, then, Molly is able to attend to the scalar complexity of the world around her, bringing things of very different scales into close relation. Here, by thinking of the ladybugs and cattle together, she is able to link their respective processes of hibernation and migration, and so consider the connection between the ranch and the wider natural environment, and her connection to both.

'Who cares about a sense of beauty?' Molly mockingly asks her older sisters, who are embarking upon a familiar journey of female development beginning with European travel and culminating in marriage proposals. 'I'd a whole lot rather have a sense of *proportion*' (176, emphasis original). For Molly, this means thinking about staying small as well as growing up. Throughout the novel she keeps a list of 'unforgivable people' who have in some way wronged or disappointed her. It occurs to her that she hates all the people on the list 'for the same reason, but she could not decide what the reason was. You could say, Because they were all fat', though she acknowledges that not all of those on the list are physically overweight. 'But fatness did have something to do with it. There was something fat about the way Mr Follansbee belched and the question Ralph had asked her had been fat' (179) – the latter referring to the moment when Ralph asks her to tell him all the dirty words she knows, a moment that marks the end of their childhood together. Molly resolves that if 'she ever got fat [. . .] she would lock herself in a bathroom and stay there until she dies [. . .] All this time she, Molly Fawcett, would be getting thinner and thinner until she was practically famous for it' (180). At other times, she imagines shrinking, wishing 'she were only four feet five' (212). Her disgust at the idea of fatness seems connected to her difficult relationship with her body as she approaches puberty. She takes a bath in her swimming costume before tightly binding herself in her towel, and pours acid on her arm in an act of self-harm. It doesn't take much to interpret this behaviour as indicative of a sexual phobia, or to relate it to Stafford's own history with food and sex, documented in the three major biographies of her life.[131] The novel even gestures to the language of psychology when we are told that 'the word "nervous" came to be as disgusting to [Molly] as "body"' (133).

And yet Stafford also ridicules any attempt at a reductive symptomatic reading of the kind sometimes in evidence in early psychoanalytic literary criticism. Molly recalls how a boy at school called Pinky Freudenburg once 'sneaked up behind her and kissed her on the cheek and at that exact moment, a front tooth fell out onto her tongue' (179) – a parody of the kind of Freudian (or 'Freudenburgian') 'case history' Brooks and Warren warn against.

Rather than take Molly's fixation with size and fatness to be symptoms, we might instead read them as part of the novel's broader undermining of its own celebrated 'lean simplicity'. What we might now call Molly's dysmorphia and disordered relationship with food are, like her finely attuned scalar imagination, part of the novel's challenge to the 'limitations' of New Critical unity and proportion. Stafford the formalist is worrying the line between shapeliness and disfigurement, discipline and self-harm, thinness and gauntness.[132]

There is also something religious in Molly's bathing and ritualistic in her self-harm, such that we might think of hers, to recall Trilling's reading of *Huckleberry Finn*, as a kind of saint's life, like that of St Teresa – Molly's story as one not of transitioning from adolescence to adulthood, but of transcending from the earthly to the spiritual. Certainly, there is something otherworldly about Molly, related to her refusal to grow up in the ways expected of her. She tells her mother's annoying friends that she had decided not to go to college 'before you were born' (124); later, she reflects that she had hated these friends 'before she was born' (179). In her untimeliness, she feels an affinity with Magdalena, Uncle Claude's African-American housekeeper, who to Molly seems 'hundreds of years old [. . .] Her wisdom was something antediluvian and cosmic and the almanac she went by dated back a million years before the fall of man' (98). The identification allows her to imagine new kinds of genealogy and kinship, including 'the idea that she looked like Magdalena' and that 'she was probably her daughter' (100). She also at different times imagines marrying Ralph, the family dog and a horse on the ranch.

Creaturely Forms

Like her redescriptions of scale and proportion, it is worth seeing whether it is possible to take seriously Molly's unorthodox picture of marriage and affiliation. To do so, we might briefly turn to Carson McCullers's *The Member of the Wedding* (1946), another midcentury bildungsroman in which a female adolescent protagonist, twelve-year-old Frankie Addams, resists the developmental narrative in which she appears to be emplotted. The New Critics never quite claimed McCullers, a Southerner, as one of their own, but they did approve of her attention to regional identity and form.¹³³ In a review in *Kenyon*, Marguerite Young highlights McCullers's use of 'intricate symbols', praising *The Member of the Wedding* for being 'as formal as a problem in geometry', and comparing it to a game of chess, wherein 'every move is a symbol and requires the reader's countermove. Many modern poems are of this order.'¹³⁴ More surprising to contemporary readers might be Joseph Frank's declaration in *Sewanee* that 'politics is left completely behind when we enter the enchanted [. . .] world' of Frankie.¹³⁵ In recent years, Frankie's fantasy of being a member of her brother's wedding, and her insistence that he and his fiancé are *'the we of me'*, has often been read as part of the novel's broader interest in reimagining the institutions that structure social relations and in interrogating categories of gender and sexual identity.¹³⁶ Over the past two decades in particular, *The Member of the Wedding* has been the subject of a number of queer readings, critics finding in the stories of Frankie and her cousin, John Henry, narratives that 'defy the imposition of normative categories of identity' and so figure new possibilities for intimacy and community.¹³⁷ Pushing against the teleology of a 'developmental narrative that leads inevitably toward heterosexuality', critics have suggested how McCullers's wayward bildungsroman grows 'sideways' – to borrow Kathryn Bond Stockton's figuration of the progress of the 'queer child' – refusing the secure futures of marriage and family.¹³⁸

In the 'queer time' of the novel, Frankie, John Henry, and the African-American housekeeper, Bernice, can, however briefly, imagine other arrangements of sexuality and sociability. Sitting around the kitchen table discussing how they would each improve society, Frankie imagines a world where 'people could instantly change back and forth from boys to girls, whichever way they felt like and wanted' (116). Bernice, meanwhile, pictures a future in which 'there would be no separate coloured people in the world, but all human beings would be light brown colour with blue eyes and black hair' (114–15). 'Queerest of all', Rachel Adams notes, is John Henry's vision of a society where everyone is 'half boy and half girl' (116) – a world of fluid sexuality and gender identity.¹³⁹ But the novel is alert to the costs involved in such radical projects of transformation. This is most starkly figured in the early death of John Henry, who comes to represent the narrative's 'inassimilable remainder', as Pam Thurschwell puts it, the shadow to the novel's exploration of the more utopian potentialities of queer life.[140] Moreover, the incompatibility of the futures imagined by Frankie, Bernice, and John Henry suggests a broader difficulty in finding a conceptual vocabulary and grammar to accommodate a plurality of sometimes competing iterations of identity and community – a difficulty already pointed to in the awkwardness of Frankie's formulation, *'they are the we of me'*. One of Frankie's early fantasies of membership involves donating blood to Allied soldiers fighting in World War II: 'her blood would be in the veins of Australians and Fighting French and Chinese [. . .] and it would be as though she were close kin to all of these people [. . .] She could hear the army doctors saying that the blood of Frankie Addams was the reddest and strongest blood that they had ever known' (31). As with her desire to join her brother's wedding, the fantasy here is not of the dissolution of personal identity, but of its affirmation in a kin-like community. And yet, in a novel set in the South, Frankie's fantasy also carries the association of the one drop rule (another kind of inassimilable remainder), adopted across the region earlier in the century. The association lingers in Frankie's discussion with Bernice and John Henry about the possibilities for reimagining the categories of race and gender. While Frankie can imagine a world of gender self-definition, Bernice cannot imagine a world in which racial difference is recognised and respected, instead dreaming of a society in which it is simply erased. John Henry, meanwhile, cannot 'think in global terms' (114) about his project of sexual fluidity, and one of the questions asked in the novel is whether the worlds imagined around the kitchen table remain conceivable at the scale of the international or universal, and indeed, what the novel form, and the bildungsroman in particular, might be able and unable to say about such scalar relations.

    Stafford pursues a congruent but distinctive experiment in the bildungsroman form in *The Mountain Lion*. A queer reading of Molly's story would also be possible; in a sense she, like John Henry, is the novel's inassimilable remainder, the deadly excess encrypted in Ralph's conventional developmental narrative.[141] Moreover, in imagining herself to be Magdalena's daughter, we might say that

Molly envisages a similar refiguring of racial identity as that conceived by Frankie or Bernice, albeit one that rests on a problematic identification of blackness with 'antediluvian' irrationality. But what to make of Molly's desire to marry a dog and a horse, if we are not simply to dismiss it as childishness? What account of personhood would we need to make such a bond imaginable? Certainly, Molly's fantasy would seem to take us beyond queer theory and perhaps into the realm of recent work associated with the 'nonhuman turn' in the humanities, focusing on the 'the multiple entanglements of human and non-human agencies'.[142] 'What would a humanities, a knowledge of and for the human, look like,' Elizabeth Grosz asks, 'if it placed the animal in its rightful place, not only before the human but also within and after the human?'[143] Rather than read Molly's desire to marry an animal as a category mistake, or a misunderstanding of the institution of marriage, we might instead read it as a querying of what constitutes the human, an effort to imagine a continuity between the human and the animal in place of the usual conceptual division. Rather than growing up into adulthood, or sideways into a queer future, Molly's wayward narrative entertains the possibility of becoming more creaturely.

We have already seen, in her study of ladybugs and her observation of cattle, that Molly is attentive to animal life and its imbrication with the human, and, more generally, there is a recognition of the nonhuman throughout the novel. Ralph becomes familiar with animals as part of his education at the ranch, where it is clear that man has dominion over other creatures, and this knowledge is tied to his growing consciousness of masculinity and male power: thus he learns the difference between a stallion and a gelding, a difference Molly refuses to acknowledge, preferring to think of them as 'two different breeds of horses' (185). Later, Molly is bewildered by the idea that the mountain lion and the family cat belong to the same species; indeed, the concept of species, like that of race, is one with which Molly struggles. Often, she herself is described as something other than fully human – she thinks of herself as not having a body, for example, but of being 'a mind inside a box' (177). While Ralph, aged about twelve, is described as 'beginning to look . . . well to put it bluntly, to look like a human being', Molly looks 'just the same as she had done when she was eight' (123), with a 'look of having been put together by an inexperienced hand' (140). After Ralph has killed her, she is said to look 'like a tall, slim monkey' (230), and is then, in an intriguing simile, 'propped up like a person' (231) by her brother and uncle.

If recent queer theory and work from the nonhuman turn offers some critical purchase on Stafford's portrayal of Molly, her creatureliness also emerges from a specifically midcentury concern with the limits of human agency and rationalism, resonating, for example, with Maritain's critique of the 'anthropocentric optimism' of modern man (and bringing to mind Alvin Folger's conversation with his dogs in *The Middle of the Journey*, and Eleanor Clark's description of Hilda's animal-like mobiles). Molly's arrested and wayward development, meanwhile, forms part of Stafford's response to and revision of the New Critical emphasis on unity, scale, and proportion. Stafford's revisionary and reflexive engagement with midcentury formalism becomes especially striking when we consider the role of the mountain lion, which, as Schorer and Heilman intuit, doesn't quite operate as the kind of organising symbol a New Critical reading would expect. A symbol, as Brooks and Warren define it in *Understanding Fiction*, is 'an object, character, or incident which stands for something else [. . .] possessing a wider significance and thus becoming expressive of the author's meaning'.[144] For this substitution to work, the symbol must be different in some way from what it stands for, and implicit is the idea that the symbol isn't significant in and of itself, but only in its possessing of a 'wider significance' and in it becoming 'expressive of the author's meaning'; that is to say, the symbol is only valuable in its relation to that which it symbolises, and to the narrative function it serves. A symbol, even a complex one, shouldn't have a life of its own. But if the human and nonhuman are not quite as distinct in this novel as they are usually taken to be, then this process of substitution and symbolic meaning making is made rather more opaque. The mountain lion's apparent narrative function – a symbol of an endangered innocence threatened by a violent world, the wider significance of which is to illuminate and magnify the meaning of Molly's death – becomes less of a given. 'The symbolic imagination conducts an action through analogy, of the human to the divine, of the natural to the supernatural, of the low to the high, of time to eternity,' Tate writes, but

Stafford's mountain lion seems to complicate or forestall such a passage of analogical progress.[145] Rather than a process of symbolic substitution, the double death of Molly and the mountain lion suggests the proximity or continuity of human and nonhuman life. Rather than a symbol, at the end of the novel the mountain lion becomes an animal.

To think of the mountain lion this way – to assert its creaturely existence beyond its symbolic function – is to think of it as part of Stafford's minor aesthetics, part of her subtle challenge to and subversion of the kind of symbolic, formalist reading in which New Criticism was invested. The novel's broader interrogation of the boundary between human and nonhuman life, meanwhile, might be taken to be her riposte to Brooks and Warren's opinion that 'the domain of fiction is [...] the world of credible human beings'.[146] Like Eleanor Clark's exploration of laughter, Stafford's animals speak to a wider midcentury preoccupation with the limits of the human. And yet Stafford does not abandon entirely the Catholic imaginary so crucial to midcentury formalism and which, as we've seen, played such a prominent role in her marriage to Lowell. To think of the mountain lion as having a life of its own might be to bring it closer to the idea of the eucharist – that is, we might think of the mountain lion not in terms of symbolism but in terms of transubstantiation (Molly and the lion are killed on Easter Sunday). This possibility is related to Molly's question, which she ponders shortly before she dies, of 'whether she would be a Catholic or a Buddhist' (215). One of the things this choice of conversions would involve is the weighing up of two very different pictures of the relationship between human and nonhuman life; and in choosing whether to believe in salvation or reincarnation, Molly would also be choosing between two contrasting accounts of what kinds of transformation, what kinds of change, a person is capable of, and so what forms a life (or a novel) might take.

Pyrotechnics: *The Catherine Wheel*

Stafford's 'underexamined' final novel, *The Catherine Wheel* (1952), stretches the recursive time of non-linear narrative and extends her interest in adolescence through the character of Andrew Shipley, a listless twelve-year-old grieving the end of a friendship with another boy that had defined the shape of his previous summers.[147] Set in the late 1930s, the novel is split between Andrew's narrative and that of Katharine, a middle-aged single woman also in a state of grief, mourning a life she hasn't quite lived. The story Katharine tells herself about her life is a story of missed events, the most haunting of which is a long-ago failed love affair with John Shipley, Andrew's father and her cousin Maeve's husband. From this 'wound', Katharine has 'never healed', and so she has 'never changed, and but for her white hair, she was the same as she had been at nineteen when her lover married someone else, at seventeen when she had sworn to marry him'.[148] To Andrew and his older sisters, who stay with 'Cousin Katharine' each summer at her country home in Maine, this 'graceful, fanciful woman, their mother's age (yet seeming, because of her white hair, to be a generation older and seeming, at the same time, because of her light heart, to be the Shipley children's contemporary)', seems to 'exist in two tenses simultaneously' (42–3), suspended between her past and present. With her 'archaic' (43) anecdotes, formal dinner parties, and horse-drawn carriage, Katharine cultivates an air of old-fashioned refinement. Her affectation is mirrored in the novel's antiquated style, a blend of *Boston Adventure*'s baroque stuffiness and the pared-back simplicity of *The Mountain Lion*.[149] The novel's setting is also quaint, Stafford's portrayal of a declining New England gentility recalling the theme of her first book and Lowell's Brahmin background. But Congreve House, Katharine's family home in which much of the novel takes place, is also said to have a 'Southern amplitude' reminiscent of 'the houses of Virginia' (63), gesturing to Stafford's engagement with Southern regionalism, and alerting us to what Joyce Carol Oates describes as Stafford's taste for a 'mode of unnerving domestic Gothicism', a taste she shared with Southern writers like Welty.[150] Katharine is steeped in a partly imagined past, failing to recover from her history, and this lends the novel an 'air of convalescence' (119) not unlike the mood of *The Middle of the Journey* – an atmosphere of 'magical boredom', as one reviewer put it, with the novel's two central characters waiting out the summer's 'endless afternoon' (199) for something to happen: Andrew, 'waiting [. . .] in the larger chambers of his being, for the world to right itself' (15), and Katharine, waiting to find the strength to in some way change the direction of her life.[151] They become co-conspirators in one another's unhappiness, an enabling, untimely odd couple. Left alone in the house one afternoon, Andrew dresses up in an old suit belonging to his Uncle George, and in these 'anachronistic clothes' (226), Katharine mistakes him for his father John, Andrew joining the 'august body of ghosts' (163) said to haunt the house.

Like Molly's not growing up, Katharine's unchangingness is posed by Stafford as a formal quandary: How might midcentury formalism cope with a middle-aged woman's inertia, and what kind of narrative might accommodate a character stranded in her own life? Stafford begins answering by showing us that Katharine's stillness is in fact a kind of decay, and that what looks like stasis is really a form of psychic decomposition, a 'cancer' (82): 'the ganglion of her being was beginning, slowly, to atrophy' (156). If we grant the novel a certain reflexiveness, then we can see that this also provides an insight into the novel's untimely style, much as Molly's preoccupation with fatness offers a way into understanding Stafford experiment with form and proportion in the earlier novel: beneath *The Catherine Wheel*'s sometimes staid and mannered artifice, there is disintegration, just as there is beneath Katharine's composure. As in *The Mountain Lion*, Stafford raises the possibility of interpreting Katharine's malaise psychoanalytically (Stafford was in her most intensive period of treatment with Shefrey during the writing of the novel).[152] 'I might go to a neurologist or even, though I should loathe so craven a capitulation to the vogue of half my friends, to a psychiatrist,' Katharine writes in her diary, but feels that 'upon a matter so indefinite, having no attendant symptoms, no preamble, no patterns of any kind, I can consult no one' (75). Psychoanalysis is not the only interpretative framework that might impose some order and meaning upon Katharine's experience. A local woman, Belulah Smithwick, is said to be able to 'foresee the future and disclose the past in a pack of filthy playing cards' (111), while Andrew comes across a book belonging to Katharine called *The Language of Flowers*, in which he learns that 'mistletoe signified "I surmount difficulties" and that "whortleberry", whatever that might be, meant "Treason"' (194–5).

Stafford satirises and cautions against giving any weight to such methods of interpretation, which may by extension include the formalist close reading of the New Critics. Yet the novel also traffics in signs and symbols. Katharine commissions the local stonemason to make her gravestone to her design, engraved with a Catherine wheel. The significance of this is discussed at some length by her neighbours, invited to Congreve House for the stone's unveiling. Mrs Shea, 'a fount of knowledge on matters ecclesiastical', informs Andrew it is 'the symbol of the martyr Catherine' (237): 'They tied her to a thing like that and set it spinning, but it broke before it killed her and then they chopped off her head' (237–8). This leads to a discussion 'over whether or not Catherine of Alexandria was included in the hierarchy of the Anglo-Catholic saints' (239), Stafford raising a series of religious images as she does towards the end of *The Mountain Lion*. Shortly after the stone is unveiled, it is discovered that Beth, Katharine's cat, has gruesomely killed one of her kittens, apparently chewing off its head. Once more, the assembled neighbours ponder the meaning of this 'mystery' (247): 'Had Beth gone berserk like a human being, like those mothers and fathers [. . .] who suddenly could not put up with the crying of their infant'; or perhaps 'the cat's mind "had lightly turned to thoughts of death" on this particular day because the tombstone had arrived' (247). Discussing whether and how Beth should be punished, 'Mr. Baker who knew a smattering of law' notes that, 'in ancient Greece, rocks that had fallen on people's heads and killed them had been tried and sentenced and executed although he was not just sure how' (247–8) – Stafford retuning, in a more comic vein, to the question of the divide between the human and nonhuman. The arrival of the tombstone and the death of the kitten foreshadow the violent end of the novel, as savage and ironic as the ending of *The Mountain Lion*, in which Katharine is engulfed in the flames of a Catherine wheel set spinning as the finale to her own grand fireworks display.

Critics admired the 'finely wrought' structure of the novel but felt that something was wrong with the ending, much as Schorer and Heilman suggested of *The Mountain Lion*.[153] Orville Prescott called it a 'technically brilliant book, almost perfect in the mechanics', but judged that 'its sudden and unexpectedly violent climax sadly handicap its overall effectiveness. It may be that Miss Stafford's melodramatic conclusion has some special symbolical significance which escapes me.'[154] Another reviewer similarly noted that the novel's 'symbolism grows too luxuriant', such that 'what happens in the story strains credibility, seeming manipulated and merely strange'; Irving Howe also wondered at 'Miss Stafford's proclivity for violent endings'.[155] The critics' sense that the novel's ending is contrived seems justified when we consider how some of the central symbols of the finale – the gravestone, the fireworks – are manoeuvred into position by the characters themselves. The final scene is 'arranged' by Katharine even if her demise is the result of a tragic accident, as though Stafford wanted us to see the novel's structural cogs turning; and this effect is strengthened by the way the neighbours – like a Greek chorus, to pick up on Mr Baker's classical allusion – comment on the symbols organised around them. The symbols themselves seem rather comically overworked and are treated with more than a dash of irony by Stafford: one of the workmen tasked with hauling the tombstone to Congreve House says of its owner, tapping his head, 'Low tide, if you ask me' (235).

The question for readers therefore becomes how to handle such overdetermined symbols, and how to treat a novel whose mechanics – or pyrotechnics – are revealed rather than concealed by its author. Rather than a failure of craft, Stafford can be seen to be pushing at the limits of the kind of well-made novel she appears to be writing, corroding or atrophying the New Critical edicts of proportion, unity, and symbolism, even as she apparently conforms to them. Like Forster's penchant for killing off his characters, Stafford's violent endings carry an element of surprise that guards against taking the novel too seriously, even as these endings also conform to the ideas of tragedy and fate central to the anti-Enlightenment tenor of midcentury thought. Stafford's novels seem drawn to the kinds of symbolic meaning-making and interpretation so important in different ways to the New Criticism, Catholicism, and psychoanalysis, and yet her fictions also exceed the bounds of these discourses, her minor aesthetics dramatising their failure or insufficiency in capturing the contours of the lives of her untimely, misfitting minor heroines, characters whose thwarted desire for transformation reflects Stafford's own circumscribed efforts to reimagine the form of the midcentury novel.

Notes

1. Jean Stafford, 'Author's Note', in *The Collected Stories of Jean Stafford* [1969] (New York: Farrar, Straus and Giroux, 2005), pp. xxi–xxii (xxi).
2. On Stafford's relation to Western writing, see Cathryn Halverson, '"A Reading Problem": Margaret Lynn, Jean Stafford, and Literary Criticism of the American West', *Legacy*, Vol. 33, No. 1 (2016), pp. 127–49.
3. Ibid., xxi–xxii.
4. Philip Rahv, 'Paleface and Redskin', *Kenyon Review*, Vol. 1, No. 3 (Summer 1939), pp. 251–6 (251, 252).
5. Ibid., 253.
6. Stafford's protagonists are often orphaned or abandoned children. Eileen Simpson recalls Stafford's fascination with her 'having been an orphan. I thought at first that Jean's questions [. . .] came from a novelist's avidity for details. Then I realized that she felt I had lived out one of her childhood fantasies.' *Poets in Their Youth: A Memoir* (New York: Random House, 1982), 131.
7. Mark McGurl, *The Program Era: Postwar Fiction and the Rise of Creative Writing* (Cambridge, MA: Harvard University Press, 2009), 60.
8. Eleanor Clark, 'Interview with Eleanor Clark and Robert Penn Warren', interview by Jay Parini, *New England Review*, Vol. 1, No. 1 (Autumn 1978), pp. 49–70 (69).
9. 'abide, v.', *OED Online*, Oxford University Press, March 2023. Available at: www.oed.com/view/Entry/293.
10. William Doreski, 'Founding a Literary Friendship: Allen Tate and Robert Lowell', *Southern Literary Journal*, Vol. 21, No. 2 (Spring 1989), pp. 72–91 (82).
11. René Wellek, 'The New Criticism: Pro and Contra', *Critical Inquiry*, Vol. 4, No. 4 (Summer 1978), pp. 611–24 (614).
12. Robert Lowell, 'Visiting the Tates', *Sewanee Review*, Vol. 67, No. 4 (Autumn 1959), pp. 557–9 (557).
13. Ibid., 559.
14. Langdon Hammer, *Hart Crane and Allen Tate: Janus-Faced Modernism* (Princeton: Princeton University Press, 1993), 215.
15. See Ann Hulbert, *The Interior Castle: The Art and Life of Jean Stafford* (Amherst: University of Massachusetts Press, 1992), 109–10.
16. John Duvall, 'New Criticism's Major Journals: *The Southern Review* (1935–42); *The Kenyon Review* (1939–70); and *The Sewanee Review* (1892–)', in Peter Brooker and Andrew Thacker (eds), *The Oxford Critical and Cultural History of Modernist Magazines, Vol. 2: North America, 1894–1960* (Oxford: Oxford University Press, 2012), pp. 928–44 (928).
17. Allen Tate, 'The Function of the Critical Quarterly', *Southern Review*, Vol. 1 (1935), pp. 551–60, quoted in Robert Buffington, 'Allen Tate and the *Sewanee Review*', *Sewanee Review*, Vol. 123, No. 2 (Spring 2015), pp. 240–51 (241).
18. See Duvall, 'New Criticism's Major Journals', 932–6.
19. Tate, 'The Function of the Critical Quarterly', 551.
20. Wellek, 'The New Criticism', 613.

21. See Allen Tate, 'The Profession of Letters in the South', *Virginia Quarterly Review*, Vol. 11, No. 2 (April 1935), pp. 161–76; 'The New Provincialism', *Virginia Quarterly Review*, Vol. 21, No. 2 (Spring 1945), pp. 262–72. For an overview, see Robert H. Brinkmeyer Jr, 'The Southern Literary Renaissance', in Richard Gray and Own Robinson (eds), *A Companion to the Literature and Culture of the American South* (Oxford: Blackwell, 2004), pp. 148–65.
22. Alexander MacLeod, '"Disagreeable Intellectual Distance": Theory and Politics in the Old Regionalism of the New Critics', in Miranda Hickman and John McIntyre (eds), *Rereading the New Criticism* (Columbus: Ohio State University Press, 2012), pp. 173–94 (178). See also Robert Penn Warren, 'Not Local Color', *Virginia Quarterly Review*, Vol. 8, No. 1 (January 1932), pp. 153–60.
23. Walter Sullivan, 'The Roman Connection: Allen Tate as Catholic Man of Letters', *Sewanee Review*, Vol. 106, No. 1 (Winter 1998), pp. 87–92 (88).
24. Ibid.
25. Mark Jancovich, *The Cultural Politics of the New Criticism* (Cambridge: Cambridge University Press, 1993), 24.
26. Allen Tate, 'Remarks on the Southern Religion' in John Crowe Ransom, et al., *I'll Take My Stand: The South and the Agrarian Tradition* [1930] (Baton Rouge: Louisiana State University Press, 1977), pp. 155–75 (173).
27. Duvall, 'New Criticism's Major Journals', 929.
28. Wellek, 'The New Criticism', 616; John Duvall, 'Eliot's Modernism and Brooks's New Criticism: Poetic and Religious Thinking', *Mississippi Quarterly*, Vol. 46, No. 1 (Winter 1992–3), pp. 23–37 (26).
29. Duvall, 'Eliot's Modernism and Brooks's New Criticism', 27.
30. See T. S. Eliot, *The Idea of a Christian Society* (New York: Harcourt, Brace and Company, 1940), vi.
31. Paul Giles, *American Catholic Arts and Fictions: Culture, Ideology, Aesthetics* (Cambridge: Cambridge University Press, 1992), 197–8.
32. William Barrett, 'What is the "Liberal" Mind?', *Partisan Review*, Vol. 16, No. 3 (June 1949), pp. 331–6 (331).
33. William Phillips and Philip Rahv, 'Editorial Statement', *Partisan Review*, Vol. 17, No. 2 (February 1950), pp. 103–6 (103).
34. Sidney Hook, 'The New Failure of Nerve', *Partisan Review*, Vol. 10, No. 1 (January–February 1943), pp. 2–23.
35. Ibid., 2. See James Schmidt, 'Inventing the "Counter-Enlightenment": Liberalism, Nihilism, and Totalitarianism', conference paper, presented at the American Historical Association, Boston, 6 January 2011, pp. 1–19.
36. Hook, 'The New Failure of Nerve', 3.
37. On Niebuhr, see Martin Halliwell, *The Constant Dialogue: Reinhold Niebuhr & American Intellectual Culture* (Lanham: Rowman & Littlefield, 2005).
38. Quoted in Mark Greif, *The Age of the Crisis of Man: Thought and Fiction in America, 1933–1973* (Princeton: Princeton University Press, 2015), 36.
39. Ibid., 36; George Cotkin, *Existential America* (Baltimore: Johns Hopkins University Press, 2003), 62.
40. Cotkin, *Existential America*, 63.

41. Greif, *The Age of the Crisis of Man*, 56.
42. Stephen Schryer, *Fantasies of the New Class: Ideologies of Professionalism in Post-World War II American Fiction* (New York: Columbia University Press, 2011), 30; Jaconovich, *The Cultural Politics of the New Critics*, 143.
43. John Sykes, *Flannery O'Connor, Walker Percy, and the Aesthetic of Revelation* (Columbia: University of Missouri Press, 2007), 14.
44. Jancovich, *The Cultural Politics of the New Critics*, 84.
45. Allen Tate, 'Narcissus as Narcissus', *Virginia Quarterly Review*, Vol. 14, No. 1 (Winter 1938), pp. 108–22 (110).
46. See Jancovich, *The Cultural Politics of the New Critics*, 143–4.
47. Ibid., 84.
48. Frank Lentricchia, *After the New Criticism* (Chicago: University of Chicago Press, 1980), 6.
49. Sykes, *Flannery O'Connor, Walker Percy, and the Aesthetic of Revelation*, 12.
50. Ibid., 26.
51. Allen Tate, 'The Symbolic Imagination: A Meditation on Dante's Three Mirrors', *Kenyon Review*, Vol. 14, No. 2 (Spring 1952), pp. 256–77 (268).
52. Ibid., 262.
53. Ibid., 260.
54. Jancovich, *The Cultural Politics of the New Critics*, 123.
55. Tate, 'The Symbolic Imagination', 262.
56. Michael Trask, *Cruising Modernism: Class and Sexuality in American Literature and Social Thought* (Ithaca: Cornell University Press, 2018), 116.
57. John Paul Russo, 'The Tranquilized Poem: The Crisis of New Criticism in the 1950s', *Texas Studies in Literature and Language*, Vol. 30, No. 2 (Summer 1988), pp. 198–229 (204).
58. Ibid., 205.
59. Jancovich, *The Cultural Politics of the New Critics*, 81.
60. Ibid., 87.
61. I refer to the summer Stafford and Lowell hosted 'an influx of poets', including John Berryman. See Charlotte Goodman, *Jean Stafford: The Savage Heart* (Austin: University of Texas Press, 1990), 155–60.
62. Allen Tate, 'Techniques of Fiction', *Sewanee Review*, Vol. 52, No. 2 (Spring 1944), pp. 210–25 (225).
63. Ibid., 211.
64. On Tate's novel, see Louis Rubin, *The Wary Fugitives: Four Poets* (Baton Rouge: Louisiana State University Press, 1978), 316–25.
65. Tate, 'The New Provincialism', 271. See, for example, George Marian O'Donnell, 'Faulkner's Mythology', *Kenyon Review*, Vol. 1, No. 3 (Summer 1939), pp. 285–99.
66. Robert Penn Warren, 'Cowley's Faulkner' [1946], in John Basett (ed.), *William Faulkner: The Critical Heritage* (London: Taylor & Francis, 2013), pp. 314–27 (317).
67. Robert Penn Warren, 'The Love and the Separateness in Miss Welty', *Kenyon Review*, Vol. 6, No. 2 (Spring 1944), pp. 246–59 (257).
68. Ibid., 256.

69. Cleanth Brooks and Robert Penn Warren (eds), *Understanding Fiction* [1943] (Englewood Cliffs, NJ: Prentice-Hall, 1971), xvii.
70. Ibid., xiii.
71. Ibid., 651, 578.
72. Michael Levenson, 'Criticism of Fiction', in A. Walton Litz, Louis Menand, and Lawrence Rainey (eds), *The Cambridge History of Literary Criticism, Vol. 7: Modernism and the New Criticism* (Cambridge: Cambridge University Press, 2000), 468–98 (486).
73. Caroline Gordon and Allen Tate (eds), *The House of Fiction: An Anthology of the Short Story with Commentary* (New York: Scribner, 1950), 632, 635, 633.
74. Ibid., 633.
75. Quoted in Levenson, 'Criticism of Fiction', 486.
76. Henry James, 'The Art of Fiction' [1888], in *The Future of the Novel*, ed. by Leon Edel (New York: Vintage, 1956), pp. 3–27 (9). In 'Techniques of Fiction', Tate calls Lubbock's book 'very nearly a model of critical procedure' (211).
77. Levenson, 'Criticism of Fiction', 485.
78. Allen Tate, 'Three Commentaries: Poe, James, and Joyce', *Sewanee Review*, Vol. 58, No. 1 (January–March 1950), pp. 1–15 (7, 9, 10).
79. Mark McGurl, *The Program Era*, 154.
80. Tate, 'The New Provincialism', 263.
81. McGurl, *The Program Era*, 154.
82. Quoted in Doreski, 'Founding a Literary Friendship', 82.
83. Robert Lowell, *Collected Prose* (Farrar, Straus and Giroux, 1987), 258. Hammer suggests that Catholicism was as 'obvious extension of Lowell's formalism' (216).
84. Hammer, *Hart Crane and Allen Tate*, 212; David Bromwich, *A Choice of Inheritance: Self and Community from Edmund Burke to Robert Frost* (Cambridge, MA: Harvard University Press, 1989), 240, quoted in Hammer, *Hart Crane and Allen Tate*, 217.
85. Hammer, *Hart Crane and Allen Tate*, 212.
86. Eileen Simpson, *Poets in their Youth*, 131; Hulbert, *The Interior Castle*, 116. Kathryn Davis describes Stafford as 'an ardent, if irritable, Catholic convert'. 'Afterword', in Jean Stafford, *The Mountain Lion* [1947] (New York: New York Review Books Classics, 2010), pp. 233–40 (237).
87. Eileen Simpson, *Poets in their Youth*, 131.
88. Hulbert, *The Interior Castle*, 120.
89. Ibid., 119.
90. Ibid., 144.
91. See Robert Giroux, 'Hard Years and "Scary Days": Remembering Jean Stafford', *New York Times Book Review*, 10 June 1984, 3.
92. Harvey Breit, 'Talk with Jean Stafford', *New York Times Book Review*, 20 January, 1952, 18.
93. Quoted in Hulbert, *The Interior Castle*, 140. Andrew Wanning described the style as 'a contemporary domestication of Proust'. 'A Variety of Fiction', review of *Boston Adventure* by Jean Stafford, *Partisan Review*, Vol. 11, No. 4 (Fall 1944), pp. 474–7 (476).

94. Breit, 'Talk with Jean Stafford'; Goodman, *Jean Stafford*, 190.
95. Elizabeth Hardwick, 'Poor Little Rich Girls', *Partisan Review*, Vol. 12, No. 3 (Summer 1945), pp. 420–2 (420).
96. David Roberts, *Jean Stafford: A Biography* (London: Chatto & Windus, 1988), 250.
97. A version of the story appeared in the *New Yorker* in 1978 told in third person, while the version included in the 2005 edition of Stafford's *Collected Stories* is in first person; I quote from the latter.
98. Jean Stafford, 'An Influx of Poets', in *The Collected Stories of Jean Stafford* (New York: Farrar, Straus and Giroux, 2005), pp. 465–88 (465). Subsequent references are given in parentheses in the text.
99. Quoted in Hulbert, *The Interior Castle*, 227.
100. See Goodman, *Jean Stafford*, 166; Kathryn Davis, 'Chronology', in Davis (ed.), *Jean Stafford: Complete Novels* (New York: Library of America, 2019), pp. 857–70 (863).
101. See Mary Jane Sherfey, 'A Theory on Female Sexuality', in Maggie Humm (ed.), *Feminisms: A Reader* (London: Taylor & Francis, 1992), pp. 264–8. Stafford also read the work of Karen Horney, another leading feminist psychoanalyst. See Goodman, *Jean Stafford*, 222–3.
102. Quoted in Roberts, *Jean Stafford*, 280.
103. Benjamin Mangrum, *Land of Tomorrow: Postwar Fiction and the Crisis of American Liberalism* (Oxford: Oxford University Press, 2019), 73.
104. Dorothy Ross, 'Freud and the Vicissitudes of Modernism in the United States, 1940–1980', in John Burnham (ed.), *After Freud Left: A Century of Psychoanalysis in America* (Chicago: University of Chicago Press, 2012), pp. 163–88; Lionel Trilling, 'Freud and Literature', in *The Liberal Imagination: Essays on Literature and Society* [1950] (New York: New York Review Books Classics, 2008), pp. 34–57 (56).
105. Mary Esteve, 'When Psychoanalysis Was in Vogue', in Steven Belletto (ed.), *American Literature in Transition, 1950–1960* (Cambridge: Cambridge University Press, 2018), pp. 46–60 (48); Trilling, 'Freud and Literature', 52.
106. Philip Blair Rice, 'Psychoanalysis: The Second Wave', *Kenyon Review*, Vol. 2, No. 2 (Spring 1940), pp. 226–8 (226, 228).
107. Brooks and Warren, *Understanding Fiction*, 170.
108. Cleanth Brooks, 'The Formalist Critics', *Kenyon Review*, Vol. 13, No. 1 (Winter 1951), pp. 72–81 (74).
109. Rice, 'Psychoanalysis: The Second Wave', 227.
110. Jean Stafford, 'The Psychological Novel', *Kenyon Review*, Vol. 10, No. 2 (Spring 1948), pp. 214–27 (214).
111. Orville Prescott, 'Books of the Times', review of *The Mountain Lion* by Jean Stafford, *New York Times*, 3 March 1947, 19.
112. Howard Mumford Jones, 'A New Jean Stafford', review of *The Mountain Lion* by Jean Stafford, *New York Times*, 2 March 1947, 189; Anon., 'Review of *The Mountain Lion* by Jean Stafford', *Washington Post*, 9 March 1947, S10.
113. Philip Rahv, Letter to Jean Stafford, 8 February 1947, quoted in Hulbert, *The Interior Castle*, 207–8.

114. Hulbert, *The Interior Castle*, 207.
115. Kathryn Davis suggests that the novel is 'part Henry James, you might say, and part Mark Twain'. Davis, 'Afterword', 235.
116. Anon., 'Review of *The Mountain Lion* by Jean Stafford', S10; Prescott, 'Books of the Times', 19; Rahv, quoted in Hulbert, *The Interior Castle* 208.
117. This interpretation was, with a change of emphasis, repeated in later feminist readings of the novel. See, for example, Charlotte Goodman, 'The Lost Brother/The Twin: Women Novelists and the Male-Female Bildungsroman', *Novel: A Forum on Fiction*, Vol. 17, No. 1 (Fall 1983), pp. 28–43.
118. Mark Schorer, 'The American Novel', review of *The Mountain Lion* by Jean Stafford, and other works, *Kenyon Review*, Vol. 9, No. 4 (Autumn 1947), pp. 628–36 (628).
119. Ibid., 629. See Schorer, 'Technique as Discovery', *Hudson Review*, Vol. 1, No. 1 (Spring 1948), pp. 67–87.
120. Schorer, 'The American Novel', 635.
121. Robert Heilman, 'Four Novels', review of *The Mountain Lion* by Jean Stafford, and other works, *Sewanee Review*, Vol. 55, No. 3 (July–September 1947), pp. 483–92 (486).
122. Ibid., 487.
123. Ibid.
124. Morris Dickstein, *Leopards in the Temple: The Transformation of American Fiction, 1945–1970* (Cambridge, MA: Harvard University Press, 2002), 83–141.
125. Eunice Glenn, 'As on a Darkling Plain', *Sewanee Review*, Vol. 56, No. 2 (Spring 1948), pp. 351–9 (352).
126. Lionel Trilling, 'Huckleberry Finn', in *The Liberal Imagination*, pp. 104–17 (105, 106).
127. Ibid., 108.
128. Leslie Fiedler, *Love and Death in the American Novel* [1960] (Funks Grove, IL: Dalkey Archive Press, 1997), 24.
129. Jean Stafford, *The Mountain Lion*, 97. Subsequent references are given in parentheses in the text.
130. On 'national time' and the bildungsroman, see Jed Esty, *Unseasonable Youth: Modernism, Colonialism, and the Fiction of Development* (Oxford: Oxford University Press, 2011), 39–70.
131. See especially Roberts's biography, described by Joyce Carol Oates as representing a 'new subspecies of the genre' she calls 'pathography', because of its focus on the 'prurient' and 'sensational'. Oates, 'Adventures in Abandonment', review of *Jean Stafford: A Biography* by David Roberts, *New York Times Book Review*, 28 August 1988, 3.
132. On fatness in the novel, see Kathryn Davis, 'Afterword', 236–7. On tropes of disfigurement and disability in Stafford's work, see Katie Collins, '"Her Ruined Head": Defacement and Disability in Jean Stafford's Life and Fiction', *Journal of Modern Literature*, Vol. 45, No. 1 (Fall 2021), pp. 121–36.
133. Brooks and Warren included McCullers's short story 'A Domestic Dilemma' (1951) in later editions of *Understanding Fiction*.

134. Marguerite Young, 'Metaphysical Fiction', review of *The Member of the Wedding* by Carson McCullers, *Kenyon Review*, Vol. 9, No. 1 (Winter 1947), pp. 151–5 (152).
135. Frank, 'Fiction Chronicle', 356.
136. Carson McCullers, *The Member of the Wedding* [1946], (London: Penguin, 2008), 52. Emphasis original. Subsequent references are given in parentheses in the text.
137. Rachel Adams, '"A Mixture of Delicious and Freak": The Queer Fiction of Carson McCullers', *American Literature*, Vol. 71, No. 3 (September 1999), pp. 551–83 (552). See also Elizabeth Freeman, '"The we of me": *The Member of the Wedding*'s Novel Alliances', *Women & Performance*, Vol. 8, No. 2 (1996), pp. 111–35; Pamela Thurschwell, 'Dead Boys and Adolescent Girls: Unjoining the Bildungsroman in Carson McCullers's *The Member of the Wedding* and Toni Morrison's *Sula*', *ESC: English Studies in Canada*, Vol. 38, No. 3–4 (September–December 2012), pp. 105–28.
138. See Kathryn Bond Stockton, *The Queer Child, or Growing Sideways in the Twentieth Century* (Durham, NC: Duke University Press, 2009).
139. Adams, '"A Mixture of Delicious and Freak"', 575.
140. Thurschwell, 'Dead Boys and Adolescent Girls', 117.
141. See Leslie Allison, 'Reading the West Sideways: Queering the Frontier in Jean Stafford's *The Mountain Lion*', *Studies in the Novel*, Vol. 49, No. 3 (Fall 2017), pp. 304–21.
142. Derek Ryan, *Virginia Woolf and the Materiality of Theory: Sex, Animal, Life* (Edinburgh: Edinburgh University Press, 2013), 13.
143. Elizabeth Grosz, *Becoming Undone: Darwinian Reflections on Life, Politics, and Art* (Durham, NC: Duke University Press, 2011), 15–16.
144. Brooks and Warren, *Understanding Fiction*, 688.
145. Tate, 'The Symbolic Imagination', 259.
146. Brooks and Warren, *Understanding Fiction*, 170.
147. Cathryn Halverson, 'Review of *Jean Stafford: Complete Novels*, ed. Kathryn Davis', *ALH Online Review*, Series XXVII (2021), pp. 1–3 (2).
148. Stafford, *The Catherine Wheel* [1952] (New York: Farrar, Straus and Giroux, 2014), 77. Subsequent reference are given in parentheses in the text.
149. See Breit, 'Talk with Jean Stafford'; Hulbert, 286; Goodman, 255.
150. Joyce Carol Oates, 'Introduction', *Collected Stories of Jean Stafford*, ix–xix (xvii). One reviewer described the novel as a 'New England Gothic tale (a kind of opposite number to the Southern Gothic of a writer like Eudora Welty)'. Alice Morris, 'When Hatred Breaks', review of *The Catherine Wheel* by Jean Stafford, *New York Times*, 13 January 1952, BR5.
151. Heinz Politzer, 'Five Novels', review of *The Catherine Wheel* by Jean Stafford, and other works, *Commentary*, 1 January 1952, pp. 510–14 (512).
152. See Goodman, 215.
153. Morris, 'When Hatred Breaks', BR5.
154. Orville Prescott, 'Books of the Times', review of *The Catherine Wheel* by Jean Stafford, *New York Times*, 15 January 1952, 25.
155. Morris, 'When Hatred Breaks', BR5; Howe, 'Sensibility Troubles', 348.

CHAPTER 4

Herzog in Venice: Richard Stern's *Stitch* and Jewish-American Literary History

Richard Stern and Saul Bellow were friends for nearly half a century. They first met in the spring of 1956, shortly after Stern had joined the English department at the University of Chicago, where he became the unofficial writer-in-residence and established a long-running undergraduate course in creative writing.[1] After earning his PhD in fiction from the University of Iowa in 1954 (where he was taught by Robert Lowell, among others), Stern became part of the first surge of Writers' Workshop graduates who 'fanned out across the country to institute at least twenty-five new [writing] programs'.[2] In the autumn of 1956, Stern invited Bellow to address his writing class, and the pair kept up a regular, intimate correspondence while Bellow was at work on *Henderson the Rain King* (1959) – which Stern praised in a piece for the *Kenyon Review* – and *Herzog* (1964).[3] Along with their mutual friend, the sociologist Edward Shils, Stern lobbied to bring Bellow to Chicago on a permanent basis; eventually, in 1962, Bellow accepted a position on the Committee on Social Thought – 'something of an academic *salon des refuses*,' Zachary Leader, Bellow's biographer, writes, and therefore 'a better fit for him than the English Department'.[4] 'Sober, reliable, immensely learned', Stern became 'a friend of Bellow's stable side' once they were both settled in the university neighbourhood of Hyde Park.[5] They offered 'each other criticism and counsel in their trials and dilemmas,' Mark Harris writes, Bellow telephoning 'the Sterns' house four or five times a day'.[6]

On the afternoon that Bellow came to address Stern's writing class, the story to be discussed was not, as usual, that of a student, but that of a young instructor in the department, Philip Roth. Roth was just beginning to get his short stories published in university literary journals, but the piece Stern picked for Bellow's visit had, Roth recalled, 'been turned down by all the classy reviews'.[7] Roth sat quietly at the back of the room while Bellow, Stern, and the students workshopped 'The Conversion of the Jews', which would appear in the *Paris Review* the following March before becoming part of Roth's National Book Award-winning first collection, *Goodbye, Columbus* (1959). After the class, Stern introduced the young writer to the famous novelist, a meeting Roth would fictionalise in *The Ghost Writer* (1979).[8] In an influential review of *Goodbye, Columbus*, published in *Commentary*, Bellow praised its twenty-six-year-old author as a 'virtuoso', his support a boost to Roth's fledgling career.[9] But it was Stern's early encouragement, and particularly his amusement at Roth's comic storytelling over their hamburger lunches at the University Tavern in Chicago, that may have played, Roth later said, 'the most important role' in guiding his youthful ambition.[10] 'I wanted to exhibit dark knowledge like Faulkner. I wanted to be deep like Dostoyevsky. I wanted to write *literature*,' Roth recalls in a tribute to Stern after his death in 2013. 'Instead I took Dick's advice and wrote *Goodbye, Columbus*.'[11] Elsewhere, Roth remembers that it had seemed to him in 1956 that he and Stern were 'working different sides of the street' as writers: 'Dick's approach seemed to me more literary than mine back then'.[12] And yet it was Stern who encouraged him 'to use the vernacular material. I didn't trust it; I didn't *see* it. I suppose I thought I ought to be *more* literary.'[13] The pair became good friends, swapping manuscripts for forty years and commenting, often with ruthless honesty, on each other's work. 'We're so close that he reads my temperature from the progress of the manuscript', as Stern put it a 1999 interview.[14]

Bellow and Roth are of course central to what has long been described as the 'breakthrough' of Jewish-American writing after 1945.[15] Their work, along with that of Bernard Malamud, so the story goes, 'changed the direction not only of Jewish literature, but of American fiction as well'.[16] Showered with prestigious national literary prizes throughout the 1950s and 1960s, their fiction was,

Josh Lambert writes, 'consecrated not just as the respectable output of an American minority subculture, aimed at a parochial, limited audience, but, more broadly, as the very best of American literature'.[17] *The Adventures of Augie March* (1953), which won Bellow the first of three National Book Awards, is often invoked as a cornerstone text of what Andrew Furman describes as 'the golden age of Jewish American writing'.[18] Morris Dickstein, for example, writes that, 'By casting Augie as a descendant of Huck Finn, Bellow had overcome the provinciality of pre-war Jewish writers to work within the American grain, filtering national motifs through an urban Jewish sensibility.'[19] In a 1971 essay, Alfred Kazin similarly suggests that, in Bellow's fiction, Jewish experience is made to seem 'the reverse of the provincial'.[20] The postwar 'renaissance' of Jewish-American writing might be said to represent one central strand of what Mark McGurl calls the rise of high cultural pluralist fiction, 'a body of fiction that joins the high literary values of modernism with a fascination with the experience of cultural difference and the authenticity of the ethnic voice'.[21] This became the mode through which minority writers gained 'literary distinction in the postwar period,' McGurl writes; Bellow and Roth may both have 'aggressively resisted' the label of Jewish-American writer, but this was the category in which their work became legible in the literary field and through which they entered the 'mainstream' of American writing.[22] What Roth admired most about *Augie March* was the way in which Bellow's style 'combines literary complexity with conversational ease', joining 'the idiom of the academy with the idiom of the streets (not all streets – certain streets)'.[23] In his reminiscences of starting out in Chicago, Roth frames his own emergence as a writer as the story of his 'letting go' of some of the values of high modernism and embracing the comic freedom of a Jewish 'vernacular', even as a notion of the 'literary' shaped by the tastes of the midcentury academy – Faulkner, Dostoevsky – still figures in his thinking.[24] Looking back in 1966, Bellow similarly suggested that in *Augie March* he threw off the 'restraints' shaping his first two novels. In *Dangling Man* (1944) and *The Victim* (1947) – both firm favourites of the *Partisan Review* crowd – Bellow had, he reflected, 'accepted a Flaubertian standard', a definition of the 'letter-perfect' novel he came to find 'repressive' (we saw in the previous chapter that the New Critics thought that it was 'through Flaubert that the novel has at last caught up poetry').[25] Rather than try to write with a 'borrowed sensibility', in *Augie March* he found a form more suited to and better able to reflect 'my upbringing in Chicago as [. . .] the son of Russian Jews'.[26]

In an interview with James Atlas (another of Bellow's biographers), Stern acknowledges that his own fiction is 'seldom included' in the 'literary cloak-and-suitery' of 'The Jewish Novel'.[27] Stern is often labelled a writer's writer, and when his fiction is mentioned by critics, it is inevitably compared to that of his two famous friends.[28] 'People frequently say, "Isn't it too bad to be in Roth's and Bellow's shadow?" I don't feel that,' Stern tells Atlas. 'The rewards are a hell of a lot greater than the indubitable pain of being overlooked.'[29] In what follows, I suggest that one of the reasons that Stern has been overlooked is that, rather than fit a narrative of high cultural pluralist 'breakthrough', his fiction figures a contrasting account of the intersection of Jewish identity, modernist aesthetics, and midcentury literary criticism. Remembering his time as a doctoral student at the Iowa Writers' Workshop, Stern recollects that he and some of his fellow writers had come to feel 'that the James-Lubbock-Brooks-Warren-Tate notion of the perfect story was finished', and that 'it was time to take off Flaubert's corset' and 'throw away Joyce's glue, shears, and colored markers'. And yet, if New Critical formalism had become too restrictive, and modernist experimentation was exhausted, then '*Augie March* looked too crude for some – "What a style!"'.[30] Rather than embrace the freedom of a Jewish vernacular, Stern's minor fiction dramatises a tension between the novel as imagined and discussed by midcentury criticism and the Jewish-American novel of high cultural pluralism taking shape in the hands of Bellow and Roth; rather than 'breakthrough', the figure that captures Stern's aesthetic project might be 'impasse'.

We can see this most clearly in the novel in which Stern's preoccupation with Jewish identity is most pronounced, and which is also perhaps his most Bellovian book. *Stitch* (1965) is about Thaddeus Stitch, an elderly, disgraced yet revered American sculptor living out his exile in Venice. Stitch bears more than a passing resemblance to Ezra Pound, whom Stern met on a number of occasions in Venice during the winter of 1962–3, when he spent a year teaching in Italy on a Fulbright fellowship. In the novel, Stitch is visited by Edward Gunther, a middle-aged Jewish-American 'burgher-adulterer' of 'minimal accomplishment and fair intelligence' (in the opinion of his second wife, Cress).[31] Upon publication, the novel was reviewed in the *New York Review of Books* by Bernard Bergonzi under the title 'Herzog in Venice' and largely dismissed as something of a pale imitation of Bellow's bestseller of the previous year.[32] If *Augie March* was Bellow's breakout book, then *Herzog* (1964) marks the start of his 'mature work', according to Morris Dickstein, and a new stage in his transition from 'distanced, ironic, carefully structured fictions toward mercurial self-portraits'.[33] But the novel is 'much more than a roman à clef', and in the letters Moses Herzog pens to deceased philosophers, Bellow found a form, Malcolm Bradbury writes, that combined the 'lyric intensity' of a 'Jewish vernacular' with 'abstract speculations' and philosophical meditation, thereby revivifying the genre of the novel of ideas.[34] Like Bellow's protagonist, Edward Gunther is a cerebral Chicagoan with a messy domestic life, *au fait* with the intellectual world of the Committee on Social Thought (Edward at one point imagines that the success of the collection of philosophical essays he is working on will lead to public debates with 'Madariaga, Polanyi, Shils' (139)). But, as the reference to Pound suggests, *Stitch*'s literary and cultural touchstones are ultimately quite different from *Herzog*'s, as indeed were Stern's from Bellow's. In what follows, I suggest how the two friends' contrasting judgements of Pound are indicative not only of a difference in attitude towards their Jewish backgrounds, but also of a difference in their conception of literary value and form. While *Herzog* was one of the novels which carried Bellow into the 'mainstream' of American literature, *Stitch* belongs to a minor current of midcentury writing carrying Stern in a quite different direction.

The Question of the Pound Award

Bellow never made a friend he didn't manage to fall out with. By his standards, his long relationship with Stern was relatively plain sailing, but they certainly had their disagreements. One came in 1988, over John Updike. Stern admired Updike's literary criticism, while Bellow felt there had been an antisemitic undertone to his negative reviews of *Humboldt's Gift* (1975) and *The Dean's December* (1982). The larger issue, Bellow wrote in a letter, was that Stern had always had a blind spot when it came to recognising antisemitism, evidenced in his admiration for Pound and now Updike, and revealing of his ambivalence about his own Jewish identity. 'A man's character is like an arch. The stones cannot be rearranged without bringing down the house,' Bellow wrote; 'I, for instance, will never understand particle physics. You will never understand the Jewish question [. . .] Has it ever occurred to you to ask *why* Updike hated and continues to hate *The Dean's December*?'[35]

Attempting to defuse the row, Stern acknowledged in his reply that 'my Jewish question' is 'unsettled'. 'There are quite a few Sauls, quite a few Richards,' he continued, 'and some continue to trip over each other'; similarly, there are 'also plenty of Updikes and Pounds. Some are [. . .] Jew-hating, Jew-resenting, some aren't. The Pound I knew wasn't the Pound I learned about. I can care for that one, hate the other.'[36] In a longer, unsent letter of response, Stern expanded:

> As for Pound, that too is not easy [. . .] the man I knew was sinking and trying to hold himself up; the man I knew had astonishing dignity [. . .] The world of hatred out of which his hatred came isn't gone, but it wasn't my world.[37]

By the time the two old friends were having this argument, Pound's reputation had, as Stern suggests, gone through a number of transformations. Pound's work was central to the canonisation of high modernism and was widely recognised as one of 'the dominant, seminal poetries of the age', in John Berryman's phrase.[38] But revelations of his fascist sympathies and wartime activities – especially his antisemitic radio broadcasts supporting Mussolini – made him an increasingly polarising figure. The controversy reached its zenith when, in 1949, Pound was awarded the inaugural Bollingen Prize for Poetry by a panel of judges including T. S. Eliot, Robert Lowell, Allen Tate, and Robert Penn Warren.[39] The Bollingen controversy is well-known as a test case of midcentury literary formalism.[40] It problematised the New Critics' emphasis upon aesthetic autonomy and challenged their conception of poetry as a distinctive form of dramatic, non-propositional discourse. In their statement announcing the award to Pound, the judges stuck to formalist principles, insisting that 'to permit other considerations than that of poetic achievement to sway the decision [. . .] would in principle deny the validity of that objective perception of value on which civilized society must rest'.[41] But for many, the award raised 'significant questions both about how politics shapes formalist critique and about the limits of formalist reading methods in the face of political extremes'.[42] In an April 1949 *Partisan Review* editorial condemning the judges' decision, William Barrett recognised the need to distinguish between 'the case of Pound the man, and the value of the particular book'. But he also suggested that the decision revealed a troubling 'attitude' within 'American literary criticism over the past decade or more', which is 'so obsessed with formal and technical questions that it has time for only a hasty glimpse at content'.[43]

Formalism's balancing act between form and content, and between the work, the author and a wider historical context, was particularly difficult for Jewish-American critics to perform during the Bollingen controversy. In the May issue of *Partisan*, several contributors responded to 'The Question of the Pound Award', and to Barrett's editorial.[44] Irving Howe worried that, 'once you consider extra literary matters in a literary judgement, where do you stop?', but concluded that he 'could not in good conscience acquiesce to *honor* [Pound] with a literary award – which if you please, must also mean to honor him as a man'.[45] Clement Greenberg began on a more personal note, stating that, 'As a Jew I myself cannot help being offended by the matter of Pound's latest poetry', making the wider point that 'life includes and is more important than art, and it judges things by their consequences'.[46] Karl Shapiro had been on the panel of judges that had made the decision but had 'voted against Pound' because, he wrote, 'I am a Jew and I cannot honor antisemites'.[47]

In his memoir, *First Loves* (2003), the writer and editor Ted Solotaroff offers a sense of how the controversy surrounding Pound generally and the Bollingen Prize in particular were not only crucial dividing lines running through the period's literary culture, but were also emblematic of a deeper dilemma facing young Jewish-American intellectuals. Solotaroff chronicles his time as a PhD student at Chicago, where he became friends with Roth (sparring good-naturedly with him in classes on Henry James) as well as Stern – 'the literary impresario of the day', a man of 'king-size appetites, talent, ambition, erudition, contacts'.[48] While at Chicago, Solotaroff would publish 'A Vocal Group: The Jewish part in American letters' (1959), an influential essay that helped define Jewish-American fiction and shape its critical reception, promoting to prominence the work of the now familiar triumvirate of Malamud, Bellow and Roth.[49] A decade earlier, however, as the Bollingen controversy was unfolding, Solotaroff was still an undergraduate at the University of Michigan trying to find his way in a literary culture dominated by the 'Christian cast of the new orthodoxy, influenced by its pope, T. S. Eliot, as well as its synod – major critics such as Cleanth Brooks, Allen Tate, John Crowe Ransom, Yvor Winters'.[50] The Bollingen Prize represented 'a difficult loyalty test,' Solotaroff recalls, because the award was 'on the one hand, deserved, and on the other, detestable. Talk about the tensions of paradox, about moral complexity!'[51] Like 'many of the young writers on campus', Solotaroff 'learned to wiggle around the evil horn of Pound's radio broadcasts' by imagining Pound as 'a kind of ultimate victim of the revenge that society takes on the modern artist'. At Michigan, Solotaroff would 'become a defender of Pound and a betrayer of my heritage', a decision he would regret and reverse by the time he reached Chicago.[52]

Bellow was in Paris when the Bollingen award was made but followed American newspaper coverage of 'the Pound controversy' closely and was 'furious' at the judges' decision.[53] In 1956, he rebuffed the entreaties of William Faulkner to get him to join an effort to secure Pound's release from St Elizabeths psychiatric hospital, where he had been admitted after pleading insanity to a federal charge of treason in relation to his wartime activities. 'Do you mean to ask me to join you in honoring a man who called for the destruction of my kinsmen?' he wrote to Faulkner. 'If sane he should be tried as a traitor; if insane he ought not to be released merely because he is a poet' (Pound was released in 1958, and returned to Italy).[54] Bellow's enmity extended to those who defended Pound, including the literary critic Hugh Kenner, author of *The Pound Era* (1971), and a good friend of Stern's. Like Updike, Kenner had made the mistake of writing a negative review of *The Dean's December*.[55]

'Kenner was openly anti-semitic,' Bellow complained to Robert Boyers in 1982. But, he continued:

> What interests me much more than what he thinks is the effect of the Eliot-Pound phenomenon, the deadly madness at the heart of 'tradition' and 'culture' as represented by those two [. . .] A poet might be great despite his obsession with Usura, Major Douglas, Mussolini, Jews. This was the line taken after the war by literary intellectuals. The inevitable corollary was that the poet's convictions could be separated from his poetry.[56]

For Stern, however, Pound's case was less clear-cut. In part this was because he had, as he told Atlas in their interview, and as I discuss later, a 'very different' relationship to his Jewish 'kinsmen' than Bellow.[57] And in part it was because the two friends came from equally different intellectual backgrounds. Stern studied English at the University of North Carolina at Chapel Hill, which in the 1940s 'was steeped in the southern literary tradition'.[58] As it was for Stafford, Stern's time in the South was formative. Stern later recalled that his fiction was 'affected by the people I read as a teenager at Chapel Hill, the New Critics and the Fugitives. I took to [the idea of] the integration of every part of the fiction in a thematic pattern.'[59] Early in his undergraduate career, Stern became friends with the poet Donald Justice, and the pair followed closely the work of Brooks, Tate, and Ransom. But they were particularly taken with the iconoclastic criticism of Yvor Winters. Stern gave Justice and his wife Jean a copy of Winters's *In Defense of Reason* (1947) as a wedding gift (along with a coffeemaker), and the book sparked Justice's deep engagement with Winters's brand of formalism.[60] 'We thought Winters was the knight of literary form,' Stern recalled, 'the enemy of the chaos into which the romantic movement had disintegrated.'[61] As Anthony Hutchison explains, 'Winters's poetry and criticism was shaped by the formal discipline of a modern classical tradition that emerged from English Renaissance poetry'; in the next chapter, I explore the influence of Winters's 'classical style' on John Williams's fiction.[62] As Stern suggests, Winters's classicism defined itself in opposition to 'modernist-Romantic' subjectivism – a label that could well describe Bellow's 'mature' work.[63] Winters maintained that literature 'approximates a real apprehension and communication of a particular kind of objective truth', and does so through the 'fusion of the dramatic with the expository'.[64] He defined poetry as 'good in so far as it makes a defensible rational statement about a given human experience [. . .] and at the same time communicates the emotion which ought to be motivated by that rational understanding of that experience'.[65] Stern would later take issue with this definition, but in the early stage of his career he and Justice were swayed by Winters's rigorous rationalism and antisubjectivism; in the 1940s, Stern recalled, 'no literary critic was more influential, either as champion or opponent, than Yvor Winters'.[66] As late as 1966 – the year after *Stitch*'s publication – Stern was echoing Winters's anti-Romanticism, telling his *Chicago Review* interviewer that there are 'two powerful notions about works of art'. The 'more recent' is 'identified with works of romantic art and can be traced at least to Rousseau's conception that a man was interesting as a man rather than in his status or accomplishments', which Stern links to the rise of autobiography in the nineteenth century; 'contemporary critics feel comfortable with this intimate relationship between a man and his work'.[67] Stern, however, says that he subscribes to the 'older notion' that 'the artist forms his experience [. . .] into works which he gradually detaches from himself and makes independent of that experience', creating 'self-reflexive' works of 'self-containment' rather than 'self-revelation'.[68]

Winters's judgement of Pound's poetry was mixed. In *In Defense of Reason*, he writes that the *Cantos* (1922–62) display 'extraordinary suavity and grace of movement' and argues that they represent 'the most ambitious attempt of our century to create a carry-all form'.[69] But he also suggests that Pound's verse at times veers into presenting 'merely a psychological progression or flux', and therefore fails to achieve the necessary synthesis of rationality and emotion, committing 'the fallacy of imitative form' and coming too close to Romantic self-revelation.[70] Stern and Justice's letters show them contending with the judgements of Winters and the New Critics and suggest the influence of midcentury criticism on their early work. After Justice sent him a story that borrowed extensively from Faulkner, for instance, Stern replied: 'I like the story, and like it well enough to repeat what Pound told Eliot about writing couplets, "Don't, unless you are going to parody Pope".'[71] While Justice went to Stanford to study with Winters, Stern completed his MA at Harvard, where he sat in on I. A. Richards's graduate course and wrote an essay on John Crowe Ransom for the college's prestigious Bowdoin Prize, placing second. His early stories of the mid-1950s were published not, like Bellow's, in *Partisan Review*, but in the *Kenyon Review*.[72] In a reminiscence, Stern recalls receiving a letter from Ransom, *Kenyon*'s editor, accepting one of his early stories for publication: 'Fifty-three years ago now, and I'm not sure anything has topped that acceptance'.[73]

At the same time that he was under the influence of the New Critics, Stern was ambivalent about his Jewish heritage. He grew up in a middle-class, secular Jewish home in Manhattan; he was not bar mitzvahed because 'one wasn't in our family' – 'it wasn't worth the expense'.[74] At Chapel Hill, he 'claimed to be half-Jewish, partly to duck Hillel functions and partly to try my luck on the other side of the street', and was content to 'dissolve' into the college's 'easy wasp soup'.[75] 'I was not,' he admitted, 'very lucid, self-reflective or self-conscious'.[76] This attitude extended to his work. It was only after his first novel, *Golk*, was published in 1961 that he realised two of its central characters were clearly Jewish.[77] That same year, Stern was among thirty-one Jewish-American intellectuals asked to respond to a questionnaire issued by *Commentary* canvassing opinion on 'the situation of the Jew in America' (Roth was also one of the respondents). Stern wrote that 'being a Jew is like being a Chicagoan, except that I pay no taxes (there may be hidden ones). I'm glad, rather than not, but I don't spend thirty minutes a year congratulating myself, or indeed, thinking of myself as a Jew.'[78]

Meeting Pound

Stern's admiration for Pound, then, can be understood in relation to his intellectual training and the early influence of the New Critics; but it also reflected his ambivalence about his Jewish background and about his uncertain place in the newly legible literary terrain marked 'Jewish-American fiction' (in 'those naïvely hierarchical days' when he was starting out as a writer at Chapel Hill,

Stern recalled, 'there seemed to be only one door to Literature, not hundreds of doors labeled "Jewish American Literature," "Black Literature," [. . .]').[79] Not prone, by his own admission, to self-reflection, Stern would be forced to face these ambivalences when he met Pound in person. Stern spent the academic year 1962–3 in Italy teaching at the Istituto Universitario di Venezia. That winter – one of the coldest on record in Venice – he regularly met Pound for tea in the apartment the poet shared with his companion, Olga Rudge.[80] Stern learned of Pound's presence through Joan Fitzgerald, an American sculptor living in the city.[81] Stern wrote to Hugh Kenner asking for a suitable entrée so that he might be granted a meeting with the poet, and Kenner suggested asking for the letters that the Jewish-American poet Louis Zukofsky had sent Pound. 'I remember wishing that there'd been another, less Semitic bridge to the old fellow,' Stern recalled, and that he felt a slight 'protocols-of-zion discomfort in the particular mission'.[82] When he did eventually broach the topic of Zukofsky's letters in their first meeting, Stern recollects that 'Pound smiled, perhaps at all good Jews getting together'.[83]

As well as fictionalising his conversations with Pound in *Stitch*, to which I turn in a moment, Stern also published three reminiscences of their encounters – in 1972, 1981, and 1998 – drawing on his contemporaneous journals.[84] The three accounts vary slightly in their details, but in each Stern records his nervous anticipation regarding Pound's reaction to his 'Jewish presence', and his relief at finding the poet to be seemingly of sound mind.[85] Stern was struck by the clarity of Pound's opinions, which he found to be 'complete and underwritten by thought, so rare that the word sanity took on new depths for me'.[86] In his journal, Stern put it less lyrically: 'If E. P. is insane, God help the rest of us'.[87] Pound's 'literary judgements, like those of the only other man of literary genius I know at all well,' Stern writes in the 1972 reminiscence, 'were almost always unexpected, oblique'.[88] The suggestion that this 'other man' is Bellow is strengthened by Stern's comment in his interview with Atlas that Bellow's 'reactions to books are unusual and telling [. . .] He reminds me a bit of Pound – perhaps he won't like that.'[89] With Pound, Stern discussed Eliot, Henry James, and Pound's recent award of *Poetry* magazine's fiftieth-anniversary Harriet Monroe Memorial Prize – evidence of the continuing evolution of Pound's postwar reputation, and that the poet still had a loyal band of admirers back in the States.[90] In each of the three accounts, their meetings reach the same emotional climax, wherein 'something said brought Pound's feelings of guilt and failure welling up'.[91] 'Wrong, wrong, wrong. I've always been wrong. Eighty-seven percent wrong,' Pound said, drawing Stern close, 'I've never recognized benevolence'.[92] Trying to comfort him, Stern told Pound that he had 'been reading [*Hugh Selwyn*] *Mauberley*; it was right on target', but the poet dolefully insisted that 'he'd left only notes, scattered notes, he hadn't made anything clear'.[93]

In a footnote to his 1972 reminiscence, Stern writes that, 'Anti-Semitism [. . .] was, in my view, not in him', rather Pound had 'fallen into what I think were wicked rhetorical habits [. . .] I doubt that he ever seriously prejudged a human being on racial grounds'.[94] In subsequent reminiscences, he is more circumspect. In the 1998 account of their meetings, Stern begins by making clear that although he 'loved' some of Pound's poetry when they met, and 'knew a bit about his place in history, and more about his scandalous attachment – as I saw it – to fascism and anti-Semitism', he had not yet read Pound's 'wild and pathetic broadcasts from Italy', except for 'those snippets quoted in the newspapers during the controversy about the Bollingen prize'.[95] Now, he writes, he feels an unease about reconciling the memory of 'the genial and touching man whom I encountered' with the fact that Pound 'had once thought like those who would have had me killed for being born my parents' son'.[96] This unease also animates *Stitch*, where the question of Pound's legacy connects to a broader reckoning with the legacy of modernism and New Critical formalism. As Stern's unlikely comparison of Pound to Bellow suggests, the question of Pound's antisemitism is also connected in the novel to Stern's uncertainty about his own Jewish identity and its relevance to his work. In this novel of the early sixties, it is as though Stern looks back to the Bollingen controversy, one of the landmark events in 1940s literary culture, so as to make sense of the postwar 'breakthrough' of Jewish American fiction, and of his own ambiguous relation to it.

Stitch

Like Pound, Thaddeus Stitch is an American artist in exile brooding over an unfinished masterpiece. The sculptor's equivalent of the *Cantos* is Sant' Ilario, an island in the lagoon on which Stitch has carved a maverick cultural history reaching back to the ancients.[97] Wandering the 'forest of stone', one comes across 'a declension of Egyptians heads', 'a shelf of green-veined marble with a Phidian Athena in high relief on a temple slab', and a 'shorthand group of Donatello Davids' (40), recalling the fragmented form of Pound's epic. In the forty years he has been at work on the island, Stitch has aimed to portray an 'ascent into light [. . .] as Dante and Homer and old Bach and Kung and François Arouet had spelled it out', but fears he has 'left only disorder, hints, scattered notes' (26). In his transposition of poetry into sculpture, Stern was following the lead of Pound himself. Pound suggested an analogy between the art forms and published extensively on the work of sculptors, while the *Cantos* frequently invoke the history of sculpture and architecture, including the history of Venice's foundation (the critic Donald Davie gave his 1964 study of Pound the subtitle *Poet as Sculptor*).[98] Among the many heads carved within the island's 'intricate amalgamation' is that of Henry James, though Stitch feels he has not quite captured the novelist's 'wonderful eyes': 'Henry's had caught more light, had a blue-gray glaze he couldn't match in stone' (22–3). Like James's Venetian artist tales, *Stitch* is a finely crafted story of literary ambition and influence, a tale of old masters ('*Le Maitre*. How many got called that and deserved it?' (23), Stitch wonders).

Much of Stitch's conversation with Edward Gunther is drawn directly from Stern's encounters with Pound and reaches the same emotional climax, Stitch declaring that he has been 'wrong, wrong, wrong [. . .] I've never been able to recognize benevolence' (62). Like Stern, Edward is also suspicious of how the artist will respond to his Jewishness. When Stitch loses his temper, accusing him of fabricating a story, Edward wonders whether it is evidence of antisemitism: 'Chicago Semite *Venitian*? Not that. That was too easy' (61, emphasis original). As readers, however, we cannot so readily dismiss the suspicion, because we hear Stitch's own inchoate reflections throughout the novel in intermittent passages of stream of consciousness, including his first impressions of Edward: 'Dazzled by celebrity, a groveler, a witness of events [. . .] A Jew of course, in essence at any rate. A secondhand dealer' (24). In these passages of private thought, we also hear the self-recrimination familiar from portraits of Pound as a 'tragic' figure in his old age.[99] He regrets the 'rant that consumed him for six years' (44) – the war years – condemning his political works as 'guff': '*Stitch on Power. Stitch on State Control* [. . .] *Stitch on the Conversion of the Jews*' (178). At other times, however, he grows defiant, defending his political actions. He admits he had 'turned fanatic, though never totally out of mind. There were essential distinctions. There were relations of passion and relations of money. Until they were sorted out, one had no right to work on an island' (45).

If Stitch is a conflicted portrait of Pound, reflecting the ambivalence Stern felt towards the poet, then Edward is a similarly complex stand-in for the author. Edward is not a novelist, but a disillusioned copywriter on sabbatical from his Chicago advertising firm. He is funding his young family's European sojourn not by way of a fellowship, but by pilfering his children's college tuition fund. As reviewers noted, Edward appears to fit a familiar literary type – the Jewish cerebral philanderer – but he also recalls Bernard Malamud's *nebbishes* on their Roman holidays, as well as a certain antisemitic caricature peddled by Eliot and Pound, to which Edward himself alludes in his reference to Eliot's 'Burbank with a Baedeker: Bleistein with a Cigar' (1919).[100] There are also a number of similarities between Edward and Stitch. Both have complicated domestic arrangements: like Pound, Stitch lives with a companion in Italy but still has 'a wife in the States' and 'a child or two by each' (6); meanwhile, Edward's first marriage has ended in divorce and his second, to Cress, is in crisis. More significantly, both hunger after greater creative achievement and fulfilment: just as Stitch rues his unfinished masterpiece, so Edward 'ache[s] with the unfinished, the barely begun' (30). But Edward knows that he is no artist. 'Unable to hold a hammer or hear a rhythm' (111), he lacks what he understands to be an artistic sensibility. 'So much of what had happened to him had washed off, unpondered, barely felt. He'd never held onto what mattered' (64). Nor is he much of an academic, although, Cress notes, he 'fawns before the university swells of Hyde Park, soaking up whatever rot came out of their mouths' (79). He clings to the idea of being a writer, but Cress is perceptive in recognising his 'self-examinations and reflections and studies' as merely a kind of 'camouflage' (33). When he does sit down to write, he dashes off a series of short, topical essays which he intends to send to 'a publisher, or to literary and philosophical quarterlies' (138) – a project rather far from the epic form and monumental ambition of Stitch's island.[101] In a suggestive aside, Edward briefly considers drawing on his own domestic situation in his essays, and imagines describing his unhappy relationship with Cress 'in terms of the 20th-century family, marriage of Jew and Gentile, the second-chance American getting ready for a third chance [. . .], the American girl in Europe [. . .] Yes, there was a great little history that could be written up' (141), though he never does. Edward is initially dismissive of his wife's suggestion that he contact her cousin, Wallie, an art historian by training who makes his living working for an arts foundation out in Santa Barbara (like Trilling's unfinished novel, *Stitch* is about the changing institutional fabric of the literary field, and about what kinds of literary careers are newly possible and foreclosed). 'According to Edward, Wallie was a plodder but he had plodded his way into all sorts of fellowships and through at least three books' (88). Eventually, however, Edward warms to the idea and to the image of himself as a foundation man, growing excited at the prospect that the 'combination of his public relations-foundation gifts and his speculative power could even lead him to popular attention', and to invitations to address 'the Rand Corporation', 'the War College', the 'Congress for Cultural Freedom' (139) – a vision of Cold War institutional power that represents a kind of American burlesque of Stitch's grand European, modernist designs.

As a partial self-portrait, Edward seems to incarnate some of Stern's uncertainties regarding his identity as a Jewish-American writer, while Stitch embodies the difficult legacy of Poundian modernist aesthetics Stern came to appreciate via the New Critics. But Stitch's and Edward's personal and artistic failings are also set against the work of Nina, the novel's third main character. Loosely based on sculptor Joan Fitzgerald, Nina is a young poet living in Venice and working on her own 'woman's epic': 'Not the adventurer founding the city or knocking one over. No justifying, no bragging. Something else' (7). With its allusions to 'Sappho, Christine de Pisan, Louise de Lyons', and its fragmentary form – 'the large scene broken into the new music' (155) – Nina's epic resembles the *Cantos*. Like the young Pound, her apprentice works are experiments in intricate and antiquated poetic forms. She reads Stitch 'a canzone she'd written in Paris', his approval representing recognition 'by someone in the great tradition' (13); later, she tries a sestina 'on the words *space, place, Venice, red, kind,* and *water*' (96). Indeed, form becomes a key concept in the novel, reflecting Stern's early brush with Winters and the New Critics. Stitch's 'mind had swum in forms for years' (126), but he now finds himself out of touch with the architectural structures and material of the modern world: 'The new forms are getting ready for space. The forms I've loved are natural, earthly' (49). He and Nina share a conception of artistic form and value derived from high modernism, or what Bellow characterised as 'the Eliot-Pound phenomenon' of 'tradition' and 'culture'. Nina insists that an artist 'must pay tribute to the overall, not wallow in the singular. I'm with Stitch [. . .] One must select, refine, bore tunnels into the great light' (111), echoing Stitch's desire for an 'ascent into light', and his search for a sculptural form that resembles 'a wall which isn't wall-like [. . .] just the sense of opening, a suggestion' (23). Like any good formalist, she knows that meaning will emerge when she pays careful, close attention to line and pattern as she surveys the island. 'Wandering, by leg and eye, Nina began to find much more that was familiar', gradually recognising how 'the broken-nosed power of Michelangelo tangled into a marble rebuke of its own power. The shape seemed to be straining toward and failing to arrive at human form' (40–1). (By contrast, when Edward goes to visit the island, he thinks it resembles 'a kind of limestone gallbladder' (102)). By the time she leaves Sant' Ilario, she appreciates it as an 'inorganic garden of high sanity' (42), recalling Stern's observation that 'the word sanity' took on a new depth of meaning after his conversations with Pound.

This search for coherent form is manifest elsewhere in the novel. When Nina is seized by artistic inspiration, she is sustained by 'the inner music', subsisting on only 'crackers' and 'staling bread' (151) – the very picture of a hunger artist.[102] By contrast, Edward's 'mounting weight' (1) and 'fattening rump' (33) would seem to testify to his overindulgence and lack of discipline, in both his personal and creative life (as in Stafford's fiction, questions of literary form are transposed into questions of appetite). He feels uncomfortably out of proportion in Stitch's small apartment, which seems to 'stretch to his bulk' (58). Resolving to lose weight, he begins exercising, 'trying to regain his real shape' (116). His 'deformed' physique seems indicative of his indistinct ambition, which leads him to settle on the idea of working for the foundation in the hope that 'his life could take form guiding his superiors' (144). As Edward gains weight, he also 'leaks' (57) money on extravagant gifts and meals. Over the course of the novel, we become acquainted with the Gunthers' 'Talman Federal Savings passbook' (32), its dwindling balance recording the family's declining fortunes in Venice. Nina, by contrast, is nearly penniless, and survives 'by the habit of charging expenses to seldom-dispatched bills' (13), shoplifting, and cadging free lunches from the likes of Edward. Behind the novel's focus on finances there is something of Pound's association of Jews and usury – Stitch wonders about how Edward is 'obscurely financed. Banker's son?' (173) – but the role of money also connects to the novel's preoccupation with the idea of aesthetic value. While Edward is more than comfortable with the prospect that his essays and a role at Wallie's foundation will connect him to the corporate world, Nina, like Stitch, is dismissive of applying for fellowships or accepting patronage: 'I've been turned down three times. Stitch says they turned him down too [. . .] They're not geared to us' (108).

Nina's understanding of literary value, along with her disciplined disavowal of material possessions, align with a modernist conception of the artist's impersonality and adversarial relation to the culture. Her epic will reflect little of her biography or personal desires; though she recognises that 'her life had to play a role, certainly [. . .] whatever went in would be placed in her map of the transient, the immutable, and the reborn' (150). This chimes with Stitch's dismissal of what he derides as the 'Kiss and tell, suffer and yell' school of literary criticism, in which the work is reductively interpreted as self-expression. 'One of them tried to make Sant' Ilario a diary. A giant Stitch from the gonads up. As if they'd never heard of Greece, Egypt. Know thyself. How that perverted them' (85). And yet Sant' Ilario contains many 'heads of Stitch himself, some cubist, some partial', which suggests that the work is at least partly autobiographical. 'I come in and out of it,' he tells Nina, 'depending what I'm thinking, or what's happening to me' (140). In his own critique of Nina's epic, Stitch suggests that her work is too self-denying, and that it lacks 'love'. He partly has in mind 'sexual passion' (157), another appetite Nina has suppressed to protect her work. But his emphasis on 'love' also recalls the mournful, personal tone of one of Pound's most famous late Cantos, published in the *Paris Review* just a few months before Stern met the poet in 1962:

> but the beauty is not the madness
> Tho my errors and wrecks lie about me.
> and I cannot make it cohere
> If love be not in the house there is nothing [. . .][103]

In the final part of the novel, we find Edward faced with his own 'errors and wrecks'. The action moves to Santa Barbara, where, separated from Cress, he is teaching at a school while waiting for a position to open up at the Foundation. Visiting the Watts Tower – 'the illiterate's Sant' Ilario' (199) – and beginning a desultory relationship with a divorcée, Edward seems to have travelled a long way from Stitch's Venice. In the novel's moving denouement, he calls to speak to his children and beg Cress to take him back, which she coolly refuses. Nina, meanwhile, has had a section of her epic published in – where else? – *Partisan Review*; she has agreed to marry Wallie, on the condition that the corpulent art historian loses 'thirty-five pounds' (195).

Interweaving the perspectives of Nina, Stitch, and Edward, the novel portrays their interrelated struggles to find a coherent form, in both their creative and personal lives. The novel mirrors this struggle in its own oscillations in style: the modernist free indirect discourse of the passages tracking Stitch's mind; the Jamesian third person perspective following the development of Nina's epic; the Herzogian comedy of Edward at work on his essays; the realism of his home life with Cress. In doing so, *Stitch* also dramatises the tension between divergent forms of the novel emerging at midcentury, and between the two conceptions of the work of art Stern discusses in his *Chicago Review* interview: the classical mode of 'self-containment', and the Romantic mode of 'self-revelation'. Its preoccupation with formal coherence and unity reflects the influence of Winters's criticism, while its sympathetic portrait of the Pound-like Stitch suggests a continuing allegiance to modernist aesthetics; yet the novel is also a kind of intricate roman à clef of the kind Stern's friends, Bellow and Roth, were beginning to make their own.[104] In Edward, Stern portrays a familiarly expansive and indulgent Herzogian Romantic-type; yet, by the novel's close, he is brought low because he fails to exercise restraint and discipline, the formal (and moral) qualities most prized by Winters. Stitch's fragmentary internal monologues, meanwhile, would seem to commit the 'fallacy of imitative form' Winters warned against; but they are not employed to suggest that the sculptor is out of his mind, à la Moses Herzog, but rather as evidence that he has achieved a 'higher sanity'. More broadly, in exploring the extent to which art can be a medium of self-expression (or 'love'), the novel returns to the formalist question of the literary object's autonomy; but, in its allusions to Pound's exile, it also returns to the Bollingen controversy which made this question so vexed for Jewish-American intellectuals in particular. Stern thus situates his novel at the intersection of modernist aesthetics and ethnic identity, an intersection which would become the site for the 'breakthrough' of Jewish-American literature and cultural pluralist fiction more broadly. But rather than embrace the freedom of a first person Jewish vernacular, or a postwar iteration of Romantic 'self-revelation', as Bellow and Roth do, Stern creates a reflexive work staging an impasse between an increasingly anachronistic modernist aesthetics (embodied in the aging figure of Stitch and taken up, in a feminist revision, by Nina) and an ethnically marked, institutionally mediated mid-century aesthetics (embodied by Edward). Stern's forgotten artist tale thus allows us to see afresh the most storied period in Jewish-American literary history. Critics often hearken back to that meeting between Bellow and Roth after Stern's writing workshop as a point of origin, because it seems so nicely to capture the idea of a line of influence forming, a genealogy being established, the beginning of the 'breakthrough'; but *Stitch* show us that other possibilities for Jewish-American writing were emerging from that same Chicago classroom.

Notes

1. Stern retired as Helen A. Regenstein Professor of English and American Literature in 2001.
2. D. G. Myers, *The Elephants Teach: Creative Writing Since 1880*, 2nd ed. (Chicago: University of Chicago Press, 2006), 165.
3. See Richard Stern, 'Henderson's Bellow', *Kenyon Review*, Vol. 21, No. 4 (Autumn 1959), pp. 655–61.
4. Zachary Leader, *The Life of Saul Bellow, Volume 1: To Fame and Fortune, 1915–1964* (New York: Random House, 2015), 615.
5. Mark Harris, *Saul Bellow, Drumlin Woodchuck* (Athens, GA: University of Georgia Press, 1980), 36–7.
6. Ibid., 40.
7. Philip Roth, 'Just a Lively Boy', in Molly McQuade (ed.), *An Unsentimental Education: Writers and Chicago* (Chicago: University of Chicago Press, 1995), pp. 123–9 (129).
8. See Leader, *To Fame and Fortune*, 524–6.
9. Saul Bellow, 'The Swamp of Prosperity', *Commentary*, July 1959, pp. 77–9 (77).
10. Philip Roth, 'In Memory of Richard Stern' [2013], in Richard Stern, *Other Men's Daughters* (New York: New York Review Books Classics, 2017), pp. vii–xii (vii). Emphasis original.
11. Ibid., viii.
12. Roth, 'Just a Lively Boy', 126–7.
13. Ibid., 127. Emphasis original.
14. Richard Stern, 'An Interview with Richard Stern', interview by James Atlas, *Chicago Review*, Vol. 45, No. 3/4 (1999), pp. 23–43 (32).
15. The cliché of a 'breakthrough' in postwar Jewish-American fiction began with Leslie Fiedler's 'The Breakthrough: The American Jewish Novelist and the Fictional Image of the Jew', *Midstream*, Vol. 4, No. 1 (Winter 1959), pp. 15–35. Recently, a number of critics – most notably, Benjamin Schreier – have challenged the 'breakthrough' narrative, arguing that it 'needs to be approached primarily as an event in Jewish American historiography, not Jewish American history', a 'discursive innovation' through which the canon and field of Jewish-American literature was organised. See Schreier, *The Rise and Fall of Jewish American Literature: Ethnic Studies and the Challenge of Identity* (Philadelphia: Pennsylvania University Press, 2020), 3, 4.
16. Victoria Aarons, 'American Jewish Fiction', in John Duvall (ed.), *The Cambridge Companion to American Fiction After 1945* (Cambridge: Cambridge University Press, 2012), pp. 129–41 (131).
17. Josh Lambert, *The Literary Mafia: Jews, Publishing, and Postwar American Literature* (New Haven: Yale University Press, 2022), 31.
18. Andrew Furman, *Contemporary Jewish American Writers and the Multicultural Dilemma: The Return of the Exiled* (Syracuse: Syracuse University Press, 2000), 4.
19. Morris Dickstein, 'Promised Lands', *Times Literary Supplement*, 15 April 2016, pp. 3–5 (3).

20. Alfred Kazin, 'The Earthly City of the Jews: Bellow, Malamud, and Roth' [1971], in Ted Solotaroff (ed.), *Alfred Kazin's America: Critical and Personal Writings* (New York: Harper Collins, 2003), pp. 255–69 (257).
21. Mark McGurl, *The Program Era: Postwar Fiction and the Rise of Creative Writing* (Cambridge, MA: Harvard University Press, 2009), 32.
22. Ibid., 57. Schreier, *The Rise and Fall of Jewish American Literature*, 58. Louis Harap's influential study of postwar Jewish American fiction is titled *In the Mainstream: The Jewish Presence in Twentieth-century American Literature, 1950s–1980s* (Westport, CT: Greenwood Press, 1987); Schreier alludes to it in the title of his essay, 'Making It into the Mainstream, 1945–1970', in Hana Wirth-Nesher (ed.), *The Cambridge History of Jewish American Literature* (Cambridge: Cambridge University Press, 2016), pp. 123–43.
23. Philip Roth, 'Writing American Fiction' [1961], in *Reading Myself and Others* (London: Vintage, 2007), pp. 165–82 (175–6).
24. Patrick Hayes argues that Roth's first novel, *Letting Go* (1962), in which James's *The Portrait of a Lady* figures prominently, is 'neither simply a continuation of an ossified 1950s literary ethos, nor a wholehearted abandonment of that legacy, but a fundamentally unresolved text – one that is indeed letting go the intellectual baggage of the previous generation, but which has by no means let go altogether'. 'Not Quite *Letting Go*: Rethinking the "tragic sense of life" in Roth's First Novel', *Philip Roth Studies*, Vol. 9, No. 2 (Fall 2013), pp. 7–22 (8).
25. Saul Bellow, 'The Art of Fiction: Saul Bellow' [1966], interview by Gordon Lloyd Harper, in Gloria Cronin and Ben Siegel (eds), *Conversations with Saul Bellow* (Jackson: University Press of Mississippi, 1994), pp. 58–76 (63); Allen Tate, 'Techniques of Fiction', *Sewanee Review*, Vol. 52, No. 2 (Spring 1944), pp. 210–25 (225).
26. Bellow, 'The Art of Fiction', 63.
27. Stern, 'An Interview with Richard Stern', 30.
28. See James Schiffer, *Richard Stern* (New York: Twayne Publishers, 1993), 23–4.
29. Stern, 'An Interview with Richard Stern', 32.
30. Richard Stern, 'Two Iowan Baudelaires Sweating Out Tetrameters', in *The Invention of the Real* (Athens, GA: University of Georgia Press, 1982), pp. 135–7 (136).
31. Richard Stern, *Stitch* [1965] (Evanston: TriQuarterly Books, 2004), 117. Subsequent references are given in parentheses in the text.
32. Bernard Bergonzi, 'Herzog in Venice', review of *Stitch* by Richard Stern, *New York Review of Books*, 9 December 1965, pp. 26–7.
33. Morris Dickstein, *Leopard in the Temple: The Transformation of American Fiction 1945–1970* (Cambridge, MA: Harvard University Press, 2002), 170, 171.
34. Ibid., 170; Malcolm Bradbury, 'Saul Bellow's *Herzog*', *Critical Quarterly*, Vol. 7, No. 3 (September 1965), pp. 269–78 (273, 272).
35. Saul Bellow, Letter to Richard Stern, 25 November 1988, Box 73, Folder 11, Saul Bellow Papers, Hanna Holborn Gray Special Collections Research Center, University of Chicago. Emphasis original.
36. Richard Stern, Letter to Saul Bellow, 29 November 1988, Box 73, Folder 11, Saul Bellow Papers.

37. Richard Stern, Letter to Saul Bellow [unsent], 29 November 1988, Box 68, Folder 1, Richard G. Stern Papers, Hanna Holborn Gray Special Collections Research Center, University of Chicago.
38. John Berryman, 'The Poetry of Ezra Pound', *Partisan Review*, Vol. 16, No. 4 (April 1949), pp. 377–94 (377).
39. For an overview, see Robert Corrigan, 'Ezra Pound and the Bollingen Prize Controversy', *Midcontinent American Studies Journal*, Vol. 8, No. 2 (Fall 1967), pp. 43–57.
40. See Greg Barnhisel, *James Laughlin, New Directions, and the Remaking of Ezra Pound* (Amherst: University of Massachusetts Press, 2005), 92–126.
41. Quoted in James Wilhelm, *Ezra Pound: The Tragic Years, 1925–1972* (University Park: Pennsylvania State University Press, 1994), 278.
42. Sarah Ehlers, 'Late Modernisms, Latent Realisms: The Politics of Literary Interpretation', in Christopher Vials (ed.), *American Literature in Transition, 1940–1950* (Cambridge: Cambridge University Press, 2017), pp. 229–45 (235).
43. William Barrett, 'A Prize for Ezra Pound', *Partisan Review*, Vol. 16, No. 4 (April 1949), pp. 344–7 (345, 347).
44. W. H. Auden, et al, 'The Question of the Pound Award', *Partisan Review*, Vol. 16, No. 5 (May 1949), pp. 512–22.
45. Ibid., 516–17. Emphasis original.
46. Ibid., 515.
47. Ibid., 518.
48. Ted Solotaroff, *First Loves: A Memoir* (New York: Seven Stories Press, 2003), 223.
49. Solotaroff recalls being inspired by 'a seminal essay by Leslie Fiedler on the "breakthrough" in America Jewish fiction' (216), published the year before. See also Solotaroff's earlier essay, 'Philip Roth and the Jewish Moralist', *Chicago Review*, Vol. 13, No. 4 (Winter 1959), pp. 87–99.
50. Solotaroff, *First Loves*, 68.
51. Ibid., 68–9.
52. Ibid., 69.
53. Saul Bellow, Letter to Henry Volkening, 10 June 1949, in Benjamin Taylor (ed.), *Saul Bellow: Letters* (New York: Penguin, 2006), pp. 83–4 (84). In an editorial note, Taylor describes Bellow as 'furious' (84) at the decision.
54. Saul Bellow, Letter to William Faulkner, 7 January 1956, in *Saul Bellow: Letters*, pp. 144–5 (144). Faulkner was chairman of 'People to People', a committee of writers established to promote American values abroad; Bellow was a member of the committee.
55. See Hugh Kenner, 'From Lower Bellowvia', *Harper's*, February 1982, pp. 62–5.
56. Saul Bellow, Letter to Robert Boyers, 12 March 1982, in *Saul Bellow: Letters*, pp. 392–4 (393).
57. Stern, 'Interview with Richard Stern', 29.
58. Elizabeth Murphy, 'Introduction', in Murphy (ed.), *A Critical Friendship: Donald Justice and Richard Stern, 1946–1961* (Lincoln: University of Nebraska Press, 2013), pp. xv–xxv (xx).

59. Richard Stern, 'Interview with James Atlas, annotated typescript', Box 74, Folder 11, Richard G. Stern Papers.
60. See Richard Stern, 'Becoming a Writer: The Forties', in *Still on Call* (Ann Arbor: University of Michigan Press, 2010), pp. 28–32 (30).
61. Richard Stern, 'Janet Lewis', in *One Person and Another: On Writers and Writing* (Dallas: Baskerville, 1993), pp. 57–66 (57).
62. Anthony Hutchison, 'Cultivating the Classical Style: The Stanford-Denver Creative Writing Axis', *Modern Fiction Studies*, Vol. 66, No. 3 (Fall 2020), pp. 474–98 (479).
63. Ibid., 473.
64. Yvor Winters, *In Defense of Reason* (Denver: Swallow Press, 1947), 11; Gerald Graff, *Poetic Statement and Critical Dogma* (Evanston: Northwestern University Press, 1970), 164.
65. Ibid., 11.
66. Stern, 'Janet Lewis', 57. Stern later called Winters's definition a 'clumsy statement'. Stern, 'Edgar Bowers', in *One Person and Another*, pp. 287–91 (288).
67. Richard Stern, 'An Interview with Richard G. Stern', interview by Robert Raeder, *Chicago Review*, Vol. 18, No. 3/4 (1966), pp. 170–5 (170, 171).
68. Ibid., 171, 173.
69. Winters, *In Defense of Reason*, 494, 144.
70. Ibid., 145.
71. Richard Stern, Letter to Donald and Jean Justice, February 1949, in Murphy (ed.), *A Critical Friendship*, pp. 71–4 (71).
72. See Richard Stern, 'Cooley's Version', *Kenyon Review*, Vol. 16, No. 2 (Spring 1954), pp. 257–67.
73. Stern, 'Becoming a Writer: The Forties', 31.
74. Richard Stern, 'Jewishness and The Young Intellectuals', *Commentary*, Vol. 31, No. 4 (1961), pp. 306–10 (309); 'An Interview with Richard Stern', 30. Stern recalled that he was 'so ashamed of not being bar-mitzvahed, I hid out in the Paramount Theater all one Saturday, and on Monday, lied to my pal Eddie Meyer about the "closed family" ceremony, even gargling some phony Hebrew for him'. *A Sistermony* (New York: Donald Fine, 1995), 66.
75. Stern, 'Jewishness and The Young Intellectuals', 309; 'An Interview with Richard Stern', 30.
76. Stern, 'An Interview with Richard Stern', 30.
77. Richard Stern, 'The Novelist on his Work', in *One Person and Another*, pp. 384–91 (387).
78. Stern, 'Jewishness and The Young Intellectuals', 310.
79. Stern, 'Becoming a Writer: The Forties', 29.
80. See Anne Coover, *Olga Rudge & Ezra Pound* (New Haven: Yale University Press, 2001), pp. 227–58.
81. Fitzgerald made two bronze busts of Pound's head: one is in the Smithsonian National Portrait Gallery; the other belonged to Stern and his Chicago colleague Wayne Booth, and for many years had pride of place in Stern's living room, before being donated to the university library.

82. Richard Stern, 'Remembering Pound', *Sewanee Review*, Vol. 106, No. 1 (Winter 1998), pp. 132–9 (133); 'A Memory or Two of Mr. Pound', *Paideuma*, Vol. 1, No. 2 (Winter 1972), pp. 215–19 (215).
83. Richard Stern, 'Extracts from a Journal', *TriQuarterly*, Vol. 50 (Winter 1981), pp. 261–73 (262).
84. The three accounts are 'A Memory or Two of Mr. Pound' (1972), 'Extracts from a Journal' (1981) and 'Remembering Pound' (1998). He also briefly discusses meeting Pound in 'Glimpse, Acquaintance, Encounter, Friendship', *Sewanee Review*, Vol. 117, No. 1 (Winter 2009), pp. 95–105, and *A Sistermony*, 102–3.
85. Stern, 'Remembering Pound', 134.
86. Stern, 'A Memory or Two of Mr. Pound', 216.
87. Stern, 'Extracts from a Journal', 263.
88. Stern, 'A Memory or Two of Mr. Pound', 216.
89. Stern, 'An Interview with Richard Stern', 32.
90. See A. David Moody, *Ezra Pound, Poet: A Portrait of the Man and his Work, Volume III: The Tragic Years, 1939–1972* (Oxford: Oxford University Press, 2015), 484.
91. Ibid., 485.
92. Stern, 'Remembering Pound', 136.
93. Stern, 'Extracts from a Journal', 266.
94. Stern, 'A Memory or Two of Mr. Pound', 218, f.n. alone.
95. Stern, 'Remembering Pound', 133.
96. Ibid., 138. Stern's growing unease regarding his judgement of Pound may have been prompted by his reading of Robert Casillo's *The Genealogy of Demons: Anti-Semitism, Fascism, and the Myths of Ezra Pound* (Evanston: Northwestern University Press, 1988). Casillo argues that Pound's antisemitism was not a case of 'suburban prejudice' but rather 'took the shape of a political and cultural ideology' that is discernible throughout his work (4). In a 1988 interview with James Schiffer, Stern says that he began to feel 'troubled by my own allegiance to Pound':

    As I was reading the Casillo book, I wanted to go down in the middle of the night and remove that bust of Pound from the living room. I said, 'My God, is this what he was doing all that time?' But then I said, 'But look, your impressions counted. He was not that way with you' [. . .] I'm just getting into this theme of [. . .] anti-Semitism, which should have been in front of my face all my life. Since it wasn't, does that mean I've betrayed something? What have I run away from? What's the evasiveness in this Jewish business? (Schiffer, *Richard* Stern, 152)

97. The depth of Stern's reading in the poet's work is suggested by the syllabus for an undergraduate course on Pound he began teaching at Chicago in spring 1964. Primary texts include the 1922 *Cantos*, *Rock-Drill* (1956) and *Personae* (1909); secondary reading includes Hugh Kenner's *The Poetry of Ezra Pound* (1951). Stern suggests that students consult the 'microfilm of the monitored radio talks' in the university library. 'English 294: Ezra Pound' [Spring 1964 course syllabus], Box 88, Folder 16, Richard G. Stern Papers.

98. Donald Davie, *Ezra Pound: Poet as Sculptor* (London: Routledge, 1964). See also Ezra Pound, *Gaudier-Brezka: A Memoir* (London: John Lane, 1916); 'Brancusi', *Little Review*, Vol. 8, No. 1 (1921), pp. 3–7. Tony Tanner explores connections between Pound's poetry and Ruskin's writing on Venice in *Venice Desired* (Cambridge, MA: Harvard University Press, 1992), 269–348.
99. Moody, for example, describes Pound's later years as 'the five act tragedy of a flawed idealist' (xiii).
100. See, for example, Bernard Malamud, 'The Last Mohican', *Partisan Review*, Vol. 25, No. 2 (Spring 1958), pp. 175–96.
101. Stern is perhaps best known for his work in another minor genre he made his own – what he called 'the orderly "miscellany"'. See 'Preface', in *What is What Was* (Chicago: University of Chicago Press, 2002), pp. ix–x (ix).
102. See Maud Ellman, *The Hunger Artists: Starving, Writing, and Imprisonment* (Cambridge, MA: Harvard University Press, 1993).
103. Ezra Pound, 'Canto CXVI', *Paris Review*, 28 (Summer/Fall 1962), pp. 14–16 (16).
104. In his review, Hugh Kenner stresses the novel's adherence to a Poundian aesthetics, suggesting that *Stitch* resembles Sant' Ilario, a 'concoction of self-sufficient fragments, scene set against scene'. Kenner, '*Stitch*: His Master's Voice', *Chicago Review*, Vol. 18, No. 3/4 (1966), pp. 176–80 (180).

CHAPTER 5

A Lost Classic: John Williams's *Stoner* and the 'Rediscovery' of the Midcentury Minor Novel

A Seminar on Tragedy

Midway through John Williams's 1965 novel *Stoner*, a scene of unexpectedly high drama takes place in a graduate seminar on 'The Latin Tradition and Renaissance Literature'.[1] The seminar is led by William Stoner, a quiet, dogged assistant professor of medieval literature at the University of Missouri, a man of modest accomplishments from a hard-scrabble background, unhappily married, devoted, in a fervent, private way, to his subject. The course, Stoner makes clear, will be limited in its scope and ambition, focusing on 'the extent to which poets and dramatists even of the middle and late Renaissance were indebted' to medieval conceptions of 'grammar, rhetoric, and dialectic' (135, 134). In an early seminar, Stoner is greatly impressed with a presentation on 'Donatus and Renaissance Tragedy' (139) given by Katherine Driscoll, an instructor in her late twenties auditing the class with whom he will later have an affair. But now it is the turn of Charles Walker, a latecomer to the course and a doctoral student writing a dissertation on Shelley under the supervision of Hollis Lomax, Stoner's powerful rival in the department. Stoner's suspicion that Walker is a charlatan is confirmed when he begins his presentation – ostensibly on 'Hellenism and the Medieval Latin Tradition' – and it quickly becomes clear 'even to the most inattentive students in the class that Walker was engaged in a performance that was entirely impromptu' (143). Watching on, Stoner finds 'a reluctant and perverse admiration stealing over him.

However florid and imprecise, the man's powers of rhetoric and invention were dismayingly impressive' (143). But he is silently furious as Walker takes aim at Driscoll's argument that the work of Shakespeare might have its roots in the ideas of an 'obscure Roman grammarian' (142). After Walker finishes, Stoner dismisses the class and demands an explanation; when Walker protests, Stoner informs the young man that 'You will, of course, receive a F' (147). 'You have not heard the last of this!' (148), Walker shouts, and indeed he hasn't, for Stoner's battle with Walker will lead to a confrontation with Lomax that will ultimately upend the medievalist's quiet life.

A good deal seems to be at stake in this seminar, and to understand how the scene connects to some of the novel's broader preoccupations – preoccupations it shares with other minor novels discussed in this book – requires a little working through. The scene reveals the strong influence on Williams's work of the formalist critic Yvor Winters, discussed briefly in the previous chapter. Winters's 'classical style' privileged 'precise language, impersonal register, and formal coherence', and defined itself in opposition to what Winters took to be the irrationalism, obscurantism, and subjectivism of Romanticism and modernism.[2] We saw that Richard Stern and Donald Justice were much taken as young men with the stridency of Winters's criticism, especially his most famous work, *In Defense of Reason* (1947), which Stern gave to Justice as a wedding gift. The same book was formative in Williams's understanding of literary history and his conception of literary form. As Charles Shields, Williams's biographer, shows, Williams worked hard to be part of the 'Winters Circle'.[3] He wrote his dissertation on Fulke Greville, the obscure Elizabethan poet whom Winters elevated to 'one of the most important lyric poets of the age', and penned a glowing review of Winters's *Collected Poems* (1952), as well as an admiring essay on the work of one of Winters's best students, the poet-critic J. V. Cunningham.[4] Particularly important was Williams's relationship with another 'ardent disciple' of Winters, Alan Swallow, a poet and Winters's publisher.[5] After studying with Robert Penn Warren and Cleanth Brooks at Louisiana State University in the late 1930s and early 1940s – around the time Jean Stafford and Robert Lowell were in Baton Rouge – Swallow went on to 'establish the University of Denver as another center of creative writing that adhered to the classical style', along with Stanford, where Winters was based.[6] Anthony Hutchison shows how 'a modern classical style in both prose and poetry [...] became institutionalized in the American West in a way that was quite distinct', thanks in large part to Swallow, who became 'the first head of the creative writing program' at Denver in 1947.[7] Williams started his undergraduate career at Denver in 1946 and soon after 'began work as an assistant at the Swallow Press', during which time he 'absorbed New Critical and classical doctrine both from his mentor and from Swallow Press reissues of critical works by figures such as Allen Tate and Winters'. After completing his PhD at the University of Missouri – the same institution as Stoner – Williams returned to Denver in 1955 as an assistant professor in English, and shortly thereafter 'took over as director of the department's creative writing program', ensuring that the university remained a 'hub' for the classical style.[8]

Winters was among those midcentury critics who thought that 'the novel in our time is nearly dead', as he put it in a 1956 essay.[9] He was also one of the first critics to outline a specifically American literary tradition, although he did so in largely negative terms. His 1936 book *Maule's Curse* was 'a milestone in critical studies of American literature' and also 'one of the most far-reaching indictments of American writing ever leveled'.[10] As Russell Riseling explains:

> *Maule's Curse* presents Winters's view of American literature as an obscurantist tradition laboring under an 'allegorical' vision derived from New England Puritanism. The major symptom of this burden is an incapacity to distinguish subjective vision from either objective fact or metaphysical reality.[11]

What Winters calls the 'New England mind' conceives of human conduct as predetermined, reducing human experience to an allegory and denying 'the importance of the whole subject of morality'.[12] A version of Winters's idea of the 'Puritan' roots of American literature became integral to key works of early American Studies, by Richard Chase, R. W. B. Lewis, and others.[13] Twenty-five years after the publication of *Maule's Curse*, we find Williams restating Winters's argument when, in a 1961 essay, he suggests that the 'New England Calvinist habit of mind' has had a 'pervasive and profound' influence on American culture.[14] According to the Puritan perspective, man's fate is 'wholly predetermined' and all experience is 'finally allegorical,' Williams writes, a 'never-ending contest between Good and Evil'.[15]

Some midcentury critics who found the 'Puritan origins' of American literature lacking in nuance and intellectual complexity, such as Trilling, looked to Henry James's cosmopolitan fiction as a counterpoint and alternative model of moral subtlety and difficulty.[16] In Winters's criticism, however, James's fiction occupies a less certain place. Winters praises James's focus on 'ethical choice and [. . .] its consequences', but also criticises his attempts in his fiction to create 'the illusion of unhampered choice' (he is discussing *The Portrait of a Lady*).[17] "There is possibly greater educative value [. . .] in suffering the consequences of an ill-judged but unhampered choice than in any other department of experience,' Winters acknowledges, but 'the person whose choice is normally unhampered may often appear to have an abominably facile existence in the eyes of him whose life is an unbroken [. . .] endurance of necessity, whose primary virtue must of necessity be fortitude'.[18] In Winters's critical schema, we have at one end Puritan predestination and at the other Jamesian 'unhampered choice'; the former leads to moral simplicity and the latter to 'obscurity'. And this obscurity is compounded, Winters writes, by the 'theory regarding the development of his plot' that emerges in James's later fiction. This theory holds that 'the omniscient author, the historical explicator, should disappear, and that the reader should proceed through the novel by way of the minds of his characters' – an early example of 'the stream-of-consciousness convention'.[19] 'The prose generated by this method is almost as impressionistic and fragmentary as possible,' writes Winters, abandoning the 'virtues' of narrative and exposition and therefore, ironically, falling foul of the same confusion of 'subjective vision' and 'objective fact' as the puritanical 'New England mind' (thus Williams in his 1961 essay can label James a 'transformed Calvinist').[20]

Winters calls for a return to the virtues of narrative and exposition. 'The convention which I should recommend [to the novelist] is that of the first-rate biography or history (Johnson's *Lives*, for example, or Hume, or Macaulay) instead of the various post-Joycean conventions now prevalent,' he writes. 'Exposition may be made an art; so may historical summary; in fact, the greatest prose in existence is that of the greatest expository writers. The novel should not forego these sources of strength.'[21] In *Stoner*, Williams takes up Winters's idea of the novel, eschewing Jamesian 'obscurity' and modernist experimentation in favour of an unadorned style and tightly structured plot. The novel's opening is a bold model of exposition and historical summary:

> William Stoner entered the University of Missouri as a freshman in the year 1910, at the age of nineteen. Eight years later, during the height of World War I, he received his Doctor of Philosophy degree and accepted an instructorship at the same University, where he taught until his death in 1956. (1)

Echoing Winters, Williams in a 1981 interview suggests that a novel 'is in a sense "A Life". The birth, living and death doesn't have to be explicit [. . .] but I think it has to be about birth, living, and death. I think any good novel ends with a kind of death.'[22] *Stoner* follows Winters's blueprint quite precisely in this regard: the novel will be the biography of, and a kind of eulogy for, its protagonist. In the seminar, the clash between Stoner and Walker stages a confrontation between a classicism derived from Winters on the one hand and Romanticism on the other; between a sensibility esteeming clarity and rationality and a 'florid and imprecise' literary mode unmoored from tradition. Other midcentury minor novels stage similar encounters between characters representing contrasting literary sensibilities, thereby dramatising the ambivalent, transitional nature of the minor novel's own aesthetic project – we might think of Vincent and Buxton, or Edward and Stitch.[23] The seminar clash is not pitched as a struggle between Good and Evil, and so is not simplistically allegorical in the way of the 'New England mind'. Stoner begrudgingly admires Walker's force of personality and power of invention, while his own motivations for failing the young man are muddied by his attraction to Driscoll; he doesn't himself seem to know where his anger comes from, and whether he is defending academic integrity or a woman's honour.

Also at stake in the seminar, and related to Williams's interest in classicism, is a particular conception of tragedy. We have seen in previous chapters how pervasive was 'thinking tragically', in Deborah Nelson's phrase, to midcentury intellectual and political culture, whether in bleak liberalism or Southern Agrarianism, and whether drawing on psychoanalysis or Christianity.[24] In different ways, midcentury intellectuals turned to tragedy to stress the limits of man's self-knowledge and freedom. Yet, ironically, Ian Afflerbach writes, 'over the same years when American intellectuals began describing liberal politics as constitutively tragic, literary critics began to worry that tragedy, as a dramatic form, was no longer possible', a worry most famously articulated in George Steiner's *The Death of Tragedy* (1961).[25] The death of tragedy and the death of the novel theses emerged as twin responses to what was perceived by many as the transformations in the structure of society and the nature of human subjectivity wrought by the expansion of the liberal federal state on the one hand and the political travesties of Stalinism and fascism on the other. As Afflerbach puts it, 'anxieties about the exhaustion of tragedy' became freighted with 'political anxieties about the exhaustion of individual agency'.[26]

Afflerbach shows how Arthur Miller's *Death of a Salesman* (1949) became 'the locus for midcentury debates about the end of tragic form'. 'From its opening run,' Afflerbach writes, 'the decisive question surrounding *Salesman* was whether Willy Loman's humble status and plight qualify him as a tragic hero.'[27] Reviewing the play in *Partisan*, Eleanor Clark was among those who found the drama 'strangely lacking in a sense either of pity or of illumination'.[28] The audience are 'expressly invited to indulge the tragic sense and to carry away a conception of man's fate as though from a production of *Oedipus Rex*,' Clark writes; 'what they have carried away instead is just [a] curious, rankling gloom'. The play 'is not a tragedy at all,' she continues, 'but an ambitious piece of confusionism' peddling a well-worn social critique familiar from 'the party line literature of the thirties': 'It is, of course, the capitalist system that has done Willy in.'[29] Perhaps, Clark wonders, 'the tragic sense with all it has undergone from the facts of recent times needs some entirely different, some unimaginably new appeal.'[30] The debate over whether the play fulfilled the classical criteria for tragedy or whether it offered an 'entirely different' conception of the form was complicated further by Miller's own revisionary theory of the tragic, outlined in an essay published during the play's first run on Broadway. Miller dismisses the Aristotelian emphasis on the nobility or 'rank of the tragic hero' as nothing more than 'a clinging to the outward forms of tragedy', arguing that 'the common man is as apt a subject for tragedy in its highest sense as kings were'.[31] More radically, Miller also counters the classical idea that tragedies are necessarily pessimistic because they provoke pathos; 'in truth,' he writes, 'tragedy implies more optimism in its author than does comedy', because in tragedy 'lies the belief [. . .] in perfectibility of man'.[32]

The seminar scene discloses how *Stoner* participates in the debates over the possibility and definition of tragedy that emerged at midcentury, and suggests how the novel might be read in light of Miller's 'heterodox' conception of the genre.[33] As others have noted, Driscoll's presentation is closely based on an essay by J. V. Cunningham on the 'Donatan Tradition' and Shakespearean tragedy, included in his study *Woe or Wonder*, published in 1951 by Alan Swallow's press.[34] Cunningham makes a careful case for the classical and medieval sources of Shakespearean tragedy, arguing that Shakespeare's emphasis on 'wonder' – 'that state of overpowering surprise, the shocked limit of feeling' – as an emotion properly roused by tragedy, alongside those familiar from Aristotle of fear and pity, builds on a rich and well-established literary tradition.[35] He also restates the classical, Aristotelian idea that 'the field of tragedy will be the state, since men of high rank are rulers of the state', and that therefore tragedy 'will involve not private life and private feeling [. . .] but public life and public feeling'.[36] The 'greatness of the tragic response' elicited by the drama will be in proportion to 'the greatness of the persons and actions,' Cunningham writes; tragedies which take an 'historical' event as their plot are best, because they will have 'the compelling absoluteness of accomplished fact'.[37] Gesturing in an aside to the broader midcentury debate regarding the shifting definition of tragedy, Cunningham suggests that '*Death of a Salesman* is not a tragedy in the old sense', because it is the largely private downfall of an unremarkable man. 'One might conjecture there is something else involved,' writes Cunningham: 'a radical difference in the nature of the tragic effect' – as, indeed, Miller himself suggests in his essay on tragedy and the common man.[38]

In his 1956 essay, Winters engages at some length with Cunningham's criteria for tragedy and considers their implications for the novel, once more twinning the death of the novel and death of tragedy theses. Cunningham's preference for tragedy based on historical events chimes with Winters's championing of historical summary and biography as resources for the midcentury novelist; 'historiographers, more than any other writers of prose narrative', are best placed to write tragedy, Winters suggests.[39] Cunningham's requirement that 'tragic characters must be great, and this means of high rank', meanwhile, leads Winters to draw a contrast between modernism's aesthetics and his own idea of the novel.[40] The 'chief virtue' of a noble tragic character, Winters suggests, 'lies in his power to generalize the subject, to extend its significance beyond the limits of particular experience'.[41] Such a character is not likely to feature in the post-Joycean novel, which is interested not in universality but 'particularity', Winters lamenting the fact that 'the particular detail and the progression from detail to detail by pure association have largely taken charge of the novel'.[42] He concludes by suggesting that Cunningham's key requirements for tragedy – a 'great' hero, a historical plot – constitute the differences between tragedy and comedy and therefore 'the essential differences [. . .] between a major and a minor form'.[43]

In the seminar, there is, Leo Robson writes, 'no doubt where Williams's sympathies lie': he is clearly on the side of Katherine, Cunningham, and classicism, and the novel as a whole adheres closely to the principles Winters outlines.[44] But Williams also departs from his mentor in ways that reflect the broader debate surrounding the changing character and continuing viability of tragedy at midcentury. Stoner is not a great man but an unremarkable one, all but forgotten by the time of his death. As the allusion to the war in the novel's opening suggests, 'public' events do encroach upon the narrative, and, if not concerned directly with matters of the state, *Stoner* is, like other minor novels considered in previous chapters, preoccupied with the university, and with the changing institutional structure of the literary field.[45] But it is ultimately a novel of private life and private feeling, of Stoner's personal battles with his wife and his colleagues, of his great love affair with his subject and with Katherine. 'There are wars and defeats and victories of the human race that are not military and that are not recorded in the annals of history' (36), Stoner's first academic mentor tells him, persuading him to keep to his studies rather than enlist. The novel will tell a small history of one man's life, a history unlikely to be chronicled by Winters's biographer or historiographer. Stoner's choices – to fail Walker and to stick to his guns when challenged by Lomax, and to pursue his affair with Katherine – will lead to the end of his career and his marriage. But they also grant him a kind of quiet, tragic nobility – displaying the virtue of 'fortitude', to use Winters's word – such that he becomes a kind of everyman character, his experience open to 'generalization' in the way Winters describes in his discussion of tragic heroes. Stoner becomes not the 'common man' of Miller's 'optimistic' tragedy but rather, as Williams puts it in a letter to his agent, 'a kind of saint'.[46] His story comes to look like a new variety of minor tragedy, one that accedes to the notion that the grandeur of traditional tragedy is no longer available, but that suggests a smaller history might still be told, that a life lived at Stoner's scale might still sustain a narrative and elicit 'wonder'. Stoner himself feels 'a sense of wonder' (104) whenever he thinks of the single, slim book he has written, a minor work of criticism based on his doctoral dissertation. At the end of the novel, when he is on his deathbed, Stoner returns to the book, and it again elicits emotions Cunningham suggests are suitable for tragedy:

> It hardly mattered to him that the book was forgotten and that it served no use, and the question of its worth at any time seemed trivial [. . .] He let his finger rifle through the pages and felt a tingling as if those pages were alive [. . .] he was minutely aware of it, and he waited until it contained him, until *the old excitement that was like terror* fixed him where he lay. (278, emphasis mine)

Rediscovered

Stoner therefore shares a number of points of contact with midcentury minor novels surveyed in earlier chapters, but I have saved discussion of it for this final chapter because it is also an outlier. No other novel previously mentioned has been rediscovered in quite the way that *Stoner* has; indeed, the most remarkable thing about the book is surely the new lease of life it has enjoyed in recent years. Between its first publication by Viking in 1965 – when it sold only 1,700 copies – and the early 2000s, the novel had 'a kind of underground life', as Williams put it in a 1981 interview, its author becoming known as a 'writer's writer', 'mildly famous for not being famous' (Richard Stern enjoyed – or endured – a similar reputation: 'I was a has-been before I'd been a been,' he quipped).[47] Only 'briefly noted' in the *New York Times*, *Stoner* was mostly ignored by critics when it first appeared, with the exception of Irving Howe, who praised the novel in the *New Republic*:

> Given the quantity of fiction published in this country each year, it seems unavoidable that most novels should be ignored and that among these a few should nonetheless be works of distinction. *Stoner*, a book that received very little notice upon its appearance several months ago, is, I think, such a work: serious, beautiful and affecting [. . .] Mr. Williams writes with discipline and strength: he is devoted to the sentence as a form, and free from the allure of imagery [. . .] I think there should be a few thousand people in this country who will find pleasure in the book.[48]

Howe's would be the first of a number of essays lamenting the novel's obscurity. As Charles Shields puts it, 'Every decade or so, the name "John Williams" and *Stoner* would reemerge, the way a summer drought sometimes reveals a forgotten edifice standing on the bottom of an ancient lake'.[49] 'Why isn't this book famous?' asked C. P. Snow in 1973, reviewing a reissued edition of *Stoner* published by Pocket Books.[50] Writing in *Ploughshares* in 1981, in a laudatory survey of Williams's career, Dan Wakefield decried the fact that the novel was again 'out of print'.[51] It was picked up once more by an admiring editor at Arkansas University Press in 1993. 'So I seem to be returning to where I began, with a smallish press,' Williams said, alluding to his early poetry and first novel, *Nothing But the Night* (1948), published by Swallow Press.[52] But that wasn't the end of the novel's journey. In 2003, *Stoner* was reissued in the UK by Vintage, and in 2006 in the US in the New York Review Books (NYRB) Classics series, whose editor, Edwin Frank, had been tipped off about the novel by an Upper East Side bookseller.[53] When it was translated into French by the novelist Anna Gavalda, it became a bestseller; the same thing happened in the Netherlands.[54] As the novel made waves in Europe, it was hailed in the US as 'The Greatest American Novel You've Never Heard Of' in the *New Yorker*; writing in the *New York Times* after the NYRB Classics edition appeared, Morris Dickstein described Williams's book as 'something rarer than a great novel – it is a perfect novel, so well told and beautifully written, so deeply moving, that it takes your breath away'.[55] To one commentator on NPR, *Stoner*'s second coming was so remarkable as to seem 'mysterious, even alchemical'.[56]

'It's not an easy book to pitch,' Frank admits; 'a midcentury, midwestern novel about a man who is a medievalist and whose life is a failure'.[57] When she received a draft manuscript in 1964, Williams's agent, Marie Roddell, agreed. 'I may be totally wrong,' she wrote to Williams, 'but I don't see this as a novel with high potential sale. Its technique of almost unrelieved narrative is out of fashion, and its theme to the average reader could well be depressing.'[58] Roddell was right that Williams's plain style was out of step with the major trends in contemporary fiction and the tastes of the literary marketplace. As discussed in the previous chapter, 1964 saw the publication of Saul Bellow's *Herzog* (also by Viking), a novel that fits into Mark McGurl's category of 'high cultural pluralist fiction' and whose professorial protagonist is, Leo Robson writes, a 'Romantic by allegiance – the author of a book on Romanticism, at work on a second – and by inclination', and therefore the polar opposite of Williams's stoic medievalist.[59] Nor did Williams's novel belong to another major strain of fiction emerging in the 1960s – postmodernism, or what McGurl more narrowly defines as 'technomodernism'.[60] Williams dismissed the metafiction of John Barth and others as a 'dead end', complaining how 'the so-called "new novel", whatever that is, almost tries to make fun of the idea of story'.[61] Rather than resort to what he called 'gimmicks and inventions', Williams conceived of narrative as 'moving primarily upon that level on which we are moved in life'.[62] The fact that Williams and Barth were pursuing very different, ultimately incomparable ideas of the novel was illustrated in 1973, when the two shared a National Book Award (for Williams's historical novel *Augustus* and Barth's metafictional trilogy *Chimera*), the first time the prize had been split.[63] Nor, despite the fact that he directed the creative writing program at

Denver, did Williams's approach fit with the literary styles McGurl suggests were being institutionalised in MFA programs across the country. His rigorous, 'rational' classical formalism didn't align with the program era's stress on indirect narrative dramatisation ('show don't tell') or on the importance of personal voice ('write what you know').[64] Another of *Stoner*'s admirers, the writer Steve Almond, recounts the experience of first reading the novel's starkly flat opening passage when it was reissued in the early 2000s. 'To understand how audacious I found this opening,' writes Almond, 'you would have to know how loyal I was, back then, to the dogma of the MFA program, the smothering exhortations to *show, don't tell*.'[65] As a teacher of creative writing, Williams took issue with the other old workshop chestnut, 'write what you know', bemoaning the fact that 'students got the idea that every work of fiction had to reflect *them*'.[66]

Stoner therefore did not adhere to the emerging categories of contemporary fiction. Nor was it suited to the kind of 'hype' campaign and publicity blitz that were, by the mid-1960s, becoming integral to the business of US publishing.[67] 'Rapidly corporatizing publishers [...] sought ever increasing returns on their investment in "literary authors",' Abram Foley explains:

> One strategy for increasing returns in corporate publishing is to publicize and promote a small handful of authors who are eager or at least willing to take on roles as literary celebrities and popular intellectuals. Consider that the two or three decades following World War II [...] produced the last profusion of what some critics have insisted on calling 'the Great American Novel.' Directly related to the idea of the great American novel is the great American novelist: Bellow, DeLillo, Ellison, Mailer, Morrison, Pynchon, and Roth, all of whom have been included as exemplary in critical books about either literary celebrity or the great American novel, and all of whom were published primarily by corporate publishing houses. The simultaneous emergence of these canonical figures and an increasingly profit-driven publishing industry is not coincidental.[68]

Notably, most of the writers on Foley's list also fit McGurl's category of 'high cultural pluralist fiction'. The exception is Pynchon (whose 'celebrity' status is also of a different order), who belongs among McGurl's technomodernists, and whose 1973 opus *Gravity's Rainbow* (also published by Viking) is representative of 'the encyclopaedic "meganovel" genre that came to dominate American fiction' and that can be classed as another iteration of the 'GAN'.[69] Dan Sinykin sketches a similar history of the 'conglomerate era' in American publishing.[70] 'Publishing houses expanded and, beginning in the 1960s, were purchased by one media conglomerate after another,' Sinykin writes, putting pressure on 'publishers to increase their profits'.[71] But cultural as well as financial capital was still crucial to the conglomerate house's business model. There remained 'pride' as well as 'profit in publishing prestigious books,' Sinykin notes, leading to 'the lionization of a particular kind of book':

> Publishers annually turn out a few such highly hyped books, whose authors have been paid outrageous advances, in the hope of achieving that ideal crossover of prestige and sales [. . .] The irrational exuberance these books inspire draws resources away from the so-called midlist, books that sell between ten thousand and a hundred thousand copies.[72]

Market conditions and changes within the structures of the publishing industry thus shaped the literary field in ways that pushed to the margins a novel like *Stoner* – albeit a comfortable margin, where Williams could make a living by teaching writing, a beneficiary of the program era if also a casualty of the conglomerate era. Such was the fate of other midcentury minor novelists – Trilling and Stern spent their entire careers teaching at Columbia and Chicago, respectively – and of the minor novel in general.

While *Stoner*'s neglect can therefore be understood in the context of postwar corporate publishing, the novel's rediscovery can be partly explained in relation to the 'backlash to conglomeration' that began in the 1990s.[73] Rather than a 'mysterious, even alchemical process', *Stoner*'s rediscovery was made possible by a set of changing dynamics and practices in the field of late twentieth-century US publishing. Lee Konstantinou and Dan Sinykin suggest that we think of the period between 1990 and 2007 as the 'independent' era of modern American publishing, in which emerged 'a movement of nonprofit publishing (Dalkey Archive, Feminist Press, Graywolf) and the rise of do-it-yourself (DIY) practices, made possible by desktop publishing and the Internet'.[74] The NYRB Classics series, which began in 1999, occupies a somewhat uncertain place in Konstantinou and Sinykin's map of independent publishing. Not a nonprofit but hardly a money-making enterprise either, the series started out in an office down the hall from the *New York Review of Books*, though it has always been editorially and financially independent of the magazine.[75] Hailed in 2008 as 'the characteristic publishing project of the decade', the series 'has made a specialty of rescuing and reviving all kinds of ignored or forgotten works in English or in translation', with a concentration on British and American mid-twentieth-century fiction and memoir, and newly commissioned translations of Easter European writers.[76] All titles in the series adhere to an unusual uniform design, composed of 'solid-colored spines and striking covers' with bold title-boxes, that 'give them a common identity,' Larry Rohter writes, 'in much the way that Blue Note Records releases look similar and encourage jazz fans to dip into the catalog' (indeed, Edwin Frank has compared the series to a vinyl record store).[77] Writing in 2015, in the twentieth-anniversary issue of *Bookforum*, Jonathan Lethem describes the 'miraculous [. . .] persistence' of the NYRB Classics series as 'the best development in the world of books and writing during the twenty-year span' of the magazine's existence; 'there's really nothing to compare to its success'.[78] Readers will have spotted that I have quoted from a number of NYRB Classics; as well as *Stoner*, the series includes titles by Trilling, Stafford, and Stern.[79] The series has, in no small way, shaped the argument of this book.

There's nothing new about republishing old books.[80] As Lethem notes, 'the shelves of used bookstores are filled with the false starts and short reigns of similar "reissue" or "reintroduction" campaigns'.[81] Occasionally, such campaigns lead to lasting reassessments of a writer's work; we have seen, for example, how important were revisionary readings of Faulkner and James to midcentury literary culture. More recently, Virago Press's Modern Classics series was central to feminist scholarship's larger project in the 1970s through to the 1990s of 'recovering lost women writers'.[82] But while the feminist mission of Virago was explicit, and the reappraisal of Faulkner and James clearly linked to the effort to canonise modernism, it's less immediately clear quite what, or who, is being recuperated in the NYRB Classics series, or how the series speaks to the concerns and anxieties of early twenty-first-century literary culture more broadly.

The editors of *n+1* magazine pondered the series' significance in a 2008 piece entitled 'The Spirit of Revival'. The editorial begins by noting that the American reader in the early 2000s has become familiar with a number of 'canons' across their lifetime:

> You've read *The Great Gatsby*, if you went through high school English. And you probably read *Beloved*, if you went through college in the last twenty-five years. If you're in a book group, you've read *The Kite Runner* [. . .] All of these canons are pretty clear, if rarely discussed: the teen angst, high school English, college English, and short-term educational bestseller canons. There's a 'major prize' canon, too: if it won a Nobel, a National Book Award, or a Pulitzer, you put it on a mental list of books you either will read or talk about meaning to [. . .][83]

The NYRB Classics series is 'creating a new canon,' the editors suggest, one that is 'utterly outside academia, indifferent to professors' interests', and that 'seems ultimately to be based on a principled idea of the truly minor, overlooked, or forgotten book'. The series brings to the surface a 'cosmopolitan minor literature' that offers an alternative to the 'official' canon represented in the long-running Library of America series.[84] Speculating as to the series' impact on contemporary writing, they wonder whether it might inspire a 'new, minor direction to American literature, to counterbalance the tradition of the big American novel', reflecting 'a present-day writerly feeling that when it comes to influences, creators must look elsewhere than to the well-known old names – Kerouac, Joyce, Morrison – associated with canons that teen angst, the university, and even the Big Prizes of recent years have bequeathed us'.[85] I have similarly argued that the minor novel arose at midcentury in part as a response by writers to the burdensome influence of modernist authors freshly canonised by newly powerful critics who at the same time proclaimed the novel to be a dying form. Just as midcentury critics queried the relation between the state of contemporary fiction and the condition of the American polis, so too do the *n+1* editors consider what the recovery by the NYRB Classics series of a 'minor literature' says about American society in the early twenty-first century, suggesting that the series' success gestures to broader anxieties about canonicity and cultural authority in the internet age.[86] Writing just at the end of what Konstaniou and Sinykin call the 'independent period' in American publishing and the beginning of what they label the 'Amazonian' era, the editors suggest that the popularity of the series might be a reaction to 'Google's plan to scan all volumes in major American libraries', a plan that 'offers a sense of a tremendous future era of recovery and reuse' but that also threatens to be 'completely chaotic': 'it's a project in which no one could know, in the midst of so many millions of titles, what exactly to look for, or what should be new common knowledge'.[87] In such a world, the series' careful curation of hard-to-come-by novels is alluring. Rather than Google's vast databases, 'it is as if the older readers (and writers) of the *New York Review of Books* were pooling their after-dinner secret favorites in an aggregation that would be impossible for any individual to hold in mind'.[88] Suspicious of 'professors' interests' and sniffy about prizes and reading groups, the *n+1* editors are happy enough to leave the task of selecting the new canon to a group whose taste in books is beyond reproach – the readers and writers of a literary magazine.

The Minor Novel in the World

Stoner is 'our best-selling book', Frank notes in a 2016 interview with the *Paris Review*, and in some ways the novel is representative of the sensibility of the series.[89] In his introduction to *The Red Thread: Twenty Years of NYRB Classics* (2019), Frank describes what kind of list he was trying to put together in 1999:

> It couldn't primarily be a list of classics [. . .] Then again it shouldn't be a list of weird cult books or books of studied smallness that get deemed lost treasures or of books important or popular in their day and quaint and curious now or of great one-offs or of books that stand out because they are absolutely like nothing else. It couldn't be any of those things, because it had in a sense to be all of them.[90]

Looking back to the series' origins, Frank frames his project in the context of conglomeration. 'Years of mergers among corporate publishers and the imperative to look after the share price' had 'reshaped' the market, leading to 'books that had done well enough over the years' being 'cast aside in favor of new books that, such was the hope, would do much better, especially with the help of the marketing muscle of superstores'. Thus a 'resource' for his new series would be 'the literature hidden away in publishers' backlists'. Frank's series, however, is composed of not just 'old books' but 'new translations', and so another resource was 'the literature of the world out there, where there were all sorts of extraordinary books that had never even been translated into English'. It is significant in this regard that Frank frames the series' emergence and impetus not only in relation to conglomeration in American publishing, but also to a wider narrative of American hegemony prevalent in the 1990s. A 'robustly complacent' sense of US 'triumphalism' had taken hold by 1999, Frank notes:

> [The] new, now-unrivaled ascendancy of the United States meant that all sorts of old bothersome problems, essentially the rest of the world, could be conveniently forgotten [. . .] and the already pronounced tendency to pay no attention to books from outside the Anglosphere, happily indulged.[91]

The series challenges this narrative in its inclusion of an array of titles by writers from the former Soviet Union and by Communist writers from across Europe. And yet Frank was keen that his list be 'recognizable as a series', despite the diverse geographic and linguistic origins of it authors. This uniformity is achieved in part through the strong, coherent design which makes no distinction between English-language and translated works. But Frank also suggests that an important aspect of the recuperative project of the series has been to 'translate' or recontextualise English-language, and especially American, writing into a European and even world literary field, pushing back against the assumed centrality of American literature and culture and blurring the boundaries between Anglophone and non-English texts – that is, to make American literature more minor.[92] In this regard, *Stoner* is again a representative text. Williams's novel is that rare breed: an American novel that has sold better in translation that in English; or, to put it another way, an American novel more at home in translation than its mother tongue. If this isn't quite the deterritorialisation of language described by Deleuze and Guattari, it does signal another way in which the series might be said to bring into being, as the *n+1* editors put it, an alternative canon of 'minor literature', one that challenges a narrative of US hegemony that stretched from the midcentury to the 1990s by casting the American novel back into the world.

Notes

1. John Williams, *Stoner* [1965] (New York: New York Review Books Classics, 2003), 130. Subsequent references are given in parentheses in the text.
2. Anthony Hutchison, 'Cultivating the Classical Style: The Stanford-Denver Creative Writing Axis', *Modern Fiction Studies*, Vol. 66, No. 3 (Fall 2020), pp. 474–98 (474).
3. Charles Shields, *The Man Who Wrote the Perfect Novel: John Williams,* Stoner, *and the Writing Life* (Austin: University of Texas Press, 2018), 78.
4. Ibid., 95. See John Williams, 'J. V. Cunningham: The Major and the Minor', *Arizona Quarterly*, Vol. 6, No. 2 (Summer 1950), pp. 132–46.
5. Leo Robson, 'John Williams and the Canon That Might Have Been', *New Yorker*, 18 March 2019.
6. Hutchison, 'Cultivating the Classical Style', 481.
7. Ibid., 481, 482.
8. Ibid., 483.
9. Yvor Winters, 'Problems for the Modern Critic of Literature', *Hudson Review*, Vol. 9, No. 3 (Autumn 1956), pp. 325–86 (352).
10. Russell Reising, *The Unusable Past: Theory and the Study of American Literature* (London: Routledge, 1986), 60. *Maule's Curse* is the second volume of Winters's critical trilogy, *In Defense of Reason* (1947).
11. Ibid., 58.
12. Yvor Winters, *Maule's Curse: Seven Studies in the History of American Obscurantism* (Norfolk, CT: New Directions, 1938), 174.
13. See Reising, *The Useable Past*, 49–91.
14. John Williams, '"The 'Western"': Definition of Myth', *The Nation*, Vol. 193, No. 17, 18 November 1961, pp. 401–6.
15. Williams, '"The 'Western"', 402.
16. Reising, *The Useable Past*, 49.
17. Winters, *Maule's Curse*, 175, 178.
18. Ibid., 177–8.
19. Winters, 'Problems for the Modern Critic of Literature', 348; Winters, *In Defense of Reason* (London: Routledge, 1947), 37.
20. Winters, 'Problems for the Modern Critic of Literature', 348; Williams, '"The 'Western"', 402.
21. Winters, *In Defense of Reason*, 38.

22. Dan Wakefield, 'John Williams, Plain Writer', *Ploughshares*, Vol. 7, No. 3/4 (1981), pp. 9–22 (19).
23. My thinking here is in dialogue with Lawrence Buell's conception of 'observer-hero narrative', a genre of first person narrative structured around an 'encounter' between the narrator and a second figure who seems 'more intensely focused and more romantic by comparison'. Buell, 'Observer-Hero Narrative', *Texas Studies in Literature and Language*, Vol. 21, No. 1 (Spring 1979), pp. 93–111 (93).
24. Deborah Nelson, *Tough Enough: Arbus, Arendt, Didion, McCarthy, Sontag, Weil* (Chicago: University of Chicago Press, 2017), 24.
25. Ian Afflerbach, *Making Liberalism New: American Intellectuals, Modern Literature, and the Rewriting of a Political Tradition* (Baltimore: Johns Hopkins University Press, 2021), 130.
26. Afflerbach, *Making Liberalism New*, 130.
27. Ibid., 130, 133.
28. Eleanor Clark, 'Theater Chronicle: Old Glamour, New Gloom', *Partisan Review*, Vol. 16, No. 6 (June 1949), pp. 631–6 (631).
29. Ibid., 632–3.
30. Ibid., 631.
31. Arthur Miller, 'Tragedy and the Common Man' [1949], in *Death of a Salesman: Text and Criticism*, ed. by Gerald Weales (Harmondsworth: Penguin, 1996), pp. 143–7 (145, 143).
32. Ibid., 146–7.
33. Afflerbach, *Making Liberalism New*, 133.
34. See Mark Asquith, *Reading the Novels of John Williams: A Flaw of Light* (Lanham: Lexington Books, 2017), 97; Robson, 'John Williams and the Canon That Might Have Been'. D. G. Myers suggests that the character of Stoner is based on Cunningham. See 'Defeats and Victories Not Recorded in the Annals of History', *Commentary*, 14 September 2011.
35. J. V. Cunningham, *Woe or Wonder: The Emotional Effect of Shakespearian Tragedy* (Denver: Swallow Press, 1951), 20.
36. Ibid., 38.
37. Ibid., 35, 39.
38. Ibid., 38.
39. Winters, 'Problems for the Modern Critic of Literature', 343.
40. Cunningham, *Woe or Wonder*, 38.
41. Winters, 'Problems for the Modern Critic of Literature', 344.
42. Ibid., 350.
43. Ibid., 343.
44. Robson, 'John Williams and the Canon that Might Have Been'.
45. On the novel's portrayal of medievalism, see Bruce Holsinger, 'Medievalization Theory: From Tocqueville to the Cold War', *American Literary History*, Vol. 22, No. 4 (Winter 2010), pp. 893–912. Holsinger describes *Stoner* as 'the novel of Cold War medievalism, a nuanced tragedy that rewrites the Middle Ages and its study into a parable of academic futility and self-defeat' (896). I touch on the revival of interest in the medieval and its importance to the New Critics in Chapter 3.
46. Quoted in Shields, *The Man Who Wrote the Perfect Novel*, 113.

47. Wakefield, 'John Williams, Plain Writer', 11; Christopher Tayler, 'I just let him have his beer', *London Review of Books*, Vol. 41, No. 24 (December 2019); Bruce Weber, 'Richard G. Stern, 84, Writer's Writer, Dies', *New York Times*, 25 January 2013, A19.
48. Irving Howe, 'The Virtues of Failure', *The New Republic*, 22 February 1966.
49. Charles Shields, *The Man Who Wrote the Perfect Novel*, 250.
50. C. P. Snow, 'Good Man and Foes', *Financial Times*, 24 May 1973.
51. Wakefield, 'John Williams, Plain Writer', 11.
52. Quoted in Shields, *The Man Who Wrote the Perfect Novel*, 243.
53. See Edwin Frank, 'How the NYRB Chooses Its Reissues: The Story of Stoner', interview by Yongxi Wu, *Lit Hub*, 4 April 2016. Available at: https://lithub.com/how-the-nyrb-chooses-its-reissues-the-story-of-stoner/.
54. See Claire Cameron, 'A Forgotten Bestseller: The Saga of John Williams's Stoner', *The Millions*, 6 June 2013. Available at: https://themillions.com/2013/06/a-forgotten-bestseller-the-saga-of-john-williamss-stoner.html.
55. Tim Kreider, 'The Greatest American Novel You've Never Heard Of', *New Yorker*, 20 October 2013; Morris Dickstein, 'The Inner Lives of Men', *New York Times*, 17 June 2007.
56. Annalisa Quinn, 'Book News: *Stoner* Created Little Buzz In 1965, But Ignites In 2013', The Two-Way, *NPR*, 9 December 2013. Available at: https://www.npr.org/sections/thetwo-way/2013/12/09/249698007/book-news-stoner-created-little-buzz-in-1965-but-ignites-in-2013.
57. Quoted in Shields, *The Man Who Wrote the Perfect Novel*, 251.
58. Quoted in Shields, *The Man Who Wrote the Perfect Novel*, 150.
59. Robson, 'John Williams And The Canon That Might Have Been'.
60. See Mark McGurl, *The Program Era: Postwar Fiction and the Rise of Creative Writing* (Cambridge, MA: Harvard University Press, 2009), 32.
61. Wakefield, 'John Williams, Plain Writer', 18.
62. Quoted in Shields, *The Man Who Wrote the Perfect Novel*, 168.
63. See Eric Pace, '2 Book Awards Split for First Time', *New York Times*, 11 April 1973, 38; Shields, *The Man Who Wrote the Perfect Novel*, 223–7.
64. See McGurl, *The Program Era*, 34, 77–182.
65. Steve Almond, 'The Man at the Top of the Stairs, On Rendering the Inner Life', *Ploughshares*, Vol. 46, No. 4 (Winter 2020–1), pp. 7–20 (10). Emphasis original.
66. Wakefield, 'John Williams, Plain Writer', 18. Emphasis original.
67. On the history of postwar publishing in the US, see Evan Brier, *A Novel Marketplace: Mass Culture, the Book Trade, and Postwar American Fiction* (Philadelphia: University of Pennsylvania Press, 2010). On twenty-first-century developments, see John Thompson, *Merchants of Culture: The Publishing Business in the Twenty-First Century* (Cambridge: Polity, 2012).
68. Foley, *The Editor Function: Literary Publishing in Postwar America* (Minneapolis: University of Minnesota Press, 2021), 8–9.
69. Brian McHale, 'Break, Period, Interregnum', *Twentieth Century Literature*, Vol. 57, No. 3/4, (Fall/Winter 2011), pp. 328–40 (331), quoted in Foley, *The Editor Function*, 14. On the history of the idea of the 'GAN', see Lawrence Buell, *The Dream of the Great American Novel* (Cambridge, MA: Harvard University Press, 2014).

70. See Dan Sinykin, 'The Conglomerate Era', *Contemporary Literature*, Vol. 58, No. 4 (Winter 2017), pp. 462–91. Sinykin dates the 'conglomerate era' from 'RCA's purchase of Random House in late 1965 to the release of the Amazon Kindle in 2007' (470). Brier dates it back to 1959, when 'Random House sold 30 percent of its shares to the public' (130).
71. Sinykin, 'The Conglomerate Era', 465.
72. Ibid., 471.
73. Lee Konstantinou and Dan Sinykin, 'Literature and Publishing, 1945–2020', *American Literary History*, Vol. 33, No. 2 (Summer 2021), pp. 225–43 (237).
74. Ibid. The period between 2007 and the present they call 'Amazonian', reflecting the impact not only of the Kindle and e-books, but also of the rise of self-published texts on the Amazon website. See Mark McGurl, *Everything and Less: The Novel in the Age of Amazon* (New York: Verso, 2021).
75. See Larry Rohter, '*New York Review of Books* Fills a Niche by Reviving Forgotten Works', *New York Times*, 7 August 2015.
76. Anon., 'The Spirit of Revival', *n+1*, Issue 6: Mainstream (Winter 2008). Available at: https://www.nplusonemag.com/issue-6/the-intellectual-situation/the-spirit-of-revival/; Rohter, '*New York Review of Books* Fills a Niche by Reviving Forgotten Works'.
77. Aida Ylanan, 'Cover to Cover: The Colors of NYRB Classics', *Los Angeles Times*, 27 December 2018. Available at: https://www.latimes.com/projects/la-et-jc-nyrb-covers/; Rohter, '*New York Review of Books* Fills a Niche by Reviving Forgotten Works'. On the series' design, see also Rick Poynor, 'Picture a Story', *Eye Magazine*, Issue 66 (Winter 2007). Available at: https://www.eyemagazine.com/opinion/article/picture-a-story-66.
78. Jonathan Lethem, 'They've Got Reissues', *Bookforum*, Vol. 21, No. 4 (December/January 2015).
79. Richard Stern's 1973 novel *Other Men's Daughters* was reissued in the series in 2017.
80. 'Selling old texts in new clothes', D.-M. Withers writes, 'is a well-established commercial practice in publishing, as old as the modern industry itself'. *Virago Reprints and Modern Classics: The Timely Business of Feminist Publishing* (Cambridge: Cambridge University Press, 2021), 1.
81. Lethem, 'They've Got Reissues'.
82. Jane Garrity, 'Found and Lost: The Politics of Modernist Recovery', *Modernism/modernity*, Vol. 15, No. 4, (November 2008), pp. 803–12 (803). See also Garrity, 'Modernist Women's Writing: Beyond the Threshold of Obsolescence', *Literature Compass*, Vol. 10, No. 1 (2013), pp. 15–29. On Virago, see Withers, *Virago Reprints and Modern Classics*. See also Urmila Seshagiri, 'Making it New: Persephone Books and the Modernist Project', *Modern Fiction Studies*, Vol. 59, No. 2 (Summer 2013), pp. 241–87.
83. Anon., 'The Spirit of Revival'.
84. In fact, the division between the two 'canons' is now less clear-cut: all of Jean Stafford's novels and three of John Williams's novels now appear both as NYRB Classics and in the Library of America.
85. Anon., 'The Spirit of Revival'. For a recent response to the editorial's conception of 'the minor', see Andrew Martin, 'The Spirit of Revival', *The Drift*, Issue 7, 14 June 2022. Available at: https://www.thedriftmag.com/the-spirit-of-revival/.

86. Discussing what the novel's resurgent popularity reveals about the contemporary academy, John Plotz speculates that *Stoner*'s 'ascendancy [. . .] hints at the pessimism that many currently have about the scholarly capacity to look beyond the campus, to shine a light outward to the world at large'. Plotz, 'Review of *The Man Who Wrote the Perfect Novel*, by Charles Shields', *Western American Literature*, Vol. 54, No. 3 (Fall 2019), pp. 331–3 (333).
87. On Google's digitisation of books, see Deanna Marcum and Roger C. Schonfeld, *Along Came Google: A History of Library Digitization* (Princeton: Princeton University Press, 2021).
88. Anon., 'The Spirit of Revival'.
89. Edwin Frank, 'What a Good Book Can Be: An Interview with Edwin Frank', interview by Susannah Hunnewell, *Paris Review*, 7 April 2016. Available at: https://www.theparisreview.org/blog/2016/04/07/what-a-good-book-can-be-an-interview-with-edwin-frank/.
90. Edwin Frank, 'Introduction', in Frank (ed.), *The Red Thread: Twenty Years of NYRB Classics: A Selection* (New York: New York Review Books Classics, 2019).
91. Ibid.
92. Of course, translation is also often associated with 'cultural as well as political homogenization,' Rebecca Walkowitz notes. But while this may sometimes be true for texts translated into English, I suggest that the series' blend of English-language and translated works makes for a new kind of heterogeneity, peripheralising, 'provincialising', or at least decentring Anglo-American texts. Walkowitz, *Born Translated: The Contemporary Novel in an Age of World Literature* (New York: Columbia University Press, 2015), 93. On 'provincialising' English, see Dipesh Chakrabarty, *Provincializing Europe: Postcolonial Thought and Historical Difference* (Princeton: Princeton University Press, 2000), also cited by Walkowitz. See also Emily Apter, *The Translation Zone: A New Comparative Literature* (Princeton: Princeton University Press, 2006).

Coda: Towards a Minor Criticism

The novelists discussed in this book pursued an odd sort of ambition. They acceded to the notion that the novel was in crisis or decline and followed closely the diagnoses and remedies provided them by influential literary critics and intellectuals. Yet, rather than finding the notion that the novel was now diminished disillusioning, they discovered within it the grounds for a certain kind of aesthetic freedom. Instead of submitting to or defiantly resisting the opinion of the critics, the novelists surveyed attempted a subtler, more reflexive dialogue with their ideas. The project of the minor novel was a paradoxical one; at midcentury, what one might hope to write, these novelists suggest, was a promising failure.

Given that the minor novel didn't aspire to great things, it would be strange if I claimed to be making in this book a major contribution to the field. Not intending to redraw the map of postwar American fiction, I have instead tried to trace an unacknowledged byway, one that in places follows the contours of well-trodden critical terrain but which also leads away from better-known routes and landmarks. The novelists discussed in this book asked, what kind of novel might be possible after we've given up on greatness, on masterpieces, on living up to expectations? In that same spirit, I have tried to consider what kind of appreciation we might afford these novels when we defer the routines of critique; or, what sort of criticism comes into view when we put to the side the ambition of the critical intervention (what other than a contribution might we make?).

'The language of the scholarly intervention has a way of ossifying hunches into convictions,' writes Pardis Dabashi.[1] In recent years, many critics have explored the possibility of critical modes more at ease with hunches, speculations, and intuition, and less committed to certainty and novelty, less guarded about appearing naïve or gauche, and less worried about the risk of getting it wrong – of a criticism that 'does not even try to clinch the case', as Wai Chee Dimock puts it.[2] These 'lower-pitched' critical modes have emerged in response to a growing disenchantment with 'certain "strong" theoretical habits of thought in literary studies', in particular those associated with symptomatic or paranoid reading – 'that is, to interpretive modes whose primary aim is to expose the ruses of ideology [. . .] or otherwise penetrate the surfaces of texts to get at their truer, occulted depths'.[3] 'Like paranoia itself,' writes Heather Love, 'paranoid criticism tends to discover the same truth everywhere'; 'the result,' according to Toril Moi, 'is a radical narrowing of the literary critic's register of attitudes'.[4] What Eve Kosofsky Sedgwick called symptomatic reading's 'drama of exposure' has come to seem to many less dramatic and less revealing in recent years.[5] As alternatives, critics have outlined a range of 'modes of reading that attend to texts rather than plumb their depths': reparative, surface, and distant reading, 'thin description', 'weak theory', a revised formalism and an expanded version of book history (including work on the sociology of publishing, sampled briefly in the previous chapter).[6] Some of these modes call for the 'closest proximity and affective attunement' to their object of study, while others – especially those affiliated with literary sociology and digital humanities approaches – 'distance themselves from texts and from practices of close reading altogether'.[7] Most try to occupy 'a paradoxical space of minimal critical agency' in contrast to 'the portrait of the critic as heroic demystifier of ideology' familiar from critique's heyday.[8] This more 'modest' critical pose goes together with a desire for 'more collaborative, more curious, less insistent modes of critical engagement' and for a generous-spirited critical environment in which argument is understood 'as trial rather than verdict, as experiment rather than product'.[9] The plurality of approaches that have emerged as part of this 'postcritical turn' suggest that the 'method wars' being waged over the past couple decades have in fact been less about method than about a wish for an 'alternative ethos, mood, or disposition'.[10] Postcritique might be a question of critical 'comportment' as much as one of reading.[11]

'The mixing of critical and at least some postcritical methods has become something [early-career academics] take for granted,' Dabashi writes, even as the scarcity of permanent posts in the humanities means that these same scholars are forced to compete in 'the race for professional distinction' and participate in 'the prestige economy that [. . .] characterizes the contemporary humanities', and in which modesty of ambition and generosity of thinking are not often rewarded.[12] 'One cannot build a publishing career and gain professional security by writing essays and book proposals whose main claim are that "X critic got it right and I'm here to remind you"', as Dabashi puts it. 'Literary scholars often have to read ungenerously, if not manufacture disagreement, in order to create elbow room for their scholarship.'[13] Perhaps unsurprisingly, therefore, postcritique's influence can be felt most keenly at the borders of and beyond the academy, where these professional imperatives are not quite so urgent, and where there's a little more elbow room. The last few years have witnessed the emergence of a rich range of experiments blending creative and critical practice and combining scholarly and personal voice, by writers sometimes securely but often more loosely affiliated with universities. These have taken the form of 'experimental' criticism, group biography, memoir, and autotheory, and have tended to appear with trade or small presses, or in a new generation of online literary magazines.[14]

Contemporary critics 'are not the first, the only, or the last to wonder whether the form of expert writing literature departments require for credentialing is actually the one best suited to capture the forms of understanding and insight that these departments foster,' Emily Ogden writes.[15] In the preceding chapters, we have seen that most of the critics associated with the discipline's professionalisation at midcentury were at best ambivalent about their involvement with the university and uncertain about the new prestige afforded to literary criticism. 'I find I can take less and less criticism,' Lionel Trilling wrote to Allen Tate in 1942, 'unless it is written out of love or anger [. . .] The whole forward-looking en-masse kind of criticism' – they had been discussing Alfred Kazin's *On Native Grounds* (1942) – 'bores me more and more.'[16] Like many midcentury intellectuals, Trilling and Tate both liked to think of themselves as creative writers first and critics second ('Fiction is what

I've always had in mind,' Trilling confided to Newton Arvin that same year).[17] Trilling's doctoral thesis was an intellectual biography of Matthew Arnold that he published as a trade book, while his essays appeared not in academic journals but in little magazines, or as introductions to paperback editions of classic novels. After the Arnold book he said he never again wanted to get bogged down in a 'long absorbing' project; he preferred essays, he said, because 'you get in and you get out fast'.[18] What he really wanted to write was a *nouvelle*, a little novel, or, failing that, a series of '*nouvelles* of biography'; Wordsworth, Keats, and Byron were the subjects he had in mind.[19] Anything but a monograph.

In this book, I have taken up some familiar tools of critique to pursue a modest ambition – to better understand some largely forgotten novels which I have suggested might be usefully grouped together as belonging to an under-appreciated strain of midcentury American fiction. Part intellectual history, part rescue mission, the book is also partly a fan letter to this group of obscure writers.[20] And in pursuing this ambition, I have also tried to demonstrate the ways in which the genre of the academic monograph – a genre falling out of favour in the new landscape of contemporary criticism – might take on something of the ethos of recent postcritical and experimental scholarship, and might also learn from the midcentury minor novel itself, a form aware of its own limited appeal and reach, and that tries to make something out of those limits. Midcentury minor novelists began with the idea that the novel was a genre with its best days behind it, and that to write a novel at midcentury was to fight a losing battle, or to embark upon a project fated for a kind of failure. To conceive of the monograph as a more minor genre would be to relinquish the idea of the major contribution or the significant intervention, and by doing so find out what other forms our ideas might take.

Notes

1. Pardis Dabashi, 'Introduction to "Cultures of Argument": The Loose Garments of Argument', *PMLA*, Vol. 135, No. 5 (2020), pp. 946–55 (951).
2. Wai Chee Dimock, 'Weak Theory: Henry James, Colm Tóibín, and W. B. Yeats', *Critical Inquiry*, Vol. 39, No. 4 (2013), pp. 732–53 (736).

3. Paul K. Saint-Amour, 'Weak Theory, Weak Modernism', *Modernism/Modernity*, Vol. 24, No. 3 (2018), pp. 437–59 (439).
4. Heather Love, 'Merely Ameliorative: Reading, Critical Affect, and the Project of Repair', in James English and Heather Love (eds), *Literary Studies and Human Flourishing* (Oxford: Oxford University Press, 2023), pp. 207–18 (208); Toril Moi, '"Nothing Is Hidden": From Confusion to Clarity; or, Wittgenstein on Critique', in Elizabeth Anker and Rita Felski (eds), *Critique and Postcritique* (Durham, NC: Duke University Press, 2017), pp. 31–49 (40).
5. Eve Kosofsky Sedgwick, 'Introduction', in *Touching Feeling: Affect, Pedagogy, Performativity* (Durham, NC: Duke University Press, 2003), 1–26 (8). See also Bruno Latour, 'Why Has Critique Run Out of Steam? From Matters of Fact to Matters of Concern', *Critical Inquiry*, Vol. 30, No. 2 (Winter 2004), pp. 225–48.
6. Stephen Best and Sharon Marcus, 'Surface Reading: An Introduction', *Representations*, Vol. 108, No. 1 (Fall 2009), pp. 1–21 (1–2). See Eve Kosofsky Sedgwick, 'Paranoid Reading and Reparative Reading, or, You're So Paranoid, You Probably Think This Essay is About You', in *Touching Feeling*, pp. 123–52; Best and Marcus, 'Surface Reading: An Introduction'; Franco Moretti, *Distant Reading* (New York: Verso, 2013); Heather Love, 'Close Reading and Thin Description', *Public Culture*, Vol. 25, No. 3 (Fall 2013), pp. 401–34; Saint-Amour, 'Weak Theory, Weak Modernism'; Marjorie Levinson, 'What Is New Formalism?', *PMLA*, Vol. 122, No. 2 (March 2007), pp. 558–69; Leah Price, 'From *The History of the Book* to a "History of the Book"', *Representations*, Vol. 108, No. 1 (November 2009), pp. 120–38.
7. James English and Heather Love, 'Introduction', in English and Love (eds), *Literary Studies and Human Flourishing*, pp. 1–24 (20); Heather Love, 'Close but Not Deep: Literary Ethics and the Descriptive Turn', *New Literary History*, Vol. 41, No. 2 (Spring 2010), pp. 371–91 (373).
8. Best and Marcus, 'Surface Reading: An Introduction', 17; Saint-Amour, 'Weak Theory, Weak Modernism', 439.
9. Maurice Lee, 'Feeling Fallible, Being Wrong', *American Literary History*, Vol. 34, No. 1 (Spring 2022), pp. 199–211 (200); Dabashi, 'Introduction to "Cultures of Argument"', 952. On the 'new modesty' of postcritical scholarship, see Jeffrey Williams, 'The New Modesty in Literary Criticism', *The Chronicle of Higher Education*, 5 January 2015.
10. Elizabeth Anker and Rita Felski, 'Introduction', in Anker and Felski (eds), *Critique and Postcritique*, pp. 1–28 (10). Heather Love describes Sedgwick's reparative reading as 'more a disposition than a method'. 'Merely Ameliorative', 208.
11. Lee, 'Feeling Fallible, Being Wrong', 208.
12. Dabashi, 'Introduction to "Cultures of Argument"', 948. On 'the race for professional distinction', see Winfried Fluck, 'The Humanities in the Age of Expressive Individualism and Cultural Radicalism', *Cultural Critique*, No. 40 (Autumn 1998), pp. 49–71, quoted in Dabashi (949).
13. Dabashi, 'Introduction to "Cultures of Argument"', 952.
14. On experimental criticism, see Beth Blum (ed.), 'Experimental Criticism', *ASAP/J*, 30 January 2023. Available at: https://asapjournal.com/tag/experimental-criticism/.

On contemporary group biographies, see Noelle Bodick, 'A Pool of One's Own: Group Biographies and the Female Friendship Vogue', *The Drift*, 28 January 2021. Available at: https://www.thedriftmag.com/a-pool-of-ones-own/. On autotheory, see Robyn Wiegman, 'Introduction: Autotheory Theory', *Arizona Quarterly*, Vol. 76, No. 1 (Spring 2020), pp. 1–14. On online literary culture, see Houman Barekat, Robert Barry and David Winters (eds), *The Digital Critic: Literary Culture Online* (New York: OR Books, 2017).

15. Emily Ogden, 'Questionnaire Answers', in Blum (ed.), 'Experimental Criticism', *ASAP/J*, 30 January 2023.
16. Lionel Trilling, Letter to Allen Tate, 27 November 1942, in Adam Kirsch (ed.), *Life in Culture: Selected Letters of Lionel Trilling* (New York: Farrar, Straus and Giroux, 2018), pp. 99–100 (100).
17. Lionel Trilling, Letter to Newton Arvin, 10 May 1942, in *Life in Culture*, pp. 92–6 (94).
18. Ibid., 94, 95.
19. Ibid., 95.
20. I have in mind Bruce Robbins's comment that postcritique makes for 'a criticism close to fandom'. Robbins, 'Not So Well Attached', *PMLA*, Vol. 132, No. 2 (2017), pp. 371–6.

BIBLIOGRAPHY

Aarons, Victoria, 'American Jewish Fiction', in John Duvall (ed.), *The Cambridge Companion to American Fiction After 1945* (Cambridge: Cambridge University Press, 2012), pp. 129–41.

Adams, Rachel, '"A Mixture of Delicious and Freak": The Queer Fiction of Carson McCullers', *American Literature*, Vol. 71, No. 3 (September 1999), pp. 551–83.

Afflerbach, Ian, 'On the Use and Abuse of Dostoevsky's *The Possessed* for Reading Tess Slesinger's *The Unpossessed*', *Notes and Queries*, Vol. 259, No. 1 (March 2014), pp. 135–6.

Afflerbach, Ian, *Making Liberalism New: American Intellectuals, Modern Literature, and the Rewriting of a Political Tradition* (Baltimore: Johns Hopkins University Press, 2021).

Aldridge, John, *After the Lost Generation: A Critical Study of the Writers of Two Wars* (New York: McGraw-Hill, 1951).

Aldridge, John, *In Search of Heresy: American Literature in an Age of Conformity* (New York: McGraw-Hill, 1956).

Allison, Leslie, 'Reading the West Sideways: Queering the Frontier in Jean Stafford's *The Mountain Lion*', *Studies in the Novel*, Vol. 49, No. 3 (Fall 2017), pp. 304–21.

Almond, Steve, 'The Man at the Top of the Stairs, On Rendering the Inner Life', *Ploughshares*, Vol. 46, No. 4 (Winter 2020–1), pp. 7–20.

Anderson, Amanda, *Bleak Liberalism* (Chicago: University of Chicago Press, 2016).

Anon., '*Con Spirito*', Vassar Encyclopedia. Available at: https://vcencyclopedia.vassar.edu/student-organizations-and-activities/student-publications/con-spirito/.

Anon., 'Eleanor Clark', Vassar Encyclopedia. Available at: https://vcencyclopedia.vassar.edu/distinguished-alumni/eleanor-clark/.

Anon., 'Review of *The Mountain Lion* by Jean Stafford', *Washington Post*, 9 March 1947, S10.

Anon., 'The Spirit of Revival', *n+1*, Issue 6: Mainstream (Winter 2008). Available at: https://www.nplusonemag.com/issue-6/the-intellectual-situation/the-spirit-of-revival/.

Apter, Emily, *The Translation Zone: A New Comparative Literature* (Princeton: Princeton University Press, 2006).

Arendt, Hannah, 'Franz Kafka: A Revaluation', *Partisan Review*, Vol. 11, No. 4 (Fall 1944), pp. 412–22.

Arendt, Hannah, 'What is Existenz Philosophy?', *Partisan Review*, Vol. 13, No. 1 (Winter 1946), pp. 34–56.

Ariail, Gregory, 'Kafka's Copycats: Imitation, Fabulism, and Late Modernism', PhD thesis, University of Michigan, 2018.

Asquith, Mark, *Reading the Novels of John Williams: A Flaw of Light* (Lanham: Lexington Books, 2017).

Auden, W. H., *The Age of Anxiety: A Baroque Eclogue* [1947] (Princeton: Princeton University Press, 2011).

Auden, W. H., Robert Gorham Davis, Clement Greenberg, Irving Howe, George Orwell, Karl Shapiro, William Barrett, Allen Tate, "The Question of the Pound Award", *Partisan Review*, Vol. 16, No. 5 (May 1949), pp. 512–22.

Barekat, Houman, Robert Barry, and David Winters (eds), *The Digital Critic: Literary Culture Online* (New York: OR Books, 2017).

Barnhisel, Greg, *James Laughlin, New Directions, and the Remaking of Ezra Pound* (Amherst: University of Massachusetts Press, 2005).

Barnhisel, Greg, *Cold War Modernists: Art, Literature, and American Cultural Diplomacy* (New York: Columbia University Press, 2015).

Barrett, William, "A Prize for Ezra Pound", *Partisan Review*, Vol. 16, No. 4 (April 1949), pp. 344–7.

Barrett, William, 'What is the "Liberal" Mind?', *Partisan Review*, Vol. 16, No. 3 (June 1949), pp. 331–6.

Baskin, Jason, *Modernism Beyond the Avant-Garde: Embodying Experience* (Cambridge: Cambridge University Press, 2018).

Battersby, Doug, *Troubling Late Modernism: Ethics, Feeling, and the Novel Form* (Oxford: Oxford University Press, 2022).

Bellow, Saul, 'Distractions of a Fiction Writer', in Granville Hicks (ed.), *The Living Novel: A Symposium* (New York: Macmillan, 1957).

Bellow, Saul, 'The Swamp of Prosperity', *Commentary*, July 1959, pp. 77–9.

Bellow, Saul, 'The Art of Fiction: Saul Bellow' [1966], interview by Gordon Lloyd Harper, in Gloria Cronin and Ben Siegel (eds), *Conversations with Saul Bellow* (Jackson: University Press of Mississippi, 1994), pp. 58–76.

Benjamin, Robert, 'Lionel Trilling's Jewish "Reverberation" of February 1944', *Studies in American Jewish Literature*, Vol. 36, No. 2 (2017), pp. 205–28.

Bergonzi, Bernard, 'Herzog in Venice', review of *Stitch* by Richard Stern, *New York Review of Books*, 9 December 1965, pp. 26–7.

Bergson, Henri, *Laughter: An Essay on the Meaning of the Comic* [1900], trans. Cloudesley Brereton and Fred Rothwell (Mineola, NY: Dover, 2005).

Berryman, John, R. P. Blackmur, Robert Gorham Davis, Leslie Fiedler, Clement Greenberg, H. L. Mencken, John Crowe Ransom, Wallace Stevens, and Lionel Trilling, 'The State of American Writing, 1948: A Symposium', *Partisan Review*, Vol. 15, No. 8 (August 1948), pp. 855–93.

Berryman, John, 'The Poetry of Ezra Pound', *Partisan Review*, Vol. 16, No. 4 (April 1949), pp. 377–94.
Best, Stephen and Sharon Marcus, 'Surface Reading: An Introduction', *Representations*, Vol. 108, No. 1 (Fall 2009), pp. 1–21.
Blotner, Joseph, *Robert Penn Warren: A Biography* (New York: Random House, 1997).
Blum, Beth (ed.), 'Experimental Criticism', *ASAP/J*, 30 January 2023. Available at: https://asapjournal.com/tag/experimental-criticism/.
Bodick, Noelle, 'A Pool of One's Own: Group Biographies and the Female Friendship Vogue', *The Drift*, 28 January 2021. Available at: https://www.thedriftmag.com/a-pool-of-ones-own/.
Bogue, Ronald, *Deleuze on Literature* (London: Routledge, 2003).
Bradbury, Malcolm, 'Saul Bellow's *Herzog*', *Critical Quarterly*, Vol. 7, No. 3 (September 1965), pp. 269–78.
Bradley, Adam, *Ralph Ellison in Progress: The Making and Unmaking of One Writer's Great American Novel* (New Haven: Yale University Press, 2010).
Breit, Harvey, 'Talk with Jean Stafford', *New York Times Book Review*, 20 January, 1952, 18.
Brier, Evan, *A Novel Marketplace: Mass Culture, the Book Trade, and Postwar American Fiction* (Philadelphia: University of Pennsylvania Press, 2010).
Brinkmeyer Jr, Robert H., 'The Southern Literary Renaissance', in Richard Gray and Own Robinson (eds), *A Companion to the Literature and Culture of the American South* (Oxford: Blackwell, 2004), pp. 148–65.
Bromwich, David, *A Choice of Inheritance: Self and Community from Edmund Burke to Robert Frost* (Cambridge, MA: Harvard University Press, 1989).
Bromwich, David, 'Ellison and the Visibility of Laughter', *Literary Imagination*, Vol. 23, No. 2, pp. 202–15.
Bronstein, Michaela, '*The Princess* Among the Polemicists: Aesthetics and Protest at Midcentury', *American Literary History*, Vol. 29, No. 1 (Spring 2017), pp. 26–49.
Brooks, Cleanth and Robert Penn Warren (eds), *Understanding Fiction* [1943] (Englewood Cliffs, NJ: Prentice-Hall, 1971).
Brooks, Cleanth, 'The Formalist Critics', *Kenyon Review*, Vol. 13, No. 1 (Winter 1951), pp. 72–81.
Buell, Lawrence, 'Observer-Hero Narrative', *Texas Studies in Literature and Language*, Vol. 21, No. 1 (Spring 1979), pp. 93–111.
Buell, Lawrence, *The Dream of the Great American Novel* (Cambridge, MA: Harvard University Press, 2014).
Buffington, Robert, 'Allen Tate and the *Sewanee Review*', *Sewanee Review*, Vol. 123, No. 2 (Spring 2015), pp. 240–51.
Callahan, John and Marc Conner (eds), *The Selected Letters of Ralph Ellison* (New York: Random House, 2019).
Cameron, Claire, 'A Forgotten Bestseller: The Saga of John Williams's Stoner', *The Millions*, 6 June 2013. Available at: https://themillions.com/2013/06/a-forgotten-bestseller-the-saga-of-john-williamss-stoner.html.
Casillo, Robert, *The Genealogy of Demons: Anti-Semitism, Fascism, and the Myths of Ezra Pound* (Evanston: Northwestern University Press, 1988).

Chakrabarty, Dipesh, *Provincializing Europe: Postcolonial Thought and Historical Difference* (Princeton: Princeton University Press, 2000).
Chase, Richard, 'Art, Nature, Politics', *Kenyon Review*, Vol. 12, No. 4 (Autumn 1950), pp. 580–94.
Chase, Richard, *The American Novel and its Tradition* (Baltimore: Johns Hopkins University Press, 1957).
Cheng, Anne Anlin, 'Ralph Ellison and the Politics of Melancholia', in Ross Posnock (ed.), *The Cambridge Companion to Ralph Ellison* (Cambridge: Cambridge University Press, 2005), pp. 121–36.
Clark, Eleanor, 'Asleep a King', *Partisan Review*, Vol. 4, No. 6 (May 1938), pp. 30–42.
Clark, Eleanor, *The Bitter Box* [1946] (London: Michael Joseph, 1947).
Clark, Eleanor, 'The Heart of the Afternoon', *Partisan Review*, Vol. 15, No. 12 (December 1948), pp. 1332–6.
Clark, Eleanor, 'Theater Chronicle: Old Glamour, New Gloom', *Partisan Review*, Vol. 16, No. 6 (June 1949), pp. 631–6.
Clark, Eleanor, 'Talk with Eleanor Clark', interview by R. W. B. Lewis, *New York Times*, 16 October 1977, 251.
Clark, Eleanor, 'Interview with Eleanor Clark and Robert Penn Warren', interview by Jay Parini, *New England Review*, Vol. 1, No. 1 (Autumn 1978), pp. 49–70.
Cole, Sarah, *Modernism, Male Friendship, and the First World War* (Cambridge: Cambridge University Press, 2003).
Colebrook, Claire, *Gilles Deleuze* (London: Routledge, 2001).
Collins, Katie, '"Her Ruined Head": Defacement and Disability in Jean Stafford's Life and Fiction', *Journal of Modern Literature*, Vol. 45, No. 1 (Fall 2021), pp. 121–36.
Conner, Marc, 'Ellison's Agon with the Fathers in *Three Days Before the Shooting. . .*', in Marc Conner and Lucas Morel (eds), *The New Territory: Ralph Ellison and the Twenty-First Century* (Jackson: University Press of Mississippi, 2016), pp. 167–93.
Cook, Richard M., *Alfred Kazin: A Biography* (New Haven: Yale University Press, 2008).
Cooney, Terry, *The Rise of The New York Intellectuals: Partisan Review and Its Circle* (Madison: University of Wisconsin Press, 1986).
Coover, Anne, *Olga Rudge & Ezra Pound* (New Haven: Yale University Press, 2001).
Corrigan, Robert, 'Ezra Pound and the Bollingen Prize Controversy', *Midcontinent American Studies Journal*, Vol. 8, No. 2 (Fall 1967), pp. 43–57.
Cotkin, George, *Existential America* (Baltimore: Johns Hopkins University Press, 2003).
Cowley, Malcolm, *The Literary Situation* (New York: Viking, 1954).
Crangle, Sara, *Prosaic Desires: Modernist Knowledge, Boredom, Laughter, and Anticipation* (Edinburgh: Edinburgh University Press, 2010).
Cunningham, J. V., *Woe or Wonder: The Emotional Effect of Shakespearian Tragedy* (Denver: Swallow Press, 1951).
Dabashi, Pardis, 'Introduction to "Cultures of Argument": The Loose Garments of Argument', *PMLA*, Vol. 135, No. 5 (2020), pp. 946–55.
Dancer, Thom, *Critical Modesty in Contemporary Fiction* (Oxford: Oxford University Press, 2021).
Davie, Donald, *Ezra Pound: Poet as Sculptor* (London: Routledge, 1964).

Davis, Kathryn, 'Afterword', in Jean Stafford, *The Mountain Lion* [1947] (New York: New York Review Books Classics, 2010), pp. 233–40.

Davis, Kathryn, 'Chronology', in Davis (ed.), *Jean Stafford: Complete Novels* (New York: Library of America, 2019), pp. 857–70.

Deleuze, Gilles, *The Logic of Sense* [French, 1969], trans. Mark Lester with Charles Stivale (New York: Columbia University Press, 1990).

Deleuze, Gilles and Félix Guattari, *Kafka: Toward a Minor Literature* [French, 1977], trans. Dana Polan (Minneapolis: University of Minnesota Press, 1986).

Deleuze, Gilles and Félix Guattari, *A Thousand Plateaus* [French, 1980], trans. Brian Massumi (Minneapolis: University of Minnesota Press, 1987).

Denning, Michael, *The Cultural Front: The Laboring of American Culture in the Twentieth Century* (London: Verso, 1996).

Dickstein, Morris, 'The Critics Who Made Us: Lionel Trilling and *The Liberal Imagination*', *Sewanee Review*, Vol. 94, No. 2 (Spring 1986), pp. 323–34.

Dickstein, Morris, *Double Agent: The Critic and Society* (Oxford: Oxford University Press, 1992).

Dickstein, Morris, *Leopards in the Temple: The Transformation of American Fiction, 1945–1970* (Cambridge, MA: Harvard University Press, 2002).

Dickstein, Morris, 'The Inner Lives of Men', *New York Times*, 17 June 2007.

Dickstein, Morris, "Promised Lands", *Times Literary Supplement*, 15 April 2016, pp. 3–5.

Dimock, Wai Chee, 'Weak Theory: Henry James, Colm Tóibín, and W. B. Yeats', *Critical Inquiry*, Vol. 39, No. 4 (2013), pp. 732–53.

Doreski, William, 'Founding a Literary Friendship: Allen Tate and Robert Lowell', *Southern Literary Journal*, Vol. 21, No. 2 (Spring 1989), pp. 72–91.

Dufourmantelle, Anne, *In Praise of Risk*, trans. Steven Miller (New York: Fordham University Press, 2019).

Duvall, John, 'Eliot's Modernism and Brooks's New Criticism: Poetic and Religious Thinking', *Mississippi Quarterly*, Vol. 46, No. 1 (Winter 1992–3), pp. 23–37.

Duvall, John, 'New Criticism's Major Journals', in Peter Brooker and Andrew Thacker (eds), *The Oxford Critical and Cultural History of Modernist Magazines: Volume II: North America 1894–1960* (Oxford: Oxford University Press, 2015), pp. 928–44.

Ehlers, Sarah, 'Late Modernisms, Latent Realisms: The Politics of Literary Interpretation', in Christopher Vials (ed.), *American Literature in Transition, 1940–1950* (Cambridge: Cambridge University Press, 2017), pp. 229–45.

Eisinger, Chester, *Fiction of the Forties* (Chicago: University of Chicago Press, 1963).

Eliot, T. S., *The Idea of a Christian Society* (New York: Harcourt, Brace and Company, 1940).

Ellman, Maud, *The Hunger Artists: Starving, Writing, and Imprisonment* (Cambridge, MA: Harvard University Press, 1993).

Ellison, Ralph, *Invisible Man* [1952] (Harmondsworth: Penguin, 2016).

Ellison, Ralph, *The Collected Essays of Ralph Ellison*, ed. John Callahan (New York: Modern Library Classics, 2003).

Esteve, Mary, 'When Psychoanalysis Was in Vogue', in Steven Belletto (ed.), *American Literature in Transition, 1950–1960* (Cambridge: Cambridge University Press, 2018), pp. 46–60.

Esteve, Mary, *Incremental Realism: Postwar American Fiction, Happiness, and Welfare-State Liberalism* (Stanford: Stanford University Press, 2021).

Esty, Jed, *A Shrinking Island: Modernism and National Culture in England* (Princeton: Princeton University Press, 2003).

Esty, Jed, *Unseasonable Youth: Modernism, Colonialism, and the Fiction of Development* (Oxford: Oxford University Press, 2011).

Esty, Jed, 'Realism Wars', *Novel: A Forum on Fiction*, Vol. 49, No. 2 (August 2016), pp. 316–42.

Fiedler, Leslie, *Love and Death in the American Novel* [1960] (Funks Grove, IL: Dalkey Archive Press, 1997).

Fiedler, Leslie, 'The Breakthrough: The American Jewish Novelist and the Fictional Image of the Jew', *Midstream*, Vol. 4, No. 1 (Winter 1959), pp. 15–35.

Fitzpatrick, Katie, 'Between Law and Justice: Legal Authority, Liberal Democracy, and Postwar Fiction', PhD thesis, Brown University, 2017.

Fitzpatrick, Katie, '"A Not-Exactly-Good Man": Lionel Trilling on Law and Judgment', *Twentieth-Century Literature*, Vol. 64, No. 2 (June 2018), pp. 129–60.

Fluck, Winfried, 'The Humanities in the Age of Expressive Individualism and Cultural Radicalism', *Cultural Critique*, No. 40 (Autumn 1998), pp. 49–71.

Foley, Abrams, *The Editor Function: Literary Publishing in Postwar America* (Minneapolis: University of Minnesota Press, 2021).

Foley, Barbara, *Radical Representations: Politics and Form in US Proletarian Fiction, 1929–1941* (Durham: Duke University Press, 1993).

Foley, Barbara, *Wrestling with the Left: The Making of Ralph Ellison's* Invisible Man (Durham, NC: Duke University Press, 2010).

Forster, E. M., *The Longest Journey* [1907] (London: Penguin, 2006).

Forster, E. M., *Aspects of the Novel* [1927] (London: Penguin, 2005).

Frank, Edwin, 'How the NYRB Chooses Its Reissues: The Story of Stoner', interview by Yongxi Wu, *Lit Hub*, 4 April 2016. Available at: https://lithub.com/how-the-nyrb-chooses-its-reissues-the-story-of-stoner/.

Frank, Edwin, 'What a Good Book Can Be: An Interview with Edwin Frank', interview by Susannah Hunnewell, *Paris Review*, 7 April 2016. Available at: https://www.theparisreview.org/blog/2016/04/07/what-a-good-book-can-be-an-interview-with-edwin-frank/.

Frank, Edwin (ed.), *The Red Thread: Twenty Years of NYRB Classics: A Selection* (New York: New York Review Books Classics, 2019).

Frank, Joseph, 'Fiction Chronicle', *Sewanee Review*, Vol. 54, No. 3 (Autumn 1946), pp. 534–9.

Freedman, Jonathan, *The Temple of Culture: Assimilation and Anti-Semitism in Literary Anglo-America* (Oxford: Oxford University Press, 2002).

Freeman, Elizabeth, '"The we of me": *The Member of the Wedding*'s Novel Alliances', *Women & Performance*, Vol. 8, No. 2 (1996), pp. 111–35.

Freud, Sigmund, *Inhibitions, Symptoms and Anxiety* [1926], trans. Alix Strachey (London: Norton, 1989).

Fromm, Erich, *Escape from Freedom* [1941] (New York: Holt, 1994).

Fulton, Ann, *Apostles of Sartre: Existentialism in America, 1945–1963* (Evanston: Northwestern University Press, 1999).

Furman, Andrew, *Contemporary Jewish American Writers and the Multicultural Dilemma: The Return of the Exiled* (Syracuse: Syracuse University Press, 2000).

Garrity, Jane, 'Found and Lost: The Politics of Modernist Recovery', *Modernism/modernity*, Vol. 15, No. 4 (November 2008), pp. 803–12.

Garrity, Jane, 'Modernist Women's Writing: Beyond the Threshold of Obsolescence', *Literature Compass*, Vol. 10, No. 1 (2013), pp. 15–29.

Genter, Robert, *Late Modernism: Art, Culture, and Politics in Cold War America* (Philadelphia: University of Pennsylvania Press, 2010).

Germana, Michael, *Ralph Ellison, Temporal Technologist* (Oxford: Oxford University Press, 2017).

Giamario, Patrick, *Laughter as Politics: Critical Theory in an Age of Hilarity* (Edinburgh: Edinburgh University Press, 2022).

Giles, Paul, *American Catholic Arts and Fictions: Culture, Ideology, Aesthetics* (Cambridge: Cambridge University Press, 1992).

Giroux, Robert, 'Hard Years and "Scary Days": Remembering Jean Stafford', *New York Times Book Review*, 10 June 1984, 3.

Glass, Loren, 'From Consensus to Conflict: Little Magazines in the 1950s', in Steven Belletto (ed.), *American Literature in Transition, 1950–1960* (Cambridge: Cambridge University Press, 2017), pp. 299–312.

Glenn, Eunice, 'As on a Darkling Plain', *Sewanee Review*, Vol. 56, No. 2 (Spring 1948), pp. 351–9.

Goodman, Charlotte, *Jean Stafford: The Savage Heart* (Austin: University of Texas Press, 1990).

Goodman, Charlotte, 'The Lost Brother/ The Twin: Women Novelists and the Male-Female Bildungsroman', *Novel: A Forum on Fiction*, Vol. 17, No. 1 (Fall 1983), pp. 28–43.

Gordon, Caroline and Allen Tate (eds), *The House of Fiction: An Anthology of the Short Story with Commentary* (New York: Scribner, 1950).

Graff, Gerald, *Poetic Statement and Critical Dogma* (Evanston: Northwestern University Press, 1970).

Graff, Gerald, *Professing Literature: An Institutional History* [1987] (Chicago: University of Chicago Press, 2008).

Greif, Mark, *The Age of the Crisis of Man: Thought and Fiction in America, 1933–1973* (Princeton: Princeton University Press, 2015).

Grosz, Elizabeth, *Becoming Undone: Darwinian Reflections on Life, Politics, and Art* (Durham, NC: Duke University Press, 2011).

Grosz, Elizabeth, *The Nick of Time: Politics, Evolution, and the Untimely* (Durham, NC: Duke University Press, 2004).

Halliwell, Martin, *The Constant Dialogue: Reinhold Niebuhr & American Intellectual Culture* (Lanham: Rowman & Littlefield, 2005).

Halverson, Cathryn, '"A Reading Problem": Margaret Lynn, Jean Stafford, and Literary Criticism of the American West', *Legacy*, Vol. 33, No. 1 (2016), pp. 127–49.

Halverson, Cathryn, 'Review of *Jean Stafford: Complete Novels*, ed. Kathryn Davis', *ALH Online Review*, Series XXVII (2021), pp. 1–3.

Hammer, Langdon, *Hart Crane and Allen Tate: Janus-Faced Modernism* (Princeton: Princeton University Press, 1993).

Harap, Louis, *In the Mainstream: The Jewish Presence in Twentieth-century American Literature, 1950s–1980s* (Westport, CT: Greenwood Press, 1987).

Hardwick, Elizabeth, 'Poor Little Rich Girls', *Partisan Review*, Vol. 12, No. 3 (Summer 1945), pp. 420–2.

Harris, Mark, *Saul Bellow, Drumlin Woodchuck* (Athens, GA: University of Georgia Press, 1980).

Hassan, Ihab, *Radical Innocence: Studies in the Contemporary American Novel* (Princeton: Princeton University Press, 1961).

Hatab, Lawrence, 'Laughter in Nietzsche's Thought: A Philosophical Tragicomedy', *International Studies in Philosophy*, Vol. 20, No. 2 (1998), pp. 67–79.

Hawthorne, Nathaniel, 'Ethan Brand', in *Young Goodman Brown and Other Tales* (Oxford: Oxford University Press, 1998), pp. 316–32.

Hayes, Patrick, 'Not Quite *Letting Go*: Rethinking the "tragic sense of life" in Roth's First Novel", *Philip Roth Studies*, Vol. 9, No. 2 (Fall 2013), pp. 7–22.

Heilman, Robert, 'Four Novels', review of *The Mountain Lion* by Jean Stafford, and other works, *Sewanee Review*, Vol. 55, No. 3 (July–September 1947), pp. 483–92.

Hikok, Bethany, *Degrees of Freedom: American Women Poets and the Women's College* (Pennsylvania: Bucknell University Press, 2008).

Hicks, Granville, 'Foreword, in Granville Hicks (ed.), *The Living Novel: A Symposium* (New York: Macmillan, 1957), pp. vii–xii.

Ho, Janice, *Nation and Citizenship in the Twentieth-Century British Novel* (Cambridge: Cambridge University Press, 2015).

Hoffman, Daniel, *Form and Fable in American Fiction* [1961] (Charlottesville: University of Virginia Press, 1994).

Hollinger, David, *In the American Province: Studies in the History and Historiography of Ideas* (Bloomington: Indiana University Press, 1985).

Holsinger, Bruce, 'Medievalization Theory: From Tocqueville to the Cold War', *American Literary History*, Vol. 22, No. 4 (Winter 2010), pp. 893–912.

Hook, Sidney, 'The New Failure of Nerve', *Partisan Review*, Vol. 10, No, 1 (January–February 1943), pp. 2–23.

Howe, Irving, 'The Age of Conformity', *Dissent*, 1 January 1954. Available at: https://www.dissentmagazine.org/online_articles/irving-howe-voice-still-heard-this-age-of-conformity.

Howe, Irving, 'The Virtues of Failure', *The New Republic*, 22 February 1966.

Hulbert, Ann, *The Interior Castle: The Art and Life of Jean Stafford* (Amherst: University of Massachusetts Press, 1992).

Hutchinson, George, *Facing the Abyss: American Literature and Culture in the 1940s* (New York: Columbia University Press, 2018).

Hutchison, Anthony, *Writing the Republic: Liberalism and Morality in American Political Fiction* (New York: Columbia University Press, 2007).

Hutchison, Anthony, 'Cultivating the Classical Style: The Stanford-Denver Creative Writing Axis', *Modern Fiction Studies*, Vol. 66, No. 3 (Fall 2020), pp. 474–98.

James, David, 'Localizing Late Modernism: Interwar Regionalism and the Genesis of the "Micro Novel"', *Journal of Modern Literature*, Vol. 32, No. 4 (Summer 2009), pp. 43–64.

James, Henry, 'The Art of Fiction' [1888], in *The Future of the Novel*, ed. by Leon Edel (New York: Vintage, 1956), pp. 3–27.

James, Henry, 'In the Cage' [1898], in *Complete Stories, 1892–1898*, ed. David Bromwich and John Hollander (New York: Library of America, 1996), pp. 835–924.

James, Henry, *Hawthorne* (New York, Doubleday, 1900).

Jancovich, Mark, *The Cultural Politics of the New Criticism* (Cambridge: Cambridge University Press, 1993).

Jones, Howard Mumford, 'A New Jean Stafford', review of *The Mountain Lion* by Jean Stafford, *New York Times*, 2 March 1947, 189.

Jordan, Julia, *Late Modernism and the Avant-Garde British Novel* (Oxford: Oxford University Press, 2020).

Kalaidjian, Walter, *American Culture Between the Wars: Revisionary Modernism & Postmodern Critique* (New York: Columbia University Press, 1993).

Kazin, Alfred, 'The Earthly City of the Jews: Bellow, Malamud, and Roth' [1971], in Ted Solotaroff (ed.), *Alfred Kazin's America: Critical and Personal Writings* (New York: Harper Collins, 2003), pp. 255–69.

Kenner, Hugh, *'Stitch*: His Master's Voice', *Chicago Review*, Vol. 18, No. 3/4 (1966), pp. 176–80.

Kenner, Hugh, 'From Lower Bellowvia', *Harper's*, February 1982, pp. 62–5.

Kierkegaard, Søren, *Repetition* [1843], trans. Howard and Edna Hong (Princeton: Princeton University Press, 1983).

Kierkegaard, Søren, *The Concept of Anxiety* [1844], trans. Reidar Thomte (Princeton: Princeton University Press, 1980).

Kimmage, Michael, *The Conservative Turn: Lionel Trilling, Whittaker Chambers, and the Lessons of Anti-Communism* (Cambridge, MA: Harvard University Press, 2009).

Kindley, Evan, 'Big Criticism', *Critical Inquiry*, Vol. 38, No. 1 (Autumn 2011), pp. 71–95.

Kirsch, Adam, *Why Trilling Matters* (New Haven: Yale University Press, 2011).

Kirsch, Adam (ed.), *Life in Culture: Selected Letters of Lionel Trilling* (New York: Farrar, Straus and Giroux, 2018).

Klein, Marcus, *After Alienation: American Novels in Mid-Century* (New York: World Publishing Company, 1964).

Konstantinou, Lee and Dan Sinykin, 'Literature and Publishing, 1945–2020', *American Literary History*, Vol. 33, No. 2 (Summer 2021), pp. 225–43.

Kreider, Tim, 'The Greatest American Novel You've Never Heard Of', *New Yorker*, 20 October 2013.

Kristol, Irving, 'The Moral Critic' (April 1944), in John Rodden (ed.), *Lionel Trilling and the Critics: Opposing Selves* (Lincoln: University of Nebraska Press, 1999), pp. 92–7.

Krupnick, Mark, *Lionel Trilling and the Fate of Cultural Criticism* (Evanston: Northwestern University Press, 1986).

Krystal, Arthur (ed.), *A Company of Readers: Uncollected Writings of W. H. Auden, Jacques Barzun, and Lionel Trilling from the Readers' Subscription and Mid-Century Book Clubs* (New York: Free Press, 2001).

Lambert, Josh, *The Literary Mafia: Jews, Publishing, and Postwar American Literature* (New Haven: Yale University Press, 2022).

Latour, Bruno, 'Why Has Critique Run Out of Steam? From Matters of Fact to Matters of Concern', *Critical Inquiry*, Vol. 30, No. 2 (Winter 2004), pp. 225–48.

Leader, Zachary, *The Life of Saul Bellow, Volume 1: To Fame and Fortune, 1915–1964* (New York: Random House, 2015).

Leaf, Munro, *The Story of Ferdinand* (New York: Viking, 1936).

Leavis, F. R., *The Great Tradition* [1948] (Harmondsworth: Penguin, 1972).

Lee, Maurice, 'Feeling Fallible, Being Wrong', *American Literary History*, Vol. 34, No. 1 (Spring 2022), pp. 199–211.

Lentricchia, Frank, *After the New Criticism* (Chicago: University of Chicago Press, 1980).

Lethem, Jonathan, 'They've Got Reissues', *Bookforum*, Vol. 21, No. 4 (December/January 2015).

Levenson, Michael, 'Earnest Ironies: Trilling's Forster', in John Rodden (ed.), *Lionel Trilling and the Critics: Opposing Selves* (Lincoln: University of Nebraska Press, 1999), pp. 104–9.

Levenson, Michael, 'Criticism of Fiction', in A. Walton Litz, Louis Menand, and Lawrence Rainey (eds), *The Cambridge History of Literary Criticism, Vol. 7: Modernism and the New Criticism* (Cambridge: Cambridge University Press, 2000), 468–98.

Levinson, Marjorie, 'What Is New Formalism?', *PMLA*, Vol. 122, No. 2 (March 2007), pp. 558–69.

Lewis, R. W. B., 'Lionel Trilling and the New Stoicism', *Hudson Review*, Vol. 3, No. 2 (Summer 1950), pp. 313–17.

Lewis, R. W. B., *The American Adam: Innocence, Tragedy, and Tradition in the Nineteenth Century* (Chicago: University of Chicago Press, 1955).

Lippitt, John, 'Nietzsche, Zarathustra and the Status of Laughter', *British Journal of Aesthetics*, Vol. 32, No. 1 (January 1992), pp. 39–49.

Love, Heather, 'Close but Not Deep: Literary Ethics and the Descriptive Turn', *New Literary History*, Vol. 41, No. 2 (Spring 2010), pp. 371–91.

Love, Heather, 'Close Reading and Thin Description', *Public Culture*, Vol. 25, No. 3 (Fall 2013), pp. 401–34.

Love, Heather, 'Merely Ameliorative: Reading, Critical Affect, and the Project of Repair', in James English and Heather Love (eds), *Literary Studies and Human Flourishing* (Oxford: Oxford University Press, 2023), pp. 207–18.

Lowell, Robert, 'Visiting the Tates', *Sewanee Review*, Vol. 67, No. 4 (Autumn 1959), pp. 557–9.

Lowell, Robert, 'Robert Lowell, The Art of Poetry', interview by Frederick Seidel, *Paris Review*, Issue 25 (Winter–Spring 1961). Available at: https://www.theparisreview.org/interviews/4664/the-art-of-poetry-no-3-robert-lowell.

Lowell, Robert, *Collected Prose* (Farrar, Straus and Giroux, 1987).

Lubbock, Percy, *The Craft of Fiction* [1921] (New York: Viking, 1957).

MacKay, Marina, *Modernism and World War II* (Cambridge: Cambridge University Press, 2007).

MacKay, Marina and Lyndsey Stonebridge (eds), *British Fiction After Modernism: The Novel at Mid-Century* (London: Routledge, 2007).

MacLeod, Alexander, '"Disagreeable Intellectual Distance": Theory and Politics in the Old Regionalism of the New Critics', in Miranda Hickman and John McIntyre (eds), *Rereading the New Criticism* (Columbus: Ohio State University Press, 2012), pp. 173–94.

Malamud, Bernard, 'The Last Mohican', *Partisan Review*, Vol. 25, No. 2 (Spring 1958), pp. 175–96.

Mangrum, Benjamin, *Land of Tomorrow: Postwar Fiction and the Crisis of American Liberalism* (Oxford: Oxford University Press, 2018).

Marcum, Deanna and Roger C. Schonfeld, *Along Came Google: A History of Library Digitization* (Princeton: Princeton University Press, 2021).

Martin, Andrew, 'The Spirit of Revival', *The Drift*, Issue 7, 14 June 2022. Available at: https://www.thedriftmag.com/the-spirit-of-revival/.

McCann, Sean, *A Pinnacle of Feeling: American Literature and Presidential Government* (Durham, NC: Duke University Press, 2008).

McCullers, Carson, *The Member of the Wedding* [1946], (London: Penguin, 2008).

McGurl, Mark, *The Program Era: Postwar Fiction and the Rise of Creative Writing* (Cambridge, MA: Harvard University Press, 2009).

McGurl, Mark, 'Philip Roth's Modest Phase', *Post45*, 12 April 2019. Available at: https://post45.org/2019/04/philip-roths-modest-phase/.

McGurl, Mark, *Everything and Less: The Novel in the Age of Amazon* (New York: Verso, 2021).

McHale, Brian, 'Break, Period, Interregnum', *Twentieth Century Literature*, Vol. 57, No. 3/4, (Fall/Winter 2011), pp. 328–40.

McQuade, Molly (ed.), *An Unsentimental Education: Writers and Chicago* (Chicago: University of Chicago Press, 1995).

Menand, Louis, 'Regrets Only', *The New Yorker*, 29 September 2008.

Menand, Louis, 'Freud, Anxiety, and the Cold War', in John Burnham (ed.), *After Freud Left: A Century of Psychoanalysis in America* (Chicago: University of Chicago Press, 2012), pp. 189–208.

Menand, Louis, *The Free World: Art and Thought in the Cold War* (New York: Farrar, Straus and Giroux, 2021).

Mendelson, Edward, *Moral Agents: Eight Twentieth-Century Writers* (New York: NYRB, 2015).

Murphy, Elizabeth (ed.), *A Critical Friendship: Donald Justice and Richard Stern, 1946–1961* (Lincoln, NE: University of Nebraska Press, 2013).

Murphy, Geraldine, 'The Politics of Reading *Billy Budd*', *American Literary History*, Vol. 1, No. 2 (Summer 1989), pp. 361–82.

Miller, Arhur, 'Tragedy and the Common Man' [1949], in *Death of a Salesman: Text and Criticism*, ed. by Gerald Weales (Harmondsworth: Penguin, 1996), pp. 143–7.

Miller, Tyrus, *Late Modernism: Politics, Fiction, and the Arts Between the World Wars* (Berkeley: University of California Press, 1999).

Mizener, Arthur, 'The Novel of Manners in America', *The Kenyon Review*, Vol. 12, No. 1, (Winter 1950), pp. 1–19.

Moi, Toril, '"Nothing Is Hidden": From Confusion to Clarity; or, Wittgenstein on Critique', in Elizabeth Anker and Rita Felski (eds), *Critique and Postcritique* (Durham, NC: Duke University Press, 2017), pp. 31–49.

Moody, A. David, *Ezra Pound, Poet: A Portrait of the Man and his Work, Volume III: The Tragic Years, 1939–1972* (Oxford: Oxford University Press, 2015).

Moretti, Franco, *Distant Reading* (New York: Verso, 2013).

Morris, Alice, 'When Hatred Breaks', review of *The Catherine Wheel* by Jean Stafford, *New York Times*, 13 January 1952, BR5.

Mundt, Hannelore, *Understanding Thomas Mann* (Columbia: University of South Carolina Press, 2004).

Murphy, Harriet, *Canetti and Nietzsche: Theories of Humor in Die Blendung* (Albany: State University of New York Press, 1997).

Myers, D. G., *The Elephants Teach: Creative Writing Since 1880*, 2nd ed. (Chicago: University of Chicago Press, 2006).

Myers, D. G., 'Defeats and Victories Not Recorded in the Annals of History', *Commentary*, 14 September 2011.

Nelson, Deborah, *Tough Enough: Arbus, Arendt, Didion, McCarthy, Sontag, Weil* (Chicago: University of Chicago Press, 2017).

Niebuhr, Reinhold, *Beyond Tragedy: A Christian Interpretation of History* (New York: Scribner and Sons, 1937).

Nietzsche, Friedrich, *Thus Spoke Zarathustra* [1883], trans. R. J. Hollingdale (Harmondsworth: Penguin, 1969).

Nietzsche, Friedrich, *Ecce Homo: How To Become What You Are* [1908], trans. Duncan Large (Oxford: Oxford University Press, 2007).

Norman, Will, *Transatlantic Aliens: Modernism, Exile, and Culture in Midcentury America* (Baltimore: Johns Hopkins University Press, 2016).

Nowlin, Michael, *Literary Ambition and the African American Novel* (Cambridge: Cambridge University Press, 2019).

O'Donnell, George Marian, 'Faulkner's Mythology', *Kenyon Review*, Vol. 1, No. 3 (Summer 1939), pp. 285–99.

O'Meally, Robert, *Antagonistic Cooperation: Jazz, Collage, Fiction, and the Shaping of African American Culture* (New York: Columbia University Press, 2022).

Oates, Joyce Carol, 'Introduction', in *The Collected Stories of Jean Stafford* [1969] (New York: Farrar, Straus and Giroux, 2005), pp. ix–xix.

Oates, Joyce Carol, 'Adventures in Abandonment', review of *Jean Stafford: A Biography* by David Roberts, *New York Times Book Review*, 28 August 1988, 3.

Ogden, Emily, 'Questionnaire Answers', in Beth Blum (ed.), 'Experimental Criticism' [online cluster], *ASAP/J*, 30 January 2023.

Pace, Eric, '2 Book Awards Split for First Time', *New York Times*, 11 April 1973, 38.

Parrish, Timothy, *Ralph Ellison and the Genius of America* (Amherst: University of Massachusetts Press, 2008).

Parvulescu, Anca, *Laughter: Notes on a Passion* (Cambridge, MA: MIT Press, 2010).

Phillips, Adam, 'Lionel Trilling's Concentrated Rush', *Raritan*, Vol. 21, No. 4 (Spring 2002), pp. 164–74.

Phillips, William and Philip Rahv, 'Editorial Statement', *Partisan Review*, Vol. 17, No. 2 (February 1950), pp. 103–6.

Plotz, John, 'Review of *The Man Who Wrote the Perfect Novel*, by Charles Shields', *Western American Literature*, Vol. 54, No. 3 (Fall 2019), pp. 331–3.

Podhoretz, Norman, 'The Arnoldian Function in American Criticism' (1952), in Rodden (ed.), *Lionel Trilling and the Critics*, pp. 175–81.

Politzer, Heinz, 'Five Novels', review of *The Catherine Wheel* by Jean Stafford, and other works, *Commentary*, 1 January 1952, pp. 510–14.

Potter, Rachel, *Obscene Modernism: Literary Censorship and Experiment 1900–1940* (Oxford: Oxford University Press, 2013).

Pound, Ezra, *Gaudier-Brezka: A Memoir* (London: John Lane, 1916).

Pound, Ezra, 'Brancusi', *Little Review*, Vol. 8, No. 1 (1921), pp. 3–7.

Pound, Ezra, 'Canto CXVI', *Paris Review*, 28 (Summer/Fall 1962), pp. 14–16.

Poynor, Rick, 'Picture a Story', *Eye Magazine*, Issue 66 (Winter 2007). Available at: https://www.eyemagazine.com/opinion/article/picture-a-story-66.

Prescott, Orville, 'Books of the Times', review of *The Mountain Lion* by Jean Stafford, *New York Times*, 3 March 1947, 19.

Prescott, Orville, 'Books of the Times', review of *The Catherine Wheel* by Jean Stafford, *New York Times*, 15 January 1952, 25.

Price, Leah, 'From *The History of the Book* to a "History of the Book"', *Representations*, Vol. 108, No. 1 (November 2009), pp. 120–38.

Quinn, Annalisa, 'Book News: *Stoner* Created Little Buzz In 1965, But Ignites In 2013', The Two-Way, *NPR*, 9 December 2013. Available at: https://www.npr.org/sections/thetwo-way/2013/12/09/249698007/book-news-stoner-created-little-buzz-in-1965-but-ignites-in-2013.

Rahv, Philip, 'Dostoevsky and Politics', *Partisan Review*, Vol. 5, No. 2 (July 1938), pp. 25–36.

Rahv, Philip, 'Paleface and Redskin', *Kenyon Review*, Vol. 1, No. 3 (Summer 1939), pp. 251–6.

Rahv, Philip, 'Henry James's America', *New York Times Book Review*, 2 March 1947, 4.

Rampersad, Arnold, *Ralph Ellison: A Biography* (New York: Knopf, 2007).

Ratner-Rosenhagen, Jennifer, *American Nietzsche: A History of an Icon and His Ideas* (Chicago: University of Chicago Press, 2011).

Reese, Sam, *The Short Story in Midcentury America: Countercultural Form in the Work of Bowles, McCarthy, Welty, and Williams* (Baton Rouge: Louisiana State University Press, 2017).

Reising, Russell, *The Unusable Past: Theory and the Study of American Literature* (London: Routledge, 1986).

Rice, Philip Blair, 'Psychoanalysis: The Second Wave', *Kenyon Review*, Vol. 2, No. 2 (Spring 1940), pp. 226–8.

Robbins, Bruce, 'Not So Well Attached', *PMLA*, Vol. 132, No. 2 (2017), pp. 371–6.

Roberts, David, *Jean Stafford: A Biography* (London: Chatto & Windus, 1988).

Robins, Natalie, *The Untold Journey: The Life of Diana Trilling* (New York: Columbia University Press, 2017).

Robson, Leo, 'John Williams and the Canon That Might Have Been', *New Yorker*, 18 March 2019.

Rohter, Larry, '*New York Review of Books* Fills a Niche by Reviving Forgotten Works', *New York Times*, 7 August 2015.

Rosenfeld, Isaac, 'Kafka and His Critics' [1947], in Mark Shechner (ed.), *Preserving the Hunger: An Isaac Rosenfeld Reader* (Detroit: Wayne State University, 1988), pp. 166–74.

Ross, Dorothy, 'Freud and the Vicissitudes of Modernism in the United States, 1940–1980', in John Burnham (ed.), *After Freud Left: A Century of Psychoanalysis in America* (Chicago: University of Chicago Press, 2012), pp. 163–88.
Roth, Philip, 'Writing American Fiction' [1961], in *Reading Myself and Others* (London: Vintage, 2007), pp. 165–82.
Roth, Philip, 'Just a Lively Boy', in Molly McQuade (ed.), *An Unsentimental Education: Writers and Chicago* (Chicago: University of Chicago Press, 1995), pp. 123–9.
Roth, Philip, 'In Memory of Richard Stern' [2013], in Richard Stern, *Other Men's Daughters* (New York: New York Review Books Classics, 2017), pp. vii–xii.
Rubin, Louis, *The Wary Fugitives: Four Poets* (Baton Rouge: Louisiana State University Press, 1978).
Russell, David, *Tact: Aesthetic Liberalism and the Essay Form in Nineteenth-Century Britain* (Princeton: Princeton University Press, 2017).
Russo, John Paul, 'The Tranquilized Poem: The Crisis of New Criticism in the 1950s', *Texas Studies in Literature and Language*, Vol. 30, No. 2 (Summer 1988), pp. 198–229.
Ryan, Derek, *Virginia Woolf and the Materiality of Theory: Sex, Animal, Life* (Edinburgh: Edinburgh University Press, 2013).
Saint-Amour, Paul K., 'Weak Theory, Weak Modernism', *Modernism/ Modernity*, Vol. 24, No. 3 (2018), pp. 437–59.
Sartre, Jean-Paul, 'Existentialist as Mobilist', *Art News*, No. 46 (December 1947), pp. 22–3.
Schaub, Thomas Hill, *American Fiction in the Cold War* (Madison: University of Wisconsin Press, 1991).
Schiffer, James, *Richard Stern* (New York: Twayne Publishers, 1993).
Schmidt, James, 'Inventing the "Counter-Enlightenment": Liberalism, Nihilism, and Totalitarianism', conference paper, presented at the American Historical Association, Boston, 6 January 2011, pp. 1–19.
Schorer, Mark, 'Technique as Discovery', *Hudson Review*, Vol. 1, No. 1 (Spring 1948), pp. 67–87.
Schorer, Mark, 'The American Novel', review of *The Mountain Lion* by Jean Stafford, and other works, *Kenyon Review*, Vol. 9, No. 4 (Autumn 1947), pp. 628–36.
Schreier, Benjamin, 'Making It into the Mainstream, 1945–1970', in Hana Wirth-Nesher (ed.), *The Cambridge History of Jewish American Literature* (Cambridge: Cambridge University Press, 2016), pp. 123–43.
Schreier, Benjamin, *The Rise and Fall of Jewish American Literature: Ethnic Studies and the Challenge of Identity* (Philadelphia: Pennsylvania University Press, 2020).
Schryer, Stephen, *Fantasies of the New Class: Ideologies of Professionalism in Post-World War II American Fiction* (New York: Columbia University Press, 2011).
Sedgwick, Eve Kosofsky, *Touching Feeling: Affect, Pedagogy, Performativity* (Durham, NC: Duke University Press, 2003).
Seguin, Robert, *Around Quitting Time: Work and Middle-Class Fantasy in American Fiction* (Durham, NC: Duke University Press, 2001).
Seiler, Claire, *Midcentury Suspension: Literature and Feeling in the Wake of World War II* (New York: Columbia University Press, 2020).

Seshagiri, Urmila, 'Making it New: Persephone Books and the Modernist Project', *Modern Fiction Studies*, Vol. 59, No. 2 (Summer 2013), pp. 241–87.

Sherfey, Mary Jane, 'A Theory on Female Sexuality', in Maggie Humm (ed.), *Feminisms: A Reader* (London: Taylor & Francis, 1992), pp. 264–8.

Shields, Charles, *The Man Who Wrote the Perfect Novel: John Williams, Stoner, and the Writing Life* (Austin: University of Texas Press, 2018).

Simpson, Eileen, *Poets in Their Youth: A Memoir* (New York: Random House, 1982).

Sinykin, Dan, 'The Conglomerate Era', *Contemporary Literature*, Vol. 58, No. 4 (Winter 2017), pp. 462–91.

Snow, C. P., 'Good Man and Foes', *Financial Times*, 24 May 1973.

Solotaroff, Ted, 'Philip Roth and the Jewish Moralist', *Chicago Review*, Vol. 13, No. 4 (Winter 1959), pp. 87–99.

Solotaroff, Ted, *First Loves: A Memoir* (New York: Seven Stories Press, 2003).

Soong, Jennifer, 'The Minor Poet: A Case of John Wieners', *Textual Practice*, 7 December 2022. Published online.

Spencer, Nicholas, 'Late Modernism and the Minor Literature of Weldon Kee's Poetry', in Daniel A. Siedell (ed.), *Weldon Kees and the Arts at Midcentury* (Lincoln: University of Nebraska Press, 2003), pp. 147–86.

Stafford, Jean, 'The Psychological Novel', *Kenyon Review*, Vol. 10, No. 2 (Spring 1948), pp. 214–27.

Stafford, Jean, *The Catherine Wheel* [1952] (New York: Farrar, Straus and Giroux, 2014).

Stafford, Jean, *The Collected Stories of Jean Stafford* [1969] (New York: Farrar, Straus and Giroux, 2005).

Stern, Richard, 'Cooley's Version', *Kenyon Review*, Vol. 16, No. 2 (Spring 1954), pp. 257–67.

Stern, Richard, "Henderson's Bellow", *Kenyon Review*, Vol. 21, No. 4 (Autumn 1959), pp. 655–61.

Stern, Richard, 'Jewishness and The Young Intellectuals', *Commentary*, Vol. 31, No. 4 (1961), pp. 306–10.

Stern, Richard, *Stitch* [1965] (Evanston: TriQuarterly Books, 2004).

Stern, Richard, 'An Interview with Richard G. Stern', interview by Robert Raeder, *Chicago Review*, Vol. 18, No. 3/4 (1966), pp. 170–5.

Stern, Richard, 'A Memory or Two of Mr. Pound', *Paideuma*, Vol. 1, No. 2 (Winter 1972), pp. 215–19.

Stern, Richard, 'Extracts from a Journal', *TriQuarterly*, Vol. 50 (Winter 1981), pp. 261–73.

Stern, Richard, *The Invention of the Real* (Athens, GA: University of Georgia Press, 1982).

Stern, Richard, *One Person and Another: On Writers and Writing* (Dallas: Baskerville, 1993).

Stern, Richard, *A Sistermony* (New York: Donald Fine, 1995).

Stern, Richard, 'Remembering Pound', *Sewanee Review*, Vol. 106, No. 1 (Winter 1998), pp. 132–9.

Stern, Richard, 'An Interview with Richard Stern', interview by James Atlas, *Chicago Review*, Vol. 45, No. 3/4 (1999), pp. 23–43.

Stern, Richard, *What is What Was* (Chicago: University of Chicago Press, 2002).
Stern, Richard, 'Glimpse, Acquaintance, Encounter, Friendship', *Sewanee Review*, Vol. 117, No. 1 (Winter 2009), pp. 95–105.
Stern, Richard, *Still on Call* (Ann Arbor: University of Michigan Press, 2010).
Stockton, Kathryn Bond, *The Queer Child, or Growing Sideways in the Twentieth Century* (Durham, NC: Duke University Press, 2009).
Sullivan, Walter, 'The Roman Connection: Allen Tate as Catholic Man of Letters', Vol. 106, No. 1 (Winter 1998), pp. 87–92.
Sykes, John, *Flannery O'Connor, Walker Percy, and the Aesthetic of Revelation* (Columbia: University of Missouri Press, 2007).
Szalay, Michael, *New Deal Modernism: American Literature and the Invention of the Welfare State* (Durham, NC: Duke University Press, 2000).
Tanner, Tony, *Venice Desired* (Cambridge, MA: Harvard University Press, 1992).
Tate, Allen, 'Remarks on the Southern Religion' in John Crowe Ransom et al., *I'll Take My Stand: The South and the Agrarian Tradition* [1930] (Baton Rouge: Louisiana State University Press, 1977), pp. 155–75.
Tate, Allen, 'The Function of the Critical Quarterly', *Southern Review*, Vol. 1 (1935), pp. 551–60.
Tate, Allen, 'The Profession of Letters in the South', *Virginia Quarterly Review*, Vol. 11, No. 2 (April 1935), pp. 161–76.
Tate, Allen, 'Narcissus as Narcissus', *Virginia Quarterly Review*, Vol. 14, No. 1 (Winter 1938), pp. 108–22.
Tate, Allen, 'Techniques of Fiction', *The Sewanee Review*, Vol. 52, No. 2 (Spring 1944), pp. 210–25.
Tate, Allen, 'The New Provincialism', *Virginia Quarterly Review*, Vol. 21, No. 2 (Spring 1945), pp. 262–72.
Tate, Allen, 'Three Commentaries: Poe, James, and Joyce', *Sewanee Review*, Vol. 58, No. 1 (January–March 1950), pp. 1–15.
Tate, Allen, 'The Symbolic Imagination: A Meditation on Dante's Three Mirrors', *Kenyon Review*, Vol. 14, No. 2 (Spring 1952), pp. 256–77.
Taylor, Benjamin (ed.), *Saul Bellow: Letters* (New York: Penguin, 2006).
Thompson, John, *Merchants of Culture: The Publishing Business in the Twenty-First Century* (Cambridge: Polity, 2012).
Thurschwell, Pamela, 'Dead Boys and Adolescent Girls: Unjoining the Bildungsroman in Carson McCullers's *The Member of the Wedding* and Toni Morrison's *Sula*', *ESC: English Studies in Canada*, Vol. 38, No. 3-4 (September–December 2012), pp. 105–28.
Trask, Michael, *Cruising Modernism: Class and Sexuality in American Literature and Social Thought* (Ithaca: Cornell University Press, 2018).
Trilling, Lionel, 'E. M. Forster', *Kenyon Review*, Vol. 4, No. 2 (Spring 1942), pp. 160–73.
Trilling, Lionel, 'Artists and the "Societal" Function', *Kenyon Review*, Vol. 4, No. 3 (Autumn 1942), pp. 425–30.
Trilling, Lionel, *E. M. Forster* [1943] (New York: New Directions, 1964).
Trilling, Lionel, 'The Life of the Novel', Vol. 8, No. 4 (Autumn 1946), pp. 658–67.
Trilling, Lionel, *The Middle of the Journey* [1947] (New York: New York Review Books Classics, 2002).

Trilling, Lionel, *The Liberal Imagination: Essays on Literature and Society* [1950] (New York: New York Review Books Classics, 2008).
Trilling, Lionel, Contribution to 'Our Country and Our Culture: A Symposium', *Partisan Review*, Vol. 19, No. 3 (May 1952), pp. 318–26.
Trilling, Lionel, *The Opposing Self: Nine Essays in Criticism* (New York: Viking, 1955).
Trilling, Lionel, *A Gathering of Fugitives* (Boston: Beacon Press, 1956).
Trilling, Lionel, 'Commentary on "The Grand Inquisitor" by Fëdor Dostoevski', in *The Experience of Literature* (New York: Holt, Rinehart and Winston, 1967), pp. 482–5.
Trilling, Lionel, *Sincerity and Authenticity* (Cambridge, MA: Harvard University Press, 1972).
Trilling, Lionel, *The Last Decade: Essays and Reviews, 1965–75* (Oxford: Oxford University Press, 1982).
Trilling, Lionel, *The Journey Abandoned: The Unfinished Novel*, ed. by Geraldine Murphy (New York: Columbia University Press, 2008).
Trilling, Lionel, 'From the Notebooks of Lionel Trilling', *Partisan Review*, Vol. 51, No. 4/Vol. 52, No. 1 (Fall 1984/Winter 1985), pp. 495–515.
Trilling, Lionel, 'From the Notebooks of Lionel Trilling, Part II', *Partisan Review*, Vol. 54, No.1 (Winter 1987), pp. 7–17.
Voelz, Johannes, *Transcendental Resistance: The New Americanists and Emerson's Challenge* (New Hampshire: Dartmouth University Press, 2010).
Wakefield, Dan, 'John Williams, Plain Writer', *Ploughshares*, Vol. 7, No. 3/4, (1981), pp. 9–22.
Wald, Alan, 'Herbert Solow: Portrait of a New York Intellectual', *Prospects*, Vol. 3 (October 1978), pp. 419–60.
Wald, Alan, *The New York Intellectuals: The Rise and Decline of the Anti-Stalinist Left From the 1930s to the 1980s* [1987], 30th Anniversary edition (Chapel Hill: North Carolina University Press, 2017).
Wald, Alan, *Writing From the Left: New Essays on Radical Culture and Politics* (London: Verso, 1994).
Wald, Alan, *American Night: The Literary Left in the Era of the Cold War* (Chapel Hill: University of North Carolina Press, 2012).
Walkowitz, Rebecca, *Born Translated: The Contemporary Novel in an Age of World Literature* (New York: Columbia University Press, 2015).
Wanning, Andrew, 'A Variety of Fiction', review of *Boston Adventure* by Jean Stafford, *Partisan Review*, Vol. 11, No. 4 (Fall 1944), pp. 474–7.
Warren, Robert Penn, 'Not Local Color', *Virginia Quarterly Review*, Vol. 8, No. 1 (January 1932), pp. 153–60.
Warren, Robert Penn, 'The Love and the Separateness in Miss Welty', *Kenyon Review*, Vol. 6, No. 2 (Spring 1944), pp. 246–59.
Warren, Robert Penn, 'Cowley's Faulkner' [1946], in John Basett (ed.), *William Faulkner: The Critical Heritage* (London: Taylor & Francis, 2013), pp. 314–27.
Warshow, Robert, 'The Legacy of the 30's: Middle-Class Mass Culture and the Intellectual's Problem', *Commentary*, December 1947, pp. 538–45.
Weber, Bruce, 'Richard G. Stern, 84, Writer's Writer, Dies', *New York Times*, 25 January 2013, A19.

Wellek, René, 'The New Criticism: Pro and Contra', *Critical Inquiry*, Vol. 4, No. 4 (Summer 1978), pp. 611–24.

West, Cornel, 'Pragmatism and the Sense of the Tragic', in *The Cornel West Reader* (New York: Basic Civitas Books, 2000), pp. 174–82.

Wiegman, Robyn, 'Introduction: Autotheory Theory', *Arizona Quarterly*, Vol. 76, No. 1 (Spring 2020), pp. 1–14.

Wieseltier, Leon (ed.), *The Moral Obligation to be Intelligent: Selected Essays of Lionel Trilling* (New York: Farrar, Straus and Giroux, 2000).

Wilhelm, James, *Ezra Pound: The Tragic Years, 1925–1972* (University Park, PA: Pennsylvania State University Press, 1994).

Williams, Jeffrey, 'The New Modesty in Literary Criticism', *The Chronicle of Higher Education*, 5 January 2015.

Williams, John, 'J. V. Cunningham: The Major and the Minor', *Arizona Quarterly*, Vol. 6, No. 2 (Summer 1950), pp. 132–46.

Williams, John, '"The 'Western'": Definition of Myth', *The Nation*, Vol. 193, No. 17 (18 November 1961), pp. 401–6.

Williams, John, *Stoner* [1965] (New York: New York Review Books Classics, 2003).

Wilson, Edmund, *The Triple Thinkers: Twelve Essays on Literary Subjects* (New York: Farrar, Straus and Giroux, 1948).

Winters, Yvor, *Maule's Curse: Seven Studies in the History of American Obscurantism* (Norfolk, CT: New Directions, 1938).

Winters, Yvor, *In Defense of Reason* (Denver: Swallow Press, 1947).

Winters, Yvor, 'Problems for the Modern Critic of Literature', *Hudson Review*, Vol. 9, No. 3 (Autumn 1956), pp. 325–86.

Withers, D.-M., *Virago Reprints and Modern Classics: The Timely Business of Feminist Publishing* (Cambridge: Cambridge University Press, 2021).

Wollaeger, Mark, 'Scholarship's Turn', in Douglas Mao, *The New Modernist Studies* (Cambridge: Cambridge University Press, 2021), pp. 41–64.

Wright, John, *Shadowing Ralph Ellison* (Jackson: University Press of Mississippi, 2006).

Ylanan, Aida, 'Cover to Cover: The Colors of NYRB Classics', *Los Angeles Times*, 27 December 2018. Available at: https://www.latimes.com/projects/la-et-jc-nyrb-covers/.

Young, Marguerite, 'Metaphysical Fiction', review of *The Member of the Wedding* by Carson McCullers, *Kenyon Review*, Vol. 9, No. 1 (Winter 1947), pp. 151–5.

INDEX

Where entries for authors have subheadings, titles of works are filed before thematic subheadings. Page numbers with the suffix 'n' indicate notes (38n104).

Adams, Rachel, 147
Afflerbach, Ian, 8, 194
African Americans, 109–15, 146
agrarianism, 127–30, 135, 194
Aldridge, John, 12, 14–15, 85
allegory, 90, 131, 134, 191–2, 193
Almond, Steve, 200
American Communist Party (CPUSA)
  Clark's depiction of, 90, 92–3, 101, 102, 103–4, 105
  Ellison's connections to, 107–8
  Ellison's depiction of, 108, 111–12
  Partisan Review, 9, 86
American identity, 109, 110, 123
American Studies, 3–4, 10, 191
Americanist critics, 2–3, 10, 12, 18, 20
Anderson, Amanda
  liberalism, 5, 7
  on Trilling, 8, 46, 54, 55, 60, 108
anti-communist novel, 84–5, 93–5, 101, 114
antisemitism, 42, 167–71, 175, 176–7, 180
anti-Stalinist intellectuals *see* New York Intellectuals (anti-Stalinist intellectuals)
anxiety
  The Bitter Box (Clark), 90, 93, 96, 99–100, 104
  Ellison, 108
  European modernism, 11, 88
  tragedy, 194
  Trilling, 90, 93, 96, 97, 99, 104
Arendt, Hannah, 11, 86–7, 101
Ariail, Gregory, 88
aristocracy, 18, 109, 195–6
Aristotle, 195

Arnold, Matthew, Trilling's biography of, 40, 82, 214
Auden, W. H., 50, 88
autobiographical writing, 137, 172, 178, 180–1, 182, 200
automatism
  Bergson, 99, 101
  The Bitter Box (Clark), 101–2, 103, 104
  bureaucracy, 87, 101
  Invisible Man (Ellison), 111–12

Barnhisel, Greg, 70
Barrett, William, 87, 129, 169
Barth, John, 199
Baskin, Jason, 111, 113, 114
Baton Rouge, 125–6, 132, 135, 190
Beckett, Samuel, 98, 99
Bellow, Saul, 163–8, 170–1
  The Adventures of Augie March, 21, 164–5, 166, 167
  Dangling Man, 84, 101, 165
  The Dean's December, 168, 170
  Henderson the Rain King, 163
  Herzog, 163, 167, 181, 182, 199
  Humboldt's Gift, 168
  The Victim, 21, 165
  midcentury criticism, overview, 12, 14, 15, 21, 24
  Partisan Review, 165, 173
  on Pound, 170–1
  and Stern, 163–4, 166, 171, 174, 182
Benveniste, Émile, 100
Bergonzi, Bernard, 'Herzog in Venice', 167
Bergson, Henri, 99, 100, 101, 105, 112

Berryman, John, 14, 168
bildungsroman, 141, 143–8
Blake, William, 'Jerusalem', 59
Bollingen Prize for Poetry, 7, 168–70, 175, 182
Bradbury, Malcolm, 167
Britten, Benjamin, *Billy Budd* (opera), 59
Brod, Max, 86, 88
Brontë, Emily, *Wuthering Heights*, 19
Brooks, Cleanth
  Understanding Fiction (with Warren), 11, 133–4, 139, 141, 145, 147, 150–1
  Understanding Poetry (with Warren), 132
  Louisiana State University, 126, 190
  Southern Review, 126, 127
bureaucracy
  banks, 92, 101
  The Bitter Box (Clark), 90, 92, 101–5
  government and state, 9, 42, 58, 71, 86–7, 104, 105
  see also universities, institutional nature of

Calder, Alexander, 104
Cambridge University, 42, 63–4
canonisation
  Great American Novel, 46, 68, 200–1, 203
  modernism, 3, 9–20, 23, 85, 138, 168, 202
  novel, 25–6
  NYRB Classics, 203–5
Casillo, Robert, 187n96
Catholicism
  Stafford, 125, 135–8, 139–40, 151, 154, 155
  Tate, 128, 131
Chambers, Whittaker, 83, 88
Chase, Richard
  The American Novel and its Tradition, 7, 19, 59, 94
  'Art, Nature, Politics', 8
  American Studies, 191
Cheng, Anne Anlin, 112
Chicago, 163–5, 167, 170, 177
Chicago, University of, 163
Clark, Eleanor, 82–5, 88–96, 98–106
  'Asleep a King', 88–9
  The Bitter Box, 82, 83–4, 90–6, 98, 99, 100–6, 110, 115, 150
  'The Heart of the Afternoon', 89–90, 93
  Con Spirito magazine, 83
  Partisan Review, 82, 84–5, 88–90, 115, 194
  review of *Death of a Salesman* (Miller), 194
  short stories, 88–90, 93, 102, 124
  Trilling's essay on *The Bitter Box*, 91–6, 110
  Trotsky Commission, 84
class, 3; *see also* aristocracy; middle class; working class
classicism, 171, 190–1, 193, 195–6, 200
close reading
  New Criticism, 8, 16, 27, 131, 133, 212
  psychoanalysis as, 139
  Stafford on, 154
Cold War, 3, 10–11, 20, 70, 178

Colebrook, Claire, 25
Colorado, 123, 141, 142, 144
Columbia University, 42, 43, 62, 66
coming-of-age narratives, 141, 143–8
Commentary, 164, 173
Committee on Social Thought, 163, 167
communism
  Trilling, 51, 52, 55, 67, 83–4
  see also American Communist Party (CPUSA)
complexity
  Ellison, 107–8, 113–14
  midcentury criticism, overview, 6, 8, 9, 18, 19, 27
  New Criticism, 133
  Trilling, 6, 18, 51, 53, 76, 96, 108
Con Spirito magazine, 83
Cotkin, George, 129
Cowley, Malcolm, 10
CPUSA (American Communist Party) *see* American Communist Party (CPUSA)
Crangle, Sara, 99
creative writing programs, 22, 71–2, 163–4, 190–1, 199–200
criticism
  professionalisation of, 15, 18, 64, 131, 213
  role of, 10–12, 15, 18, 211–14
Cunningham, J. V., 190, 195–6, 197

Dabashi, Pardis, 211, 213
Dancer, Thom, 28–9
Dante, 131, 140
Davie, Donald, 176
Davis, Robert Gorham, 15
'death of the novel' discourse
  Ellison, 108, 113
  midcentury criticism, overview, 13–16, 24, 26, 194
  Trilling, 13, 46, 68, 91
  Winters, 191, 196
Deleuze, Gilles and Guattari, Félix, 24–5, 28, 143, 205
democracy
  Ellison, 108, 110, 113, 114
  and literature, 7, 10–12
  totalitarian nature of, 6
  Trilling, 41–2, 59, 71, 72
Denver, University of, 190–1, 200
deterritorialisation, 25–6, 205
Dickstein, Morris, 43, 143, 165, 167, 199
Dimock, Wai Chee, 212
Dostoevsky, Fyodor
  The Brothers Karamazov, 92
  Notes from Underground, 88, 92, 106
  The Possessed, 51–2, 87
  anti-Stalinist revival of, 9, 47, 52, 87, 88, 90
  Trilling on, 41, 51–2, 91
Dreiser, Theodore, 47
Dufourmantelle, Anne, 105

Eisinger, Chester, 38n104
Eliot, T. S.

'The Dry Salvages', 143
antisemitism, 177
Bollingen Prize judge, 168–9
New Criticism influenced by, 127, 128, 129, 131, 135, 171
Ellison, Ralph, 106–15
  'Change the Joke and Slip the Yoke', 109, 111
  'The Extravagance of Laughter', 109, 111
  Invisible Man, 84, 106–8, 109–15
  'Society, Morality, and the Novel', 21, 108–9, 110
  complexity, 107–8, 113–14
  high cultural pluralism, 23, 106
  midcentury criticism, overview, 12, 21
Esteve, Mary, 27–8, 138
ethnicity, 23, 25, 42, 114, 165, 182; *see also* African Americans; Jewish identity; race
European modernism, 9–11, 47, 86–8, 90, 91
existentialism, 11, 84, 87–90, 93, 97–8, 107
exposition, 172, 192–3

family institutions, 147
fascism, 6, 168, 175, 194
Faulkner, William, 10, 110, 132–3, 170, 202
feminism, 138, 182, 202
Fiedler, Leslie, 20, 144, 183n15, 185n49
first person narration, 21–3, 136, 182
Fitzgerald, F. Scott, 48
Fitzgerald, Joan, 174, 178
Fitzpatrick, Katie, 53, 61–2
Flaubert, Gustave, 17, 21, 24, 132, 165, 166
Foley, Abram, 200
Foley, Barbara, 3, 107
Ford Foundation, 67, 70
formalism
  midcentury criticism, overview, 6, 8–10, 13, 16–17, 20–1
  revised, 212
  Stitch (Stern), 179–82
  Williams, 190, 200
  see also close reading; New Criticism; proportion; scale; unity; Winters, Yvor
Forster, E. M.
  Aspects of the Novel, 44
  Billy Budd (opera libretto), 59
  The Longest Journey, 41
  Trilling's fiction influenced by, 54, 55–6, 64, 65, 76
  Trilling's monograph on, 40, 43–4, 66, 96
Frank, Edwin, 198–9, 202, 204–5
freedom (aesthetic/formal), 2, 22, 125, 165, 166, 182
freedom (individual/political)
  The Bitter Box (Clark), 92, 96, 101–5, 110
  European modernism, 86, 88
  Invisible Man (Ellison), 110, 113
  midcentury criticism, overview, 7–8, 194
  Niebuhr, 129
  Trilling, 53
Freudianism *see* psychoanalysis
friendship, 41–2, 43, 64–5, 76

Fugitives, 127, 128, 171
Furman, Andrew, 165

Gandhi, Leela, 28–9
gender, 3, 147–8, 149
Giles, Paul, 128
Gordon, Caroline, 27, 133
government and state
  bureaucracy, 9, 42, 58, 71, 86–7, 104, 105
  see also democracy; fascism; totalitarianism
Great American Novel, 25–6, 46, 68, 200–1, 203
greatness, 44–6, 48, 65, 76, 143–4, 211; *see also* heroism; major novel
Greenberg, Clement, 15, 169
Greif, Mark, 6, 11, 129
Grosz, Elizabeth, 97, 149
Guattari, Félix *see* Deleuze, Gilles and Guattari, Félix

Hardwick, Elizabeth, 136–7
Harris, Mark, 163
Harvard University, 126, 173
Hassan, Ihab, 12
Hawthorne, Nathaniel, 101, 109
Hayes, Patrick, 184n24
Heilman, Robert, 142–3, 150
Hemingway, Ernest, 45
heroism, 46, 48, 66–9, 195, 196–7
Hicks, Granville, *The Living Novel*, 13
high cultural pluralism
  Ellison's writing, 23, 106
  Jewish-American writing, 165, 166, 182
  minority writers, 26
  The Program Era (McGurl), 23, 25, 114, 165, 199–200
high modernism
  canonisation of, 12, 14, 23, 85, 138, 168
  high cultural pluralism emerges after, 23, 113, 164
  Kafka, 84, 85, 86, 90, 124
  limits of, 98, 100
  New York Intellectuals (anti-Stalinist intellectuals), 12, 83–6, 90, 94, 113
Hollinger, David, 8, 16, 18
Hook, Sidney, 129
Howe, Irving, 155, 169, 198
Hulbert, Ann, 136
human agency *see* non-human agency
Hutchison, Anthony, 51, 54–5, 171, 191

idealism, 11, 41, 52, 54, 109, 128
ideas, 42, 46–7, 52, 69; *see also* novel of ideas
identity, 24–5, 54, 108, 143, 147–9; *see also* American identity; ethnicity; Jewish identity; regional identity
ideology
  midcentury criticism, overview, 7, 10, 20
  Trilling, 51, 53–4, 59, 72, 76
institutions *see* bureaucracy; family institutions; Ford Foundation;

professionalisation; universities, institutional nature of intellectual class
psychoanalysis, 138
tragedy, 194
Trilling, 42, 55, 63, 70, 72, 83, 97, 143
see also Jewish-American intellectuals; New York Intellectuals (anti-Stalinist intellectuals)
Iowa, University of, 163, 166

James, Henry
The Ambassadors, 22
'The Art of Fiction', 134
'The Beast in the Jungle', 134
'In the Cage', 120n116
Hawthorne, 109
The Portrait of a Lady, 192
The Princess Casamassima, 19, 45, 48, 68
Rahv's 'paleskin' reference to, 123, 141
revival of, 10, 91, 202
Stafford influenced by, 123–4, 139
Stern influenced by, 176, 181
Trilling's essay, 'The Princess Casamassima', 18–19, 41, 45–6, 48, 53, 60
Trilling's fiction influenced by, 65, 68, 69–70, 73, 192
Winters on, 192
Jancovich, Mark, 131
Jarrell, Randall, 15
Jewish-American intellectuals, 169–70, 173, 182
Jewish-American writing, 45, 164–8, 169–70, 173–5, 178, 182
Jewish identity, 166–8, 171, 173–5, 177–8
Jewish vernacular, 164, 165, 166, 167, 182
John Reed Club, 86
Jones, Howard Mumford, 140
Joyce, James, 85, 93, 108, 124, 166
Justice, Donald, 171–3

Kafka, Franz
Clark's fiction influenced by, 85–6, 89–90, 93, 101, 115, 124
deterritorialisation, 25, 86–7
Ellison, 106, 113
high modernism, 84, 85, 86, 90, 124
'Little Man' stories, 87
Partisan Review, 9, 47, 86, 88, 90, 95–6
Kazin, Alfred
On Native Grounds, 66, 213
on Bellow, 165
Keats, John, 44
Kenner, Hugh, 170, 174
Kenyon College, 126
Kenyon Review
'The Life of the Novel' (Trilling), 91–6
midcentury criticism, overview, 11
New Criticism, 126–7
psychoanalysis, 138–9
Schorer's review of Stafford, 141–3, 150

Stern, 163, 173
Young's review of McCullers, 147
Kierkegaard, Søren, 87, 96, 107
Kindley, Evan, 69–70, 71
Kirsch, Adam, 45, 49
Klein, Marcus, 12, 15
Konstantinou, Lee, 201–2, 204
Kristol, Irving, 44
Krupnick, Mark, 53

Lambert, Josh, 165
Landor, Walter Savage, 68
late modernism, 4–5, 98–9, 100, 101, 104, 105
laughter
The Bitter Box (Clark), 102–6, 110, 115
Invisible Man (Ellison), 109–15
Nietzsche, 97–8, 106, 110
Trilling, 96–100, 104, 105, 106, 110
Leader, Zachary, 163
Leaf, Munro, 56
Leavis, F. R., 19, 63
Lethem, Jonathan, 202
Levenson, Michael, 133, 134
Lewis, R. W. B., 13, 96, 191
Lewis, Wyndham, 98, 99
The Liberal Imagination (Trilling)
'Art and Fortune', 13, 18, 46, 47
Clark's editorial role, 82
'Huckleberry Finn', 143, 146
'The Immortality Ode', 75
'Manners, Morals, and the Novel', 6, 15, 18, 41, 108–9
'The Meaning of a Literary Idea', 16, 47
Preface, 18, 42, 46, 48
'The Princess Casamassima', 18–19, 41, 45–6, 48, 53, 60
'Reality in America', 7, 40, 41, 47, 94
liberalism
Ellison, 108
midcentury criticism, overview, 4–8, 10, 18, 20–1, 24, 27–8
New Criticism, 125, 127, 133
and tragedy, 6, 8, 10, 41, 53, 65, 125, 194
Trilling, 40–1, 42, 47, 51–3, 59, 65
Library of America series, 203
literary criticism *see* criticism, role of
Lockwood, Helen, 83
Louisiana State University, 126, 190
Love, Heather, 212
Lowell, Robert
Bollingen Prize judge, 168–9
New Criticism, 11–12, 125–6, 135, 136
Stafford's depiction of, 137
Stern's teacher, 163
Lubbock, Percy, *The Craft of Fiction*, 44, 134

McCarthy, Mary, 83
McCullers, Carson, *The Member of the Wedding*, 146–8
McGurl, Mark

The Program Era, 22–3, 114, 134, 165, 199–200
  high cultural pluralism, 23, 25, 114, 165, 199–200
  on Roth, 23, 28
  technomodernism, 23, 199, 201
  major novel, 25–6, 44, 113–14; *see also* Great American Novel; greatness
Malamud, Bernard, 164, 177
Malraux, André, 107
Mangrum, Benjamin, 9, 16, 97–8
Maritain, Jacques, *The Dream of Descartes*, 128, 129, 150
marriage, institution of, 147
mass/popular culture, 21, 23, 26, 60, 138
Matthiessen, F. O., 59
medievalism, 128, 129–30, 131, 189–90, 195, 199
Melville, Herman, *Billy Budd*, 59–60, 61
Menand, Louis, 88
Mendelson, Edward, 50
Michigan, University of, 170
midcentury studies, 4–5
middle class, 18, 42, 63–4, 70, 88, 144, 173
Miller, Arthur, *Death of a Salesman*, 194–5
Miller, Tyrus, 4, 5, 98–9, 100, 101, 105
minor characters
  adolescents, 143–4
  The Bitter Box (Clark), 90, 101, 115
  Death of a Salesman (Miller), 195
  Invisible Man (Ellison), 113
  Kafkaesque 'Little Man' stories, 87
  The Mountain Lion (Stafford), 143
  Stoner (Williams), 196–7
minor literature, definition (Deleuze and Guattari), 24–5
minor novel
  The Bitter Box (Clark), 90, 100, 106
  definition and overview, 2, 19, 26–9, 211
  The Journey Abandoned (Trilling), 67–8, 76
  The Middle of the Journey (Trilling), 54, 65
  NYRB Classics, 203
  The Princess Casamassima (James), 48
  Stafford's fiction, 125, 151, 155
  Stoner (Williams), 193, 196–7, 201
  translated works, 204–5
minority writers, 22–3, 26, 114, 174; *see also* Jewish-American writing
Missouri, University of, 189, 191, 193
Mizener, Arthur, 17
modernism
  canon, 3, 9–20, 23, 85, 138, 168, 202
  Ellison, 108
  New Criticism, 127, 134, 166
  new modernist studies, 3–5, 23
  Schaub, 21–2, 23, 94
  Stern, 178, 180, 182
  Trilling, 47, 52, 68
  Winters, 171–2, 190, 191–3, 196
  see also European modernism; high modernism; late modernism

Moi, Toril, 212
moral realism, 18, 21, 24, 47, 93
morality
  Ellison, 108–9
  midcentury criticism, overview, 6, 16, 27
  Trilling, 6, 16, 42, 46–7, 49–50, 61–2, 91, 108–9
  Winters, 191–2
Murphy, Geraldine, 53, 59, 71
Murphy, Harriet, 97
Murray, Gilbert, 129
mythology, 10, 38n104, 114, 128, 132–3, 138

n+1 magazine, 203–4, 205
narration *see* first person narration; third person narration
National Book Awards, 165, 199
National Committee for the Defense of Political Prisoners (NCDPP), 83
nationalism, 10–11, 42, 98
naturalism
  Ellison, 107
  midcentury criticism, overview, 7, 10, 20, 21
  New Criticism, 134
  Rahv, 123
  Trilling, 47, 93–6, 100, 115
Nelson, Deborah, 60, 194
New Americanist critics, 2–3, 10
New Criticism
  key terms, 132, 133
  midcentury criticism, overview, 2–4, 8–12, 16–17, 20, 26–7
  poetry, 8, 11, 17, 126–7, 130–7, 168–9
  predecessor groups, 125–30
  Stafford's fiction in tension with, 124–5, 132, 135–6, 140–6, 150–1, 154–5
  Stern, 171–3
  symbolism, 27, 131, 133–6, 138, 140, 150–1
  Williams, 191
new modernist studies, 3–5, 23
New York Intellectuals (anti-Stalinist intellectuals)
  Clark, 82–5, 90, 91
  Ellison, 108, 113
  high modernism, 12, 83–6, 90, 94, 113
  Kenyon Review, 127
  midcentury criticism, overview, 2–4, 6–12, 18, 20, 26
  see also Partisan Review; Trilling, Lionel
New York Review Books (NYRB) Classics, 198–9, 201–5
New York Review of Books, 167, 202, 204
Niebuhr, Reinhold, 6, 129
Nietzsche, Friedrich, 97–8, 106, 110
nihilism, 93, 97, 98, 112, 129
non-human agency, 88, 102, 104, 149–51, 154; *see also* automatism
North Carolina at Chapel Hill, University of, 171, 173
novel
  as 'primitive' form, 18, 29, 48, 66, 76

and society, 7–9, 17–18, 21
  see also anti-communist novel; 'death of the novel' discourse; Great American Novel; major novel; minor novel
novel of ideas, 7, 18, 53–9, 65–6, 69, 167
novel of manners, 18–19, 21, 24, 54, 91–2, 108–9
NYRB (New York Review Books) Classics, 198–9, 201–5

Oates, Joyce Carol, 152
obscurity, 190–3, 198
Ogden, Emily, 213

Paris Review, 181, 204
Partisan Review
  Bellow, 165, 173
  Bollingen Prize controversy, 169
  Clark, 82, 84–5, 88–90, 115, 194
  Ellison, 106
  modernism, 86, 91, 95, 100
  New York Intellectuals (anti-Stalinist intellectuals), 3, 9–12
  'Our Country and Our Culture' (1952 symposium), 70
  'Religion and the Intellectuals' (1950 symposium), 129
  Stafford, 136–7
  'The State of American Writing' (1948 symposium), 12, 14, 15, 95
  Stern, 181
  Trilling's connections to, 18, 47, 70, 82, 91, 95
  Trilling's private journals published in, 42, 45–6, 48, 61, 62
Parvulescu, Anca, 100, 106
Phillips, Adam, 46
Phillips, William, 43, 86
pluralism, 148; *see also* high cultural pluralism
Podhoretz, Norman, 48
poetry
  New Criticism, 8, 11, 17, 126–7, 130–7, 168–9
  Trilling, 68, 73, 74–5
  Winters, 171–2, 190
Popular Front, 9, 10, 71, 86
popular/mass culture, 21, 23, 26, 60, 138
positivism, 127, 130
postcritique, 212–14
postmodernism, 4, 5, 100, 199, 201
Pound, Ezra
  Cantos, 172, 176, 179, 181
  Bellow on, 170–1
  Bollingen Prize for Poetry, 7, 168–70, 175, 182
  Stern on, 166–8, 171, 174–81
  Winters on, 172
Prescott, Orville, 140, 141, 154–5
professionalisation
  of criticism, 15, 18, 64, 131, 213

middle class, 42, 63–4, 70
progressive politics, 9, 47, 51–2, 59, 96, 112–13
proportion
  New Criticism, 125, 133–4
  Stafford's fiction, 135, 142, 145, 146, 150, 153, 155
  Stitch (Stern), 180
Protestantism, 128, 129; *see also* Puritanism
Proust, Marcel, 136, 139
psychoanalysis
  Stafford, 137–8, 139–40, 145, 153, 155
  tragedy, 194
  Trilling's Freudianism, 50, 55, 93, 99, 138–9
publishing industry, 200–5
Puritanism, 191–2, 193
Pynchon, Thomas, *Gravity's Rainbow*, 201

queer theory, 147–50

race, 3, 108, 148–9; *see also* African Americans; antisemitism; ethnicity; Jewish identity
Rahv, Philip
  'Paleface and Redskin', 123–4, 141
  Partisan Review, 10, 47, 52, 86, 87, 106
  Stafford praised by, 140, 141
Ransom, John Crowe, 12, 42, 126, 130, 173
rationalism
  midcentury criticism, overview, 6, 9
  New Criticism, 125, 130–1
Sartre, 87
Southern Agrarians, 127, 128
Stafford, 150
Trilling, 42, 46, 47, 51, 91, 94–5, 96
Williams, 200
Winters, 172, 193
Ratner-Rosenhagen, Jennifer, 98
realism, 10, 27–8, 85, 90, 124, 181; *see also* moral realism; socialist realism
regional identity, 125, 127, 134, 147
regionalism, 27, 123–5, 127, 144, 152, 171
religion, 127–30, 133–4, 143, 154, 194; *see also* Catholicism; Protestantism; Puritanism
Richards, I. A., 173
Riesman, David, 47
Riseling, Russell, 191
Roddell, Marie, 199
Rohter, Larry, 202
roman à clef, 167, 182
Romanticism, 68, 127, 171–2, 180–2, 190, 193, 199
Rosenfeld, Isaac, 86
Ross, Dorothy, 138
Roth, Philip
  'The Conversion of the Jews', 164
  The Ghost Writer, 164
  Goodbye, Columbus, 164
  Letting Go, 184n24
  'Nemeses' quartet, 28

high cultural pluralism, 23, 182
Jewish identity, 173
Russell, David, 8
Russo, John Paul, 131

Sartre, Jean-Paul, 87, 98, 107, 120n120
scale
 Ellison, 107
 New Criticism, 133-4
 Stafford's fiction, 136, 142, 144, 148, 150
 Stoner (Williams), 197
 Trilling, 65
Schaub, Thomas Hill, *American Fiction in the Cold War*, 20-2, 23, 94, 104, 113
Schorer, Mark
 'Technique as Discovery', 12, 17, 141
 reviews of Stafford, 141-3, 150
Schreier, Benjamin, 183n15
Schryer, Stephen, 3, 63-4, 70
Sedgwick, Eve Kosofsky, 212
Seiler, Claire, 4-5, 89, 99-100
Sewanee Review, 126, 142-3, 147, 150
sexuality, 3, 138, 145, 147-8, 181
Shakespeare, William, 195
Shapiro, Karl, 169
Sherfey, Mary Jane, 138
Shields, Charles, 190
Shils, Edward, 163
short stories
 Clark, 88-90, 93, 102, 124
 New Criticism, 124-5, 127, 133, 134, 136-7, 142, 144
 Roth, 164
 Southern regionalism, 27, 124
 Stafford, 125, 136, 137, 139-40, 142, 144, 158n61
 Welty, 133
Sinykin, Dan, 201-2, 204
Slesinger, Tess, *The Unpossessed*, 84, 87
Snow, C. P., 198
social class *see* class
social reality, 7, 20, 130
socialist realism, 83, 86
society
 novel form's relationship with, 7-9, 17-18, 21
 'Society, Morality, and the Novel' (Ellison), 21, 108-9, 110
Solotaroff, Ted
 First Loves, 169-70
 'A Vocal Group: The Jewish part in American letters', 170
Solow, Herbert, 83-4
Southern Agrarians, 127-30, 135, 194
Southern critics *see* New Criticism
Southern regionalism, 27, 124-5, 127, 152, 171
Southern Review, 11, 126-7
Spengler, Oswald, *The Decline of the West*, 60-1
Stafford, Jean, 123-6, 135-55

Boston Adventure, 136-8, 139, 152
The Catherine Wheel, 124-5, 151-5
Collected Stories, foreword, 123-4
'An Influx of Poets', 137, 139-40, 158n61
'The Interior Castle', 136
The Mountain Lion, 124-5, 137, 140-6, 148-51, 155
'The Psychological Novel', 139
Catholicism, 125, 135-8, 139-40, 151, 154, 155
New Criticism, her fiction in tension with, 124-5, 132, 135, 140-4, 146, 150-1, 154-5
NYRB Classics, 202
psychoanalysis, 137-8, 139-40, 145, 153, 155
Southern Review, 126
Stalinism, 6, 194
Stanford University, 173, 191
state *see* government and state
Steinbeck, John, 7, 47
Steiner, George, *The Death of Tragedy*, 194
Stendhal (Marie-Henri Beyle), 97
Stern, Richard
 Golk, 173
 Stitch, 166-7, 174, 175-81
 and Bellow, 163-4, 166, 171, 174, 182
 Jewish identity, 166-8, 171, 173-5, 177-8
 NYRB Classics, 202
 on Pound, 166-8, 171, 174-81
 reputation, 198
 and Winters, 171-3
Stockton, Kathryn Bond, 147
subjectivity
 Afflerbach, 8, 194
 laughter, 99, 100, 104, 114
 Winters's antisubjectivism, 171-2, 190, 192
 see also autobiographical writing; non-human agency
Swallow, Alan, 190, 191
Swallow Press, 191, 195, 198
Sykes, John, 130
symbolism
 McCullers's fiction, 147
 New Criticism, 27, 131, 133-6, 138, 140, 150-1
 Rahv, 123
 Stafford's fiction, 125, 140, 141, 142, 150-1, 154-5
 'The Symbolic Imagination' (Tate), 131, 140, 150-1
Szalay, Michael, 3, 28

Tate, Allen
 The Fathers, 132
 The House of Fiction (with Gordon), 133
 'The Symbolic Imagination', 131, 140, 150-1
 'Techniques of Fiction', 17, 132, 134, 166

Bollingen Prize judge, 168–9
New Criticism, 27, 126–8, 129–31, 132, 133–4, 168
technomodernism, 23, 199, 201
Teresa of Ávila, Saint, *The Interior Castle*, 136
third person narration, 2, 23–4, 134, 181
Thurschwell, Pam, 148
totalitarianism, 6, 8, 11, 92, 98, 101, 104
tragedy
   Cunningham, 195–6, 197
   Death of a Salesman (Miller), 194–5
   Ellison, 108, 109, 113
   laughter, 96, 97
   liberalism, 6, 8, 10, 41, 53, 65, 125, 194
   New Criticism, 134
   psychoanalysis, 138
   Stafford, 125, 141
   Stoner (Williams), 193, 195, 197
   tragic limitation, 6, 41, 65, 125
   Trilling on, 41, 48, 76, 96, 138
   in Trilling's fiction, 52–3, 60–1, 64–5, 67–9, 73
translated works, 198, 202, 205–6
Trask, Michael, 131
Trilling, Lionel, 40–76
   'Artists and the "Societal" Function', 7
   E. M. Forster, 40, 43–4, 66, 96
   The Journey Abandoned, 49, 66–76
   The Last Decade: Essays and Reviews, 49, 83, 84
   'The Life of the Novel' (essay on Clark's *The Bitter Box*), 91–6, 110
   Matthew Arnold, 40, 66, 82, 214
   The Middle of the Journey, 49, 51–62, 64–5, 69, 70, 83, 96, 104, 150, 152
   communism, 51, 52, 55, 67, 83–4
   creative writing preferred to criticism, 49, 213
   Forster's influence on his fiction, 54, 55–6, 64, 65, 76
   Freudianism, 50, 55, 93, 99, 138–9
   James's influence on his fiction, 65, 68, 69–70, 73, 192
   laughter, 96–100, 104, 105, 106, 110
   liberalism, 40–1, 42, 47, 51–3, 59, 65
   morality, 42, 46–7, 49, 50, 61–2, 91, 108–9
   NYRB Classics, 202
   Partisan Review, connections to, 18, 47, 70, 82, 91, 95
   Partisan Review, publication of private journals, 42, 45–6, 48, 61, 62
   universities, institutional nature of, 42, 43, 62–5, 69–72
   see also The Liberal Imagination (Trilling)
Trotsky Commission, 84
Twain, Mark
   Huckleberry Finn, 143, 146
   Rahv's 'redskin' reference to, 123–4, 141

unity
   New Criticism, 8, 125, 130, 132–4

Stafford's fiction, 135, 140, 142–3, 146, 150
Stitch (Stern), 182
universalism, 10–11, 88, 113–14, 196
universities, institutional nature of
   Stern, 178, 182
   Trilling, 42, 43, 62–5, 69–72
   Williams, 191, 196, 200
   see also creative writing programs
Updike, John, 167–8

Vanderbilt University, 127
Vassar College, 83
Venice, Italy, 166, 174, 176
vernacular material *see* Jewish vernacular
Viking Press, 198, 199, 200
Virago Press, 202

Wakefield, Dan, 198
Wald, Alan, 3, 84
Warren, Robert Penn
   All the King's Men, 106
   Night Rider, 132
   Understanding Fiction (with Brooks), 11, 133–4, 139, 141, 145, 147, 150–1
   Understanding Poetry (with Brooks), 132
   Bollingen Prize judge, 168–9
   Louisiana State University, 190
   New Criticism, predecessor groups, 127, 130
   Southern Review, 126, 127
Warshow, Robert, 53
Welty, Eudora, 133, 152
Western writers, 123, 124, 141
Williams, John
   Augustus, 199
   Nothing But the Night, 198
   Stoner, 189–90, 193, 195, 196–9, 201, 204, 205
   and Winters, 190, 193
Wilson, Edmund, 91
Winters, Yvor
   In Defense of Reason, 171–2, 190
   Maule's Curse, 191
   classicism, 171, 190, 191, 193
   formalism, 13, 171–2, 182, 190
   on the novel form, 192–3, 196, 197
   on Pound, 172
   and Stern, 171–2, 182
   tragedy, 196
Wordsworth, William, 74–5
working class, 41, 88
Wright, John, 109
Wright, Richard, 'The Man Who Lived Underground', 107, 113

Young, Marguerite, 147

Zilboorg, Gregory, 137–8
Zola, Émile, 94
Zukofsky, Louis, 174

EU Authorised Representative:
Easy Access System Europe Mustamäe tee 50, 10621 Tallinn, Estonia
gpsr.requests@easproject.com

Printed and bound by CPI Group (UK) Ltd, Croydon, CR0 4YY
02/03/2026
02063692-0003